ABOUT THIS PUBLICATION

FOR SERVICE ASSISTANCE

Customer Service
1.704.898.0770

North Carolina General Statues is published by The Muliti-Media Group of Greater Charlotte in Charlotte, North Carolina. Copyright 2015 by the Multi-Media Group of Greater Charlotte. This book or parts thereof may not be reproduced in any form, stored in a retrieval system, or transmitted in any form by any means—electronic, mechanical, photocopy, recording or otherwise—without prior written permission of the publisher, except as provided by United States of America copyright law.

The records required by U.S. Code 2257(a) through (c) and the pertinent regulations 28 C.F.R. Cli. 1, Part 75 with respect to this publication and all materials associated with such records are maintained by The Multi-Media Group of Greater Charlotte, Publisher and available for review by Attorney General.

www.visionbooks.org

Copyright © 2015 by MMGGC
All rights reserved!

TID: 5109306
ISBN (10) digit: 1503254658
ISBN (13) digit: 978-1503254657

123-4-56789-01239-Paperback
123-4-56789-01239-Hardback

First Edition

090520140547

Printed in the United States of America

2015 EDITION

North Carolina Criminal Law And Procedure-Pamphlet # 88

Printed In conjunction with the Administration of the Courts

North Carolina Criminal Law and Procedure
Pamphlet Reference Guide

Chapters	Pamphlet
Chapter 1 Civil Procedure	1
Chapter 1 Civil Procedure (Continue)	2
Chapter 1A Rules of Civil Procedure	2
Chapter 1B Contribution.	2
Chapter 1C Enforcement of Judgments.	2
Chapter 1D Punitive Damages.	2
Chapter 1E Eastern Band of Cherokee Indians.	2
Chapter 1F North Carolina Uniform Interstate Depositions and Discovery Act.	2
Chapter 2 - Clerk of Superior Court [Repealed and Transferred.]	3
Chapter 3 - Commissioners of Affidavits and Deeds [Repealed.]	3
Chapter 4 - Common Law	3
Chapter 5 - Contempt [Repealed.]	3
Chapter 5A - Contempt	3
Chapter 6 - Liability for Court Costs	3
Chapter 7 - Courts [Repealed and Transferred.]	3
Chapter 7A – Judicial Department	3
Chapter 7A – Continuation (Judicial Department)	4
Chapter 7A – Continuation (Judicial Department)	5
Chapter 7B - Juvenile Code	5
Chapter 8 - Evidence	6
Chapter 8A - Interpreters for Deaf Persons [Recodified.]	6
Chapter 8B - Interpreters for Deaf Persons	6
Chapter 8C - Evidence Code	6
Chapter 9 - Jurors	6
Chapter 10 - Notaries [Repealed.]	6
Chapter 10A - Notaries [Recodified.]	6
Chapter 10B - Notaries	6
Chapter 11 - Oaths	6
Chapter 12 - Statutory Construction	6
Chapter 13 - Citizenship Restored	6
Chapter 14 - Criminal Law	7
Chapter 14 –Criminal Law (Continuation)	8
Chapter 15 - Criminal Procedure	9
Chapter 15A - Criminal Procedure Act (Continuation)	10
Chapter 15A - Criminal Procedure Act (Continuation)	11
Chapter 15B - Victims Compensation	11
Chapter 15C - Address Confidentiality Program	11
Chapter 16 - Gaming Contracts and Futures	11
Chapter 17 - Habeas Corpus	11

Chapter 17A - Law-Enforcement Officers [Recodified.]	11
Chapter 17B - North Carolina Criminal Justice Education and Training System [Recodified.] Chapter 17C - North Carolina Criminal Justice Education and Training Standards Commission	11 11
Chapter 17D - North Carolina Justice Academy	11
Chapter 17E - North Carolina Sheriffs' Education and Training Standards Commission	11
Chapter 18 - Regulation of Intoxicating Liquors [Repealed.]	12
Chapter 18A - Regulation of Intoxicating Liquors [Repealed.]	12
Chapter 18B - Regulation of Alcoholic Beverages	12
Chapter 18C - North Carolina State Lottery	12
Chapter 19 - Offenses against Public Morals	12
Chapter 19A - Protection of Animals	12
Chapter 20 - Motor Vehicles	13
Chapter 20 - Motor Vehicles (Continuation)	14
Chapter 20 - Motor Vehicles (Continuation)	15
Chapter 20 - Motor Vehicles (Continuation)	16
Chapter 21 - Bills of Lading	17
Chapter 22 - Contracts Requiring Writing	17
Chapter 22A - Signatures	17
Chapter 22B - Contracts Against Public Policy	17
Chapter 22C - Payments to Subcontractors	17
Chapter 23 - Debtor and Creditor	17
Chapter 24 – Interest	17
Chapter 25 – Uniform Commercial Code	18
Chapter 25 – Uniform Commercial Code (Continuation)	19
Chapter 25A – Retail Installment Sales Act	20
Chapter 25B - Credit	20
Chapter 25C - Sales of Artwork	20
Chapter 26 - Suretyship	20
Chapter 27 - Warehouse Receipts [Repealed.]	20
Chapter 28 - Administration [Repealed.]	20
Chapter 28A - Administration of Decedents' Estates	20
Chapter 28B - Estates of Absentees in Military Service	20
Chapter 28C - Estates of Missing Persons	20
Chapter 29 - Intestate Succession	21
Chapter 30 - Surviving Spouses	21
Chapter 31 - Wills	21
Chapter 31A - Acts Barring Property Rights	21
Chapter 31B - Renunciation of Property and Renunciation of Fiduciary Powers Act	21
Chapter 31C - Uniform Disposition of Community Property Rights at Death Act	21
Chapter 32 - Fiduciaries	21
Chapter 32A - Powers of Attorney	21
Chapter 33 - Guardian and Ward [Repealed and Recodified.]	21

Chapter 33A - North Carolina Uniform Transfers to Minors Act	21
Chapter 33B - North Carolina Uniform Custodial Trust Act	21
Chapter 34 - Veterans' Guardianship Act	22
Chapter 35 - Sterilization Procedures	22
Chapter 35A - Incompetency and Guardianship	22
Chapter 36 - Trusts and Trustees [Repealed.]	22
Chapter 36A - Trusts and Trustees	22
Chapter 36B - Uniform Management of Institutional Funds Act [Repealed.]	22
Chapter 36C - North Carolina Uniform Trust Code	22
Chapter 36D - North Carolina Community Third Party Trusts, Pooled Trusts	23
Chapter 36E - Uniform Prudent Management of Institutional Funds Act	23
Chapter 37 - Allocation of Principal and Income [Repealed.]	23
Chapter 37A - Uniform Principal and Income Act	23
Chapter 38 - Boundaries	23
Chapter 38A - Landowner Liability	23
Chapter 39 - Conveyances	23
Chapter 39A - Transfer Fee Covenants Prohibited	23
Chapter 40 - Eminent Domain [Repealed.]	23
Chapter 40A - Eminent Domain	23
Chapter 41 - Estates	23
Chapter 41A - State Fair Housing Act	23
Chapter 42 - Landlord and Tenant	23
Chapter 42A - Vacation Rental Act	23
Chapter 43 - Land Registration	23
Chapter 44 - Liens	24
Chapter 44A - Statutory Liens and Charges	24
Chapter 45 - Mortgages and Deeds of Trust	24
Chapter 45A - Good Funds Settlement Act	24
Chapter 46 - Partition	24
Chapter 47 - Probate and Registration	25
Chapter 47A - Unit Ownership	25
Chapter 47B - Real Property Marketable Title Act	25
Chapter 47C - North Carolina Condominium Act	25
Chapter 47D - Notice of Settlement Act [Expired.]	25
Chapter 47E - Residential Property Disclosure Act	25
Chapter 47F - North Carolina Planned Community Act	25
Chapter 47G - Option to Purchase Contracts	25
Chapter 47H - Contracts for Deed	25
Chapter 48 - Adoptions	26
Chapter 48A - Minors	26
Chapter 49 - Bastardy	26
Chapter 49A - Rights of Children	26
Chapter 50 - Divorce and Alimony	26
Chapter 50A - Uniform Child-Custody Jurisdiction and	

Enforcement Act	26
Chapter 50B - Domestic Violence	26
Chapter 50C - Civil No-Contact Orders	26
Chapter 51 - Marriage	26
Chapter 52 - Powers and Liabilities of Married Persons	27
Chapter 52A - Uniform Reciprocal Enforcement of Support Act [Repealed.]	27
Chapter 52B - Uniform Premarital Agreement Act	27
Chapter 52C - Uniform Interstate Family Support Act	27
Chapter 53 - Banks	27
Chapter 53A - Business Development Corporations and North Carolina Capital Resource Corporations	28
Chapter 53B - Financial Privacy Act	28
Chapter 54 - Cooperative Organizations	28
Chapter 54A - Capital Stock Savings and Loan Associations [Repealed.]	28
Chapter 54B - Savings and Loan Associations	29
Chapter 54C - Savings Banks	29
Chapter 55 - North Carolina Business Corporation Act	30
Chapter 55A - North Carolina Nonprofit Corporation Act	31
Chapter 55B - Professional Corporation Act	31
Chapter 55C - Foreign Trade Zones	31
Chapter 55D - Filings, Names, and Registered Agents for Corporations, Nonprofit Corporations, and Partnerships	31
Chapter 56 - Electric, Telegraph and Power Companies [Repealed.]	31
Chapter 57 - Hospital, Medical and Dental Service Corporations [Recodified.]	31
Chapter 57A - Health Maintenance Organization Act [Recodified.]	31
Chapter 57B - Health Maintenance Organization Act [Recodified.]	31
Chapter 57C - North Carolina Limited Liability Company Act.	31
Chapter 58 - Insurance.	32
Chapter 58 - Insurance (Continuation)	33
Chapter 58 - Insurance (Continuation)	34
Chapter 58 - Insurance (Continuation)	35
Chapter 58 - Insurance (Continuation)	36
Chapter 58 - Insurance (Continuation)	37
Chapter 58 - Insurance (Continuation)	38
Chapter 58A - North Carolina Health Insurance Trust Commission [Recodified.]	38
Chapter 59 - Partnership.	39
Chapter 59B - Uniform Unincorporated Nonprofit Association Act.	39
Chapter 60 - Railroads and Other Carriers [Repealed and Transferred.]	39
Chapter 61 - Religious Societies	39
Chapter 62 - Public Utilities	39

Chapter 62 - Public Utilities (Continuation)	40
Chapter 62A - Public Safety Telephone Service And Wireless Telephone Service	40
Chapter 63 - Aeronautics	40
Chapter 63A - North Carolina Global TransPark Authority	40
Chapter 64 - Aliens	40
Chapter 65 – Cemeteries	40
Chapter 66 - Commerce and Business	41
Chapter 67 - Dogs	41
Chapter 68 - Fences and Stock Law	41
Chapter 69 - Fire Protection	41
Chapter 70 - Indian Antiquities, Archaeological Resources and Unmarked Human Skeletal Remains Protection	42
Chapter 71 - Indians [Repealed.]	42
Chapter 71A - Indians	42
Chapter 72 - Inns, Hotels and Restaurants	42
Chapter 73 - Mills	42
Chapter 74 - Mines and Quarries	42
Chapter 74A - Company Police [Repealed.]	42
Chapter 74B - Private Protective Services Act [Repealed.]	42
Chapter 74C - Private Protective Services	42
Chapter 74D - Alarm Systems	42
Chapter 74E - Company Police Act	42
Chapter 74F - Locksmith Licensing Act	42
Chapter 74G - Campus Police Act	42
Chapter 75 - Monopolies, Trusts and Consumer Protection	42
Chapter 75A - Boating and Water Safety	43
Chapter 75B - Discrimination in Business	43
Chapter 75C - Motion Picture Fair Competition Act	43
Chapter 75D - Racketeer Influenced and Corrupt Organizations	43
Chapter 75E - Unlawful Activities in Connection With Certain Corporate Transactions	43
Chapter 76 - Navigation	43
Chapter 76A - Navigation and Pilotage Commissions	43
Chapter 77 - Rivers, Creeks, and Coastal Waters	43
Chapter 78 - Securities Law [Repealed.]	43
Chapter 78A - North Carolina Securities Act	43
Chapter 78B - Tender Offer Disclosure Act [Repealed.]	43
Chapter 78C - Investment Advisers	43
Chapter 78D - Commodities Act	43
Chapter 79 - Strays [Repealed.]	43
Chapter 80 - Trademarks, Brands, etc.	44
Chapter 81 - Weights and Measures [Recodified.]	44
Chapter 81A - Weights and Measures Act of 1975.	44
Chapter 82 - Wrecks [Repealed.]	44
Chapter 83 - Architects [Recodified.]	44

Chapter 83A - Architects	44
Chapter 84 - Attorneys-at-Law	44
Chapter 84A - Foreign Legal Consultants	44
Chapter 85 - Auctions and Auctioneers [Repealed.]	44
Chapter 85A - Bail Bondsmen and Runners [Recodified.]	44
Chapter 85B - Auctions and Auctioneers	44
Chapter 85C - Bail Bondsmen and Runners [Recodified.]	44
Chapter 86 - Barbers [Recodified.]	44
Chapter 86A - Barbers	44
Chapter 87 - Contractors	44
Chapter 88 - Cosmetic Art [Repealed.]	44
Chapter 88A - Electrolysis Practice Act	44
Chapter 88B - Cosmetic Art	45
Chapter 89 - Engineering and Land Surveying [Recodified.]	45
Chapter 89A - Landscape Architects	45
Chapter 89B - Foresters	45
Chapter 89C - Engineering and Land Surveying	45
Chapter 89D - Landscape Contractors	45
Chapter 89E - Geologists Licensing Act	45
Chapter 89F - North Carolina Soil Scientist Licensing Act	45
Chapter 89G - Irrigation Contractors	45
Chapter 90 - Medicine and Allied Occupations	45
Chapter 90 - Medicine and Allied Occupations (Continuation)	46
Chapter 90 - Medicine and Allied Occupations (Continuation)	47
Chapter 90 - Medicine and Allied Occupations (Continuation)	48
Chapter 90A - Sanitarians and Water and Wastewater Treatment Facility Operators	48
Chapter 90B - Social Worker Certification and Licensure Act	48
Chapter 90C - North Carolina Recreational Therapy Licensure Act	48
Chapter 90D - Interpreters and Transliterators	48
Chapter 91 - Pawnbrokers [Repealed.]	48
Chapter 91A - Pawnbrokers Modernization Act of 1989	48
Chapter 92 - Photographers [Deleted.]	48
Chapter 93 - Certified Public Accountants	48
Chapter 93A - Real Estate License Law	49
Chapter 93B - Occupational Licensing Boards	49
Chapter 93C - Watchmakers [Repealed.]	49
Chapter 93D - North Carolina State Hearing Aid Dealers and Fitters Board.	49
Chapter 93E - North Carolina Appraisers Act	49
Chapter 94 - Apprenticeship	49
Chapter 95 - Department of Labor and Labor Regulations	49
Chapter 95 - Department of Labor and Labor Regulations (Continuation)	50
Chapter 96 - Employment Security	50
Chapter 97 - Workers' Compensation Act	50
Chapter 97 - Workers' Compensation Act (Continuation)	51

Chapter 98 - Burnt and Lost Records	51
Chapter 99 - Libel and Slander	51
Chapter 99A - Civil Remedies for Criminal Actions	51
Chapter 99B - Products Liability	51
Chapter 99C - Actions Relating to Winter Sports Safety and Accidents	51
Chapter 99D - Civil Rights	51
Chapter 99E - Special Liability Provisions	51
Chapter 100 - Monuments, Memorials and Parks	51
Chapter 101 - Names of Persons	51
Chapter 102 - Official Survey Base	51
Chapter 103 - Sundays, Holidays and Special Days	51
Chapter 104 - United States Lands	51
Chapter 104A - Degrees of Kinship	51
Chapter 104B - Hurricanes or Other Acts of Nature	51
Chapter 104C - Atomic Energy, Radioactivity and Ionizing Radiation [Repealed and Recodified.]	51
Chapter 104D - Southern States Energy Compact	51
Chapter 104E - North Carolina Radiation Protection Act	51
Chapter 104F - Southeast Interstate Low-Level Radioactive Waste Management Compact [Repealed]	51
Chapter 104G - North Carolina Low-Level Radioactive Waste Management Authority Act of 1987 [Repealed]	51
Chapter 105 - Taxation	51
Chapter 105 - Taxation (Continuation)	52
Chapter 105 - Taxation (Continuation)	53
Chapter 105 - Taxation (Continuation)	54
Chapter 105A - Setoff Debt Collection Act	55
Chapter 105B - Defaulted Student Loan Recovery Act	55
Chapter 106 - Agriculture	55
Chapter 106 - Agriculture (Continue)	56
Chapter 106 - Agriculture (Continue)	57
Chapter 107 - Agricultural Development Districts [Repealed.]	57
Chapter 108 - Social Services [Repealed and Recodified.]	57
Chapter 108A - Social Services	57
Chapter 108B - Community Action Programs	58
Chapter 108C Medicaid and Health Choice Provider Requirements.	58
Chapter 108D Medicaid Managed Care for Behavioral Health Services.	58
Chapter 109 - Bonds [Recodified.]	58
Chapter 110 - Child Welfare	58
Chapter 111 - Aid to the Blind	58
Chapter 112 - Confederate Homes and Pensions [Repealed.]	58
Chapter 113 - Conservation and Development	58
Chapter 113 - Conservation and Development (Continuation)	59

Chapter 113A - Pollution Control and Environment	59
Chapter 113A - Pollution Control and Environment (Continuation)	60
Chapter 113B - North Carolina Energy Policy Act of 1975	60
Chapter 114 - Department of Justice	60
Chapter 115 - Elementary and Secondary Education [Repealed.]	60
Chapter 115A - Community Colleges, Technical Institutes, and Industrial Education Centers [Repealed.]	60
Chapter 115B - Tuition and Fee Waivers	60
Chapter 115C - Elementary and Secondary Education	60
Chapter 115C - Elementary and Secondary Education (Continuation)	61
Chapter 115C - Elementary and Secondary Education (Continuation)	62
Chapter 115C - Elementary and Secondary Education (Continuation)	63
Chapter 115D - Community Colleges	63
Chapter 115E - Private Educational Facilities Finance Act [Recodified]	63
Chapter 116 - Higher Education	63
Chapter 116 - Higher Education (Continuation)	63
Chapter 116A - Escheats and Abandoned Property [Repealed.]	64
Chapter 116B - Escheats and Abandoned Property	64
Chapter 116C - Continuum of Education Programs	64
Chapter 116D - Higher Education Bonds	64
Chapter 116E -Education Longitudinal Data System	64
Chapter 117 - Electrification	64
Chapter 118 - Firemen's and Rescue Squad Workers' Relief and Pension Funds [Recodified.]	64
Chapter 118A - Firemen's Death Benefit Act [Repealed.]	64
Chapter 118B - Members of a Rescue Squad Death Benefit Act [Repealed.]	64
Chapter 119 - Gasoline and Oil Inspection and Regulation	64
Chapter 120 - General Assembly	65
Chapter 120 - General Assembly (Continuation)	66
Chapter 120 - General Assembly (Continuation)	67
Chapter 120C - Lobbying	67
Chapter 121 - Archives and History	67
Chapter 122 - Hospitals for the Mentally Disordered [Repealed.]	67
Chapter 122A - North Carolina Housing Finance Agency	67
Chapter 122B - North Carolina Agricultural Facilities Finance Act [Repealed.]	67
Chapter 122C - Mental Health, Developmental Disabilities, and Substance Abuse Act of 1985	67
Chapter 122C - Mental Health, Developmental Disabilities, and Substance Abuse Act of 1985 (Continuation)	68

Chapter 122D - North Carolina Agricultural Finance Act	68
Chapter 122E - North Carolina Housing Trust and Oil Overcharge Act	68
Chapter 123 - Impeachment	69
Chapter 123A - Industrial Development [Repealed.]	69
Chapter 124 - Internal Improvements	69
Chapter 125 - Libraries	69
Chapter 126 - State Personnel System	69
Chapter 127 - Militia [Repealed.]	69
Chapter 127A - Militia	69
Chapter 127B - Military Affairs	69
Chapter 127C - Advisory Commission on Military Affairs	69
Chapter 128 - Offices and Public Officers	69
Chapter 128 - Offices and Public Officers (Continuation)	70
Chapter 129 - Public Buildings and Grounds	70
Chapter 130 - Public Health [Repealed.]	70
Chapter 130A - Public Health	70
Chapter 130A - Public Health (Continuation)	71
Chapter 130A - Public Health (Continuation)	72
Chapter 130B - Hazardous Waste Management Commission [Repealed.]	72
Chapter 131 - Public Hospitals [Repealed.]	72
Chapter 131A - Health Care Facilities Finance Act	72
Chapter 131B - Licensing of Ambulatory Surgical Facilities [Repealed.]	72
Chapter 131C - Charitable Solicitation Licensure Act [Repealed.]	72
Chapter 131D - Inspection and Licensing of Facilities	72
Chapter 131E - Health Care Facilities and Services	72
Chapter 131E - Health Care Facilities and Services (Continuation)	73
Chapter 131F - Solicitation of Contributions	73
Chapter 132 - Public Records	73
Chapter 133 - Public Works	74
Chapter 134 - Youth Development [Recodified.]	74
Chapter 134A - Youth Services [Repealed.]	74
Chapter 135 - Retirement System for Teachers and State Employees; Social Security; Health Insurance Program for Children	74
Chapter 135 - Retirement System for Teachers and State Employees; Social Security; Health Insurance Program for Children	75
Chapter 136 - Transportation	75
Chapter 136 - Transportation (Continuation)	76
Chapter 137 - Rural Rehabilitation [Repealed.]	76
Chapter 138 - Salaries, Fees and Allowances	76
Chapter 138A - State Government Ethics Act	76

Chapter 139 - Soil and Water Conservation Districts	76
Chapter 140 - State Art Museum; Symphony and Art Societies	76
Chapter 140A - State Awards System	76
Chapter 141 - State Boundaries	76
Chapter 142 - State Debt	76
Chapter 143 - State Departments, Institutions, and Commissions	77
Chapter 143 - State Departments, Institutions, and Commissions (Continuation)	78
Chapter 143 - State Departments, Institutions, and Commissions (Continuation)	79
Chapter 143 - State Departments, Institutions, and Commissions (Continuation)	80
Chapter 143A - State Government Reorganization	80
Chapter 143B - Executive Organization Act of 1973	80
Chapter 143B - Executive Organization Act of 1973 (Continuation)	81
Chapter 143B - Executive Organization Act of 1973 (Continuation)	82
Chapter 143C - State Budget Act	83
Chapter 143D - The State Governmental Accountability and Internal Control Act	83
Chapter 144 - State Flag, Official Governmental Flags, Motto, and Colors	83
Chapter 145 - State Symbols and Other Official Adoptions.	83
Chapter 146 - State Lands	83
Chapter 147 - State Officers	83
Chapter 148 - State Prison System	84
Chapter 149 - State Song and Toast	84
Chapter 150 - Uniform Revocation of Licenses [Repealed.]	84
Chapter 150A - Administrative Procedure Act [Recodified.]	84
Chapter 150B - Administrative Procedure Act	84
Chapter 151 - Constables [Repealed.]	84
Chapter 152 - Coroners	84
Chapter 152A - County Medical Examiner [Repealed.]	84
Chapter 152A - County Medical Examiner [Repealed.] (Continuation)	84
Chapter 153 - Counties and County Commissioners [Repealed.]	84
Chapter 153A - Counties	84
Chapter 153A - Counties (Continue)	85
Chapter 153B - Mountain Resources Planning Act	85
Chapter 153C - Uwharrie Regional Resources Act	85
Chapter 154 - County Surveyor [Repealed.]	85
Chapter 155 - County Treasurer [Repealed.]	85

Chapter 156 - Drainage	85
Chapter 156 – Drainage (Continuation)	86
Chapter 157 - Housing Authorities and Projects	86
Chapter 157A - Historic Properties Commissions [Transferred.]	86
Chapter 158 - Local Development	86
Chapter 159 - Local Government Finance	86
Chapter 159 - Local Government Finance (Continuation)	87
Chapter 159A - Pollution Abatement and Industrial Facilities Financing Act [Unconstitutional.]	87
Chapter 159B - Joint Municipal Electric Power and Energy Act	87
Chapter 159C - Industrial and Pollution Control Facilities Financing Act	87
Chapter 159D - The North Carolina Capital Facilities Financing Act	87
Chapter 159E - Registered Public Obligations Act	87
Chapter 159F - North Carolina Energy Development Authority [Repealed.]	87
Chapter 159G - Water Infrastructure	87
Chapter 159H - [Reserved.]	87
Chapter 159I - Solid Waste Management Loan Program and Local Government Special Obligation Bonds	87
Chapter 160 - Municipal Corporations [Repealed And Transferred.]	87
Chapter 160A - Cities and Towns	88
Chapter 160A - Cities and Towns (Continuation)	89
Chapter 160B - Consolidated City-County Act	89
Chapter 160C - Baseball Park Districts [Repealed.]	90
Chapter 161 - Register of Deeds	90
Chapter 162 - Sheriff	90
Chapter 162A - Water and Sewer Systems	90
Chapter 162B Continuity of Local Government in Emergency.	90
Chapter 163 Elections and Election Laws.	90
Chapter 163 Elections and Election Laws. (Continuation)	91
Chapter 164 Concerning the General Statutes of North Carolina.	92
Chapter 165 Veterans.	92
Chapter 166 Civil Preparedness Agencies [Repealed.]	92
Chapter 166A North Carolina Emergency Management Act.	92
Chapter 167 State Civil Air Patrol [Repealed.]	92
Chapter 168 Persons with Disabilities.	92
Chapter 168A Persons With Disabilities Protection Act.	92

Chapter 160A.

Cities and Towns.

Article 1.

Definitions and Statutory Construction.

§ 160A-1. Application and meaning of terms.

Unless otherwise specifically provided, or unless otherwise clearly required by the context, the words and phrases defined in this section shall have the meaning indicated when used in this Chapter.

(1)   "Charter" means the entire body of local acts currently in force applicable to a particular city, including articles of incorporation issued to a city by an administrative agency of the State, and any amendments thereto adopted pursuant to 1917 Public Laws, Chapter 136, Subchapter 16, Part VIII, sections 1 and 2, or Article 5, Part 4, of this Chapter.

(2)   "City" means a municipal corporation organized under the laws of this State for the better government of the people within its jurisdiction and having the powers, duties, privileges, and immunities conferred by law on cities, towns, and villages. The term "city" does not include counties or municipal corporations organized for a special purpose. "City" is interchangeable with the terms "town" and "village," is used throughout this Chapter in preference to those terms, and shall mean any city as defined in this subdivision without regard to the terminology employed in charters, local acts, other portions of the General Statutes, or local customary usage. The terms "city" or "incorporated municipality" do not include a municipal corporation that, without regard to its date of incorporation, would be disqualified from receiving gasoline tax allocations by G.S. 136-41.2(a), except that the end of status as a city under this sentence shall not affect the levy or collection of any tax or assessment, or any criminal or civil liability, and shall not serve to escheat any property until five years after the end of such status as a city, or until September 1, 1991, whichever comes later.

(3)   "Council" means the governing board of a city. "Council" is interchangeable with the terms "board of aldermen" and "board of commissioners," is used throughout this Chapter in preference to those terms, and shall mean any city council as defined in this subdivision without regard to

the terminology employed in charters, local acts, other portions of the General Statutes, or local customary usage.

(4)   "General law" means an act of the General Assembly applying to all units of local government, to all cities, or to all cities within a class defined by population or other criteria, including a law that meets the foregoing standards but contains a clause or section exempting from its effect one or more cities or all cities in one or more counties.

(5)   "Local act" means an act of the General Assembly applying to one or more specific cities by name, or to all cities within one or more specifically named counties. "Local act" is interchangeable with the terms "special act," "public-local act," and "private act," is used throughout this Chapter in preference to those terms, and shall mean a local act as defined in this subdivision without regard to the terminology employed in charters, local acts, or other portions of the General Statutes.

(6)   "Mayor" means the chief executive officer of a city by whatever title known.

(7)   "Publish," "publication," and other forms of the verb "to publish" mean insertion in a newspaper qualified under G.S. 1-597 to publish legal advertisements in the county or counties in which the city is located.

(8)   "Rural Fire Department" means, for the purpose of Articles 4A or 14 of this Chapter, a bona fide department which, as determined by the Commissioner of Insurance, is classified as not less than class "9" in accordance with rating methods, schedules, classifications, underwriting rules, bylaws or regulations effective or applied with respect to the establishment of rates or premiums used or charged pursuant to Article 36 or Article 40 of Chapter 58 of the General Statutes, and which operates fire apparatus and equipment of the value of five thousand dollars ($5,000) or more; but it does not include a municipal fire department. (1971, c. 698, s. 1; 1973, c. 426, s. 3; 1983, c. 636, s. 17.1; 1985 (Reg. Sess., 1986), c. 934, s. 1.)

§ 160A-2. Effect upon prior laws.

Nothing in this Chapter shall repeal or amend any city charter in effect as of January 1, 1972, or any portion thereof, unless this Chapter or a subsequent enactment of the General Assembly shall clearly show a legislative intent to repeal or supersede all local acts. The provisions of this Chapter, insofar as they are the same in substance as laws in effect as of December 31, 1971, are intended to continue such laws in effect and not to be new enactments. The enactment of this Chapter shall not require the readoption of any city ordinance enacted pursuant to laws that were in effect before January 1, 1972, and are restated or revised herein. The provisions of this Chapter shall not affect any act heretofore done, any liability incurred, any right accrued or vested, or any suit or prosecution begun or cause of action accrued as of January 1, 1972. (1971, c. 698, s. 1.)

§ 160A-3. General laws supplementary to charters.

(a)   When a procedure that purports to prescribe all acts necessary for the performance or execution of any power, duty, function, privilege, or immunity is provided by both a general law and a city charter, the two procedures may be used as alternatives, and a city may elect to follow either one.

(b)   When a procedure for the performance or execution of any power, duty, function, privilege, or immunity is provided by both a general law and a city charter, but the charter procedure does not purport to contain all acts necessary to carry the power, duty, function, privilege, or immunity into execution, the charter procedure shall be supplemented by the general law procedure; but in case of conflict or inconsistency between the two procedures, the charter procedure shall control.

(c)   When a power, duty, function, privilege, or immunity is conferred on cities by a general law, and a charter enacted earlier than the general law omits or expressly denies or limits the same power, duty, function, privilege or immunity, the general laws shall supersede the charter. (1971, c. 698, s. 1.)

§ 160A-4. Broad construction.

It is the policy of the General Assembly that the cities of this State should have adequate authority to execute the powers, duties, privileges, and immunities conferred upon them by law. To this end, the provisions of this Chapter and of city charters shall be broadly construed and grants of power shall be construed to include any additional and supplementary powers that are reasonably necessary or expedient to carry them into execution and effect: Provided, that the exercise of such additional or supplementary powers shall not be contrary to State or federal law or to the public policy of this State. (1971, c. 698, s. 1.)

§ 160A-4.1. Notice of new fees and fee increases; public comment period.

(a) A city shall provide notice to interested parties of the imposition of or increase in fees or charges applicable solely to the construction of development subject to the provisions of Part 2 of Article 19 of this Chapter at least seven days prior to the first meeting where the imposition of or increase in the fees or charges is on the agenda for consideration. The city shall employ at least two of the following means of communication in order to provide the notice required by this section:

(1) Notice of the meeting in a prominent location on a Web site managed or maintained by the city.

(2) Notice of the meeting in a prominent physical location, including, but not limited to, any government building, library, or courthouse within the city.

(3) Notice of the meeting by electronic mail to a list of interested parties that is created by the city for the purpose of notification as required by this section.

(4) Notice of the meeting by facsimile to a list of interested parties that is created by the city for the purpose of notification as required by this section.

(a1) If a city does not maintain its own Web site, it may employ the notice option provided by subdivision (1) of subsection (a) of this section by submitting a request to a county or counties in which the city is located to post such notice in a prominent location on a Web site that is maintained by the county or counties. Any city that elects to provide such notice shall make its request to the county or counties at least 15 days prior to the date of the first meeting where the imposition of or increase in the fees or charges is on the agenda for consideration.

(b) During the consideration of the imposition of or increase in fees or charges as provided in subsection (a) of this section, the governing body of the city shall permit a period of public comment.

(c) This section shall not apply if the imposition of or increase in fees or charges is contained in a budget filed in accordance with the requirements of G.S. 159-12. (2009-436, s. 2; 2010-180, s. 11(b).)

§ 160A-5. Statutory references deemed amended to conform to Chapter.

Whenever a reference is made in another portion of the General Statutes or any local act, or any city ordinance, resolution, or order, to a portion of Chapter 160 of the General Statutes that is repealed or superseded by this Chapter, the reference shall be deemed amended to refer to that portion of this Chapter which most nearly corresponds to the repealed or superseded portion of Chapter 160. (1971, c. 698, s. 1; 1973, c. 426, s. 2.)

Article 1A.

Municipal Board of Control.

§§ 160A-6 through 160A-10. Repealed by Session Laws 1981 (Regular Session, 1982), c. 1191, s. 63.

Article 2.

General Corporate Powers.

§ 160A-11. Corporate powers.

The inhabitants of each city heretofore or hereafter incorporated by act of the General Assembly or by the Municipal Board of Control shall be and remain a municipal corporation by the name specified in the city charter. Under that name they shall be vested with all of the property and rights in property belonging to the corporation; shall have perpetual succession; may sue and be sued; may contract and be contracted with; may acquire and hold any property, real and personal, devised, sold, or in any manner conveyed, dedicated to, or otherwise acquired by them, and from time to time may hold, invest, sell, or dispose of the same; may have a common seal and alter and renew the same at will; and shall have and may exercise in conformity with the city charter and the general laws of this State all municipal powers, functions, rights, privileges, and immunities of every name and nature whatsoever.

All documents required or permitted by law to be executed by municipal corporations will be legally valid and binding in this respect when a legible corporate stamp, which is a facsimile of its seal, is used in lieu of an imprinted or embossed corporate or common seal. (Code, ss. 704, 3117; 1901, c. 283; 1905, c. 526; Rev., s. 2916; 1907, c. 978; P.L. 1917, c. 223; C.S., s. 2623; Ex. Sess. 1921, c. 58; 1927, c. 14; 1933, c. 69; 1949, c. 938; 1955, c. 77; 1959, c. 391; 1961, c. 308; 1967, c. 100, s. 2; c. 1122, s. 1; 1969, c. 944; 1971, c. 698, s. 1; 1973, c. 170; c. 426, s. 7; 2011-284, s. 110.)

§ 160A-12. Exercise of corporate power.

All powers, functions, rights, privileges, and immunities of the corporation shall be exercised by the city council and carried into execution as provided by the charter or the general law. A power, function, right, privilege, or immunity that is conferred or imposed by charter or general law without directions or restrictions as to how it is to be exercised or performed shall be carried into execution as provided by ordinance or resolution of the city council. (Code, s. 703; Rev., s. 2917; C.S., s. 2624; 1971, c. 698, s. 1.)

§§ 160A-13 through 160A-15. Reserved for future codification purposes.

Article 3.

Contracts.

§ 160A-16. Contracts to be in writing; exception.

All contracts made by or on behalf of a city shall be in writing. A contract made in violation of this section shall be void and unenforceable unless it is expressly ratified by the council. (1917, c. 136, subch. 13, s. 8; C.S., s. 2831; 1971, c. 698, s. 1.)

§ 160A-17. Continuing contracts.

A city is authorized to enter into continuing contracts, some portion or all of which are to be performed in ensuing fiscal years. Sufficient funds shall be appropriated to meet any amount to be paid under the contract in the fiscal year in which it is made, and in each ensuing fiscal year, the council shall appropriate sufficient funds to meet the amounts to be paid during the fiscal year under continuing contracts previously entered into. (1971, c. 698, s. 1.)

§ 160A-17.1. Grants from other governments.

(a) Federal and State. - The governing body of any city or county is hereby authorized to make contracts for and to accept grants-in-aid and loans from the federal and State governments and their agencies for constructing, expanding, maintaining, and operating any project or facility, or performing any function, which such city or county may be authorized by general law or local act to provide or perform.

In order to exercise the authority granted by this section, the governing body of any city or county may:

(1) Enter into and carry out contracts with the State or federal government or any agency or institution thereof under which such government, agency, or institution grants financial or other assistance to the city or county;

(2) Accept such assistance or funds as may be granted or loaned by the State or federal government with or without such a contract;

(3) Agree to and comply with any lawful and reasonable conditions which are imposed upon such grants or loans;

(3a) Agree to and comply with minimum minority business enterprise participation requirements established by the federal government and its agencies in projects financed by federal grants-in-aid or loans, by including such minimum requirements in the specifications for contracts to perform all or part of such projects and awarding bids pursuant to G.S. 143-129 and 143-131, if applicable, to the lowest responsible bidder or bidders meeting these and any other specifications.

(4) Make expenditures from any funds so granted.

(b)   Expired effective December 31, 2010. (1971, c. 896, s. 10; c. 937, ss. 1, 1.5; 1973, c. 426, s. 8; 1981, c. 827; 2007-91, s. 1.)

§ 160A-18. Certain deeds validated.

(a)   All deeds made, executed, and delivered by any city before July 1, 1970, for a good and valuable consideration are hereby in all respects validated, ratified, and confirmed notwithstanding any lack of authority to make the deed or any irregularities in the procedures by which conveyance of the land or premises described therein was authorized by the city council.

(b)   All conveyances and sales of any interest in real property by private sale, including conveyances in fee and releases of vested or contingent future interests, made by the governing body of any city, school district, or school administrative unit before July 1, 1970, are hereby validated, ratified, and confirmed notwithstanding the fact that such conveyances or releases were made by private sale and not after notice and public outcry.

(b1)   All conveyances of any interest in real property by private sale, including conveyance in fee, made by the governing body of any county before January 1, 1977, are hereby validated, ratified, and confirmed notwithstanding the fact that such conveyances were made by private sale, without advertisement, and not after notice and public outcry.

(c)   Nothing in this section shall affect any action or proceeding begun before January 1, 1977. (Ex. Sess. 1924, c. 95; 1951, c. 44; 1959, c. 487; 1971, c. 698, s. 1; 1977, c. 1103.)

§ 160A-19. Leases.

A city is authorized to lease as lessee, with or without option to purchase, any real or personal property for any authorized public purpose. A lease of personal property with an option to purchase is subject to Article 8 of Chapter 143 of the General Statutes. (1973, c. 426, s. 9.)

§ 160A-20. Security interests.

(a) Purchase. - A unit of local government may purchase, or finance or refinance the purchase of, real or personal property by installment contracts that create in some or all of the property purchased a security interest to secure payment of the purchase price to the seller or to an individual or entity advancing moneys or supplying financing for the purchase transaction.

(b) Improvements. - A unit of local government may finance or refinance the construction or repair of fixtures or improvements on real property by contracts that create in some or all of the fixtures or improvements, or in all or some portion of the property on which the fixtures or improvements are located, or in both, a security interest to secure repayment of moneys advanced or made available for the construction or repair.

(c) Accounts. - A unit of local government may use escrow accounts in connection with the advance funding of transactions authorized by this section, whereby the proceeds of the advance funding are invested pending disbursement. A unit of local government may also use other accounts, such as debt service payment accounts and debt service reserve accounts, to facilitate transactions authorized by this section. To secure transactions authorized by this section, a unit of local government may also create security interests in these accounts.

(d) Nonsubstitution. - No contract entered into under this section may contain a nonsubstitution clause that restricts the right of a unit of local government to:

(1) Continue to provide a service or activity; or

(2) Replace or provide a substitute for any fixture, improvement, project, or property financed, refinanced, or purchased pursuant to the contract.

(e) Oversight. - A contract entered into under this section is subject to approval by the Local Government Commission under Article 8 of Chapter 159 of the General Statutes if it:

(1) Meets the standards set out in G.S. 159-148(a)(1), 159-148(a)(2), and 159-148(a)(3), or involves the construction or repair of fixtures or improvements on real property; and

(2) Is not exempted from the provisions of that Article by one of the exemptions contained in G.S. 159-148(b).

(e1)   Public Hospitals. - A nonprofit entity operating or leasing a public hospital may enter into a contract pursuant to this section only if the nonprofit entity will have an ownership interest in the property being financed or refinanced, including a leasehold interest. The security interest granted in the property shall be only to the extent of the nonprofit entity's property interest. In addition, any contract entered into by a nonprofit entity operating or leasing a public hospital pursuant to this section is subject to the approval of the city, county, hospital district, or hospital authority that owns the hospital. Approval of the city, county, hospital district, or hospital authority may be withheld only under one or more of the following circumstances:

(1)   The contract would cause the city, county, hospital district, or hospital authority to breach or violate any covenant in an existing financing instrument entered into by the nonprofit entity.

(2)   The contract would restrict the ability of the city, county, hospital district, or hospital authority to incur anticipated bank-eligible indebtedness under federal tax laws.

(3)   The entering into of the contract would have a material, adverse impact on the credit ratings of the city, county, hospital district, or hospital authority or would otherwise materially interfere with an anticipated financing by the nonprofit entity.

(f)   Limit of Security. - No deficiency judgment may be rendered against any unit of local government in any action for breach of a contractual obligation authorized by this section. The taxing power of a unit of local government is not and may not be pledged directly or indirectly to secure any moneys due under a contract authorized by this section.

(g)   Public Hearing. - Before entering into a contract under this section involving real property, a unit of local government shall hold a public hearing on the contract. A notice of the public hearing shall be published once at least 10 days before the date fixed for the hearing.

(h)   Local Government Defined. - As used in this section, the term "unit of local government" means any of the following:

(1)   A county.

(2)   A city.

(3)   A water and sewer authority created under Article 1 of Chapter 162A of the General Statutes.

(3a)   A metropolitan sewerage district created under Article 5 of Chapter 162A of the General Statutes.

(3b)   A sanitary district created under Part 2 of Article 2 of Chapter 130A of the General Statutes.

(3c)   A county water and sewer district created under Article 6 of Chapter 162A of the General Statutes.

(4)   An airport authority whose situs is entirely within a county that has (i) a population of over 120,000 according to the most recent federal decennial census and (ii) an area of less than 200 square miles.

(5)   An airport authority in a county in which there are two incorporated municipalities with a population of more than 65,000 according to the most recent federal decennial census.

(5a)   An airport board or commission authorized by agreement between two cities pursuant to G.S. 63-56, one of which is located partially but not wholly in the county in which the jointly owned airport is located, and where the board or commission provided water and wastewater services off the airport premises before January 1, 1995, except that the authority granted by this subdivision may be exercised by such a board or commission with respect to water and wastewater systems or improvements only.

(5b)   A local airport authority that was created pursuant to a local act of the General Assembly.

(6)   A local school administrative unit whose board of education is authorized to levy a school tax.

(6a)   Any other local school administrative unit, but only for the purpose of financing energy conservation measures acquired pursuant to Part 2 of Article 3B of Chapter 143 of the General Statutes.

(6b)   A community college, but only for the purpose of financing energy conservation measures acquired pursuant to Part 2 of Article 3B of Chapter 143 of the General Statutes.

(7) An area mental health, developmental disabilities, and substance abuse authority, acting in accordance with G.S. 122C-147.

(8) A consolidated city-county, as defined by G.S. 160B-2(1).

(9) Repealed by Session Laws 2001-414, s. 52, effective September 14, 2001.

(10) A regional natural gas district, as defined by Article 28 of this Chapter.

(11) A regional public transportation authority or a regional transportation authority created pursuant to Article 26 or Article 27 of this Chapter.

(12) A nonprofit corporation or association operating or leasing a public hospital as defined in G.S. 159-39.

(13) A public health authority created under Part 1B of Article 2 of Chapter 130A of the General Statutes.

(14) A special district created under Article 43 of Chapter 105 of the General Statutes. (1979, c. 743; 1987 (Reg. Sess., 1988), c. 981, s. 1; 1989, c. 708; 1991, c. 741, s. 1; 1993 (Reg. Sess., 1994), c. 592, s. 2; 1995, c. 461, s. 6; 1995 (Reg. Sess., 1996), c. 644, s. 2; 1997-380, s. 3; 1997-426, s. 7; 1997-426, s. 7.1; 1998-70, s. 1; 1998-117, s. 1; 1999-386, ss. 1, 2; 2001-414, s. 52; 2002-161, s. 10; 2003-259, s. 1; 2003-388, s. 3; 2007-226, s. 1; 2007-229, s. 3; 2009-527, s. 2(g).)

§ 160A-20.1. Contracts with private entities; contractors must use E-Verify.

(a) Authority. – A city may contract with and appropriate money to any person, association, or corporation, in order to carry out any public purpose that the city is authorized by law to engage in. A city may not require a private contractor under this section to abide by any restriction that the city could not impose on all employers in the city, such as paying minimum wage or providing paid sick leave to its employees, as a condition of bidding on a contract.

(b) Contractors Must Use E-Verify. – No city may enter into a contract unless the contractor and the contractor's subcontractors comply with the requirements of Article 2 of Chapter 64 of the General Statutes. (1985, c. 271, s. 1; 2013-413, s. 5(d); 2013-418, s. 2(b).)

Article 4.

Corporate Limits.

Part 1. General Provisions.

§ 160A-21. Existing boundaries.

The boundaries of each city shall be those specified in its charter with any alterations that are made from time to time in the manner provided by law or by local act of the General Assembly. (1971, c. 698, s. 1.)

§ 160A-22. Map of corporate limits.

The current city boundaries shall at all times be drawn on a map, or set out in a written description, or shown by a combination of these techniques. This delineation shall be retained permanently in the office of the city clerk. Alterations in these established boundaries shall be indicated by appropriate entries upon or additions to the map or description made by or under the direction of the officer charged with that duty by the city charter or by the council. Copies of the map or description reproduced by any method of reproduction that gives legible and permanent copies, when certified by the city clerk, shall be admissible in evidence in all courts and shall have the same force and effect as would the original map or description. The council may provide for revisions in any map or other description of the city boundaries. A revised map or description shall supersede for all purposes the earlier map or description that it is designated to replace. (1971, c. 698, s. 1; 1973, c. 426, s. 10.)

§ 160A-23. District map; reapportionment.

(a) If the city is divided into electoral districts for the purpose of electing the members of the council, the map or description required by G.S. 160A-22 shall also show the boundaries of the several districts.

(b) The council shall have authority to revise electoral district boundaries from time to time. If district boundaries are set out in the city charter and the charter does not provide a method for revising them, the council may revise them only for the purpose of (i) accounting for territory annexed to or excluded from the city, and (ii) correcting population imbalances among the districts shown by a new federal census or caused by exclusions or annexations. When district boundaries have been established in conformity with the federal Constitution, the council shall not be required to revise them again until a new federal census of population is taken or territory is annexed to or excluded from the city, whichever event first occurs. In establishing district boundaries, the council may use data derived from the most recent federal census and shall not be required to use any other population estimates. (1969, c. 629; 1971, c. 698, s. 1.)

§ 160A-23.1. Special rules for redistricting after a federal decennial census.

(a) As soon as possible after receipt of federal decennial census information, the council of any city which elects the members of its governing board on a district basis, or where candidates for such office must reside in a district in order to run, shall evaluate the existing district boundaries to determine whether it would be lawful to hold the next election without revising districts to correct population imbalances. If such revision is necessary, the council shall consider whether it will be possible to adopt the changes (and obtain approval from the United States Department of Justice, if necessary) before the third day before opening of the filing period for the municipal election. The council shall take into consideration the time that will be required to afford ample opportunities for public input. If the council determines that it most likely will not be possible to adopt the changes (and obtain federal approval, if necessary) before the third business day before opening of the filing period, and determines further that the population imbalances are so significant that it would not be lawful to hold the next election using the current electoral districts, it may adopt a resolution delaying the election so that it will be held on the timetable provided by subsection (d) of this section. Before adopting such a resolution, the council shall hold a public hearing on it. The notice of public hearing shall summarize the proposed resolution and shall be published at least once in a newspaper of general circulation, not less than seven days before the date fixed for the hearing. Notwithstanding adoption of such a resolution, if the council proceeds to adopt the changes, (and federal approval is obtained, if necessary) by the end of the third business day before the opening of the filing period, the election shall be held on the regular schedule under the revised electoral districts. Any resolution adopted under this subsection, and any changes in electoral district boundaries made under this section shall be submitted to the United States Department of Justice (if the city is covered under Section 5 of the Voting Rights Act of 1965), the State Board of Elections, and to the board conducting the elections for that city.

(b)   In adopting any revisal under this section, if the council determines that in order for the plan to conform to the Voting Rights Act of 1965, the number of district seats needs to be increased or decreased, it may do so by following the procedures set forth in Part 4 of Article 5 of Chapter 160A of the General Statutes, except that the ordinance under G.S. 160A-102 may be adopted at the same meeting as the public hearing, and any referendum on the change under G.S. 160A-103 shall not apply to the municipal election in the two years following a federal decennial census.

(c)   If the resolution provided for in subsection (a) of this section is not adopted and:

(1)   Proposed changes to the electoral districts are not adopted, or

(2)   Such changes are adopted, but approval under the Voting Rights Act of 1965, as amended, is required, and notice of such approval is not received,

by the end of the third business day before the opening of the filing period, the election shall be held on the regular schedule using the current electoral districts.

(d)   If the council adopts the resolution provided for in subsection (a) of this section and does not adopt the changes, or does adopt the changes, but approval under the Voting Rights Act of 1965, as amended, is required, and notice of such approval is not received, by the end of the third day before the opening of the filing period, the municipal election shall be rescheduled as provided in this subsection and current officeholders shall hold over until their successors are elected and qualified. For cities using the:

(1)   Partisan primary and election method under G.S. 163-291, the primary shall be held on the primary election date for county officers in the second year following a federal decennial census, the second primary, if necessary, shall be held on the second primary election date for county officers in that year, and the general election shall be held on the general election date for county officers in that year.

(2) Nonpartisan primary and election method under G.S. 163-294, the primary shall be held on the primary election date for county officers in the second year following a federal decennial census, and the election shall be held on the date for the second primary for county officers in that year.

(3) Nonpartisan plurality election method under G.S. 163-292, the election shall be held on the primary election date for county officers in the second year following a federal decennial census.

(4) Election and runoff method under G.S. 163-293, the election shall be held on the primary election date for county officers in the second year following a federal decennial census, and the runoffs, if necessary, shall be held on the date for the second primary for county officers in that year.

The organizational meeting of the new council may be held at any time after the results of the election have been officially determined and published, but not later than the time and date of the first regular meeting of the council in November of the second year following a federal decennial census, except in the case of partisan municipal elections, when the organizational meeting shall be held not later than the time and date of the first regular meeting of the council in December of the second year following a federal decennial census.

(e) This section does not apply to any municipality that, under its charter, is not scheduled to hold an election in the year following a federal decennial census. (1989 (Reg. Sess., 1990), c. 1012, s. 2; 1999-227, s. 4; 2000-140, s. 34; 2002-159, s. 52; 2009-414, s. 1.)

Article 4A.

Extension of Corporate Limits.

Part 1. Extension by Petition.

§§ 160A-24 through 160A-28: Repealed by Session Laws 1983, c. 636, s. 26.

§ 160A-29. Map of annexed area, copy of ordinance and election results recorded in the office of register of deeds.

Whenever the limits of any municipal corporation are enlarged, in accordance with the provisions of this Article, it shall be the duty of the mayor of the city or town to cause an accurate map of such annexed territory, together with a copy of the ordinance duly certified, and the official results of the election, if conducted, to be recorded in the office of the register of deeds of the county or counties in which such territory is situated and in the office of the Secretary of State. The documents required to be filed with the Secretary of State under this section shall be filed not later than 30 days following the effective date of the annexation ordinance. All documents shall have an identifying number affixed thereto and shall conform in size in accordance with rules prescribed by the Secretary. Failure to file within 30 days shall not affect the validity of the annexation. Any annexation shall be reported as part of the Boundary and Annexation Survey of the United States Bureau of the Census. (1947, c. 725, s. 6; 1973, c. 426, s. 74; 1987, c. 715, s. 6, c. 879, s. 3; 1989, c. 440, s. 7; 1991, c. 586, s. 1.)

§ 160A-30. Surveys of proposed new areas.

The governing bodies of the cities and towns after five days' written notice to the owner of record or persons in possession of the premises are hereby authorized to enter upon any lands to make surveys or examinations as may be necessary in carrying out the mapping requirements of proposed annexations under any provision of Article 4A of Chapter 160A; provided, the city or town authorizing such entry shall make reimbursement for any damage resulting from such activity. (1947, c. 725, s. 7; 1973, c. 426, s. 74; 1975, c. 312.)

§ 160A-31. Annexation by petition.

(a) The governing board of any municipality may annex by ordinance any area contiguous to its boundaries upon presentation to the governing board of a petition signed by the owners of all the real property located within such area. The petition shall be signed by each owner of real property in the area and shall contain the address of each such owner.

(b) The petition shall be prepared in substantially the following form:

DATE:

To the _____ (name of governing board) of the (City or Town) of
_____

1. We the undersigned owners of real property respectfully request that the area described in paragraph 2 below be annexed to the (City or Town) of _____

2. The area to be annexed is contiguous to the (City or Town) of _____ and the boundaries of such territory are as follows:

(b1) Notwithstanding the provisions of subsections (a) and (b) of this section, if fifty-one percent (51%) of the households in an area petitioning for annexation pursuant to this section have incomes that are two hundred percent (200%) or less than the most recently published United States Census Bureau poverty thresholds, the governing board of any municipality shall annex by ordinance any area the population of which is no more than ten percent (10%) of that of the municipality and one-eighth of the aggregate external boundaries of which are contiguous to its boundaries, upon presentation to the governing board of a petition signed by the owners of at least seventy-five percent (75%) of the parcels of real property in that area. A municipality shall not be required to adopt more than one ordinance under this subsection within a 36-month period.

(b2) The petition under subsection (b1) of this section shall be prepared in substantially the following form:

DATE:

To the _____ (name of governing board) of the (City or Town) of
_____

1. We the undersigned owners of real property believe that the area described in paragraph 2 below meets the requirements of G.S. 160A-31(b1) and respectfully request that the area described in paragraph 2 below be annexed to the (City or Town) of _____.

2. The area to be annexed is contiguous to the (City or Town) of _____, and the boundaries of such territory are as follows:

(c) Upon receipt of the petition, the municipal governing board shall cause the clerk of the municipality to investigate the sufficiency thereof and to certify the result of the investigation. For petitions received under subsection (b1) or (j) of this section, the clerk shall receive the evidence provided under subsection (l) of this section before certifying the sufficiency of the petition. Upon receipt of the certification, the municipal governing board shall fix a date for a public hearing on the question of annexation, and shall cause notice of the public hearing to be published once in a newspaper having general circulation in the municipality at least 10 days prior to the date of the public hearing; provided, if there be no such paper, the governing board shall have notices posted in three or more public places within the area to be annexed and three or more public places within the municipality.

(d)   At the public hearing persons resident or owning property in the area described in the petition and persons resident or owning property in the municipality shall be given an opportunity to be heard. The governing board shall then determine whether the petition meets the requirements of this section. Upon a finding that the petition that was not submitted under subsection (b1) or (j) of this section meets the requirements of this section, the governing board shall have authority to pass an ordinance annexing the territory described in the petition. The governing board shall have authority to make the annexing ordinance effective immediately or on the June 30 after the date of the passage of the ordinance or the June 30 of the following year after the date of passage of the ordinance.

(d1)   Upon a finding that a petition submitted under subsection (j) of this section meets the requirements of this section, the governing body shall have the authority to adopt an annexation ordinance for the area with an effective date no later than 24 months after the adoption of the ordinance.

(d2)   Upon a finding that a petition submitted under subsection (b1) of this section meets the requirements of this section, the governing body shall, within 60 days of the finding, estimate the capital cost to the municipality of extending water and sewer lines to all parcels within the area covered by the petition and estimate the annual debt service payment that would be required if those costs were financed by a 20-year revenue bond. If the estimated annual debt service payment is less than five percent (5%) of the municipality's annual water and sewer systems revenue for the most recent fiscal year, then the governing body shall within 30 days adopt an annexation ordinance for the area with an effective date no later than 24 months after the adoption of the ordinance. If the estimated annual debt service payment is greater than or equal to five percent (5%) of the municipality's annual water and sewer systems revenue for the most recent fiscal year, then the governing body may adopt a resolution declining to annex the area. If such a resolution is adopted, the governing body shall immediately submit a request to the Local Government Commission to certify that its estimate of the annual debt service payment is reasonable based on established governmental accounting principles.

(1)   If the Local Government Commission certifies the estimate, the municipality is not required to annex the area and no petition to annex the area may be submitted under subsection (b1) of this section for 36 months following the certification. During the 36-month period, the municipality shall make ongoing, annual good faith efforts to secure Community Development Block Grants or other grant funding for extending water and sewer service to all parcels in the areas covered by the petition. If sufficient funding is secured so that the estimated capital cost to the municipality for extending water and sewer service, less the funds secured, would result in an annual debt service payment cost to the municipality of less than five percent (5%) of the municipality's annual water and sewer systems revenue for the most recent fiscal year, then the governing body shall within 30 days adopt an annexation ordinance for the area with an effective date no later than 24 months after the adoption of the ordinance.

(2)   If the Local Government Commission notifies the governing board that the estimates are not reasonable based on established governmental accounting principles and that a reasonable estimate of the annual debt service payment is less than five percent (5%) of the municipality's annual water and sewer systems revenue for the most recent fiscal year, then the governing body shall within 30 days of the notification adopt an annexation ordinance for the area with an effective date no later than 24 months after the adoption of the ordinance.

(d3)   Municipal services shall be provided to an area annexed under subsections (b1) and (j) of this section in accordance with the requirements of Part 7 of this Article.

(e)   From and after the effective date of the annexation ordinance, the territory and its citizens and property shall be subject to all debts, laws, ordinances and regulations in force in such municipality and shall be entitled to the same privileges and benefits as other parts of such municipality. Real and personal property in the newly annexed territory on the January 1 immediately preceding the beginning of the fiscal year in which the annexation becomes effective is subject to municipal taxes as provided in G.S. 160A-58.10. If the effective date of annexation falls between June 1 and June 30, and the effective date of the privilege license tax ordinance of the annexing municipality is June

1, then businesses in the area to be annexed shall be liable for taxes imposed in such ordinance from and after the effective date of annexation.

(f) For purposes of this section, an area shall be deemed "contiguous" if, at the time the petition is submitted, such area either abuts directly on the municipal boundary or is separated from the municipal boundary by the width of a street or street right-of-way, a creek or river, or the right-of-way of a railroad or other public service corporation, lands owned by the municipality or some other political subdivision, or lands owned by the State of North Carolina. A connecting corridor consisting solely of a street or street right-of-way may not be used to establish contiguity. In describing the area to be annexed in the annexation ordinance, the municipal governing board may include within the description any territory described in this subsection which separates the municipal boundary from the area petitioning for annexation.

(g) The governing board may initiate annexation of contiguous property owned by the municipality by adopting a resolution stating its intent to annex the property, in lieu of filing a petition. The resolution shall contain an adequate description of the property, state that the property is contiguous to the municipal boundaries and fix a date for a public hearing on the question of annexation. Notice of the public hearing shall be published as provided in subsection (c) of this section. The governing board may hold the public hearing and adopt the annexation ordinance as provided in subsection (d) of this section.

(h) A city council which receives a petition for annexation under this section may by ordinance require that the petitioners file a signed statement declaring whether or not vested rights with respect to the properties subject to the petition have been established under G.S. 160A-385.1 or G.S. 153A-344.1. If the statement declares that such rights have been established, the city may require petitioners to provide proof of such rights. A statement which declares that no vested rights have been established under G.S. 160A-385.1 or G.S. 153A-344.1 shall be binding on the landowner and any such vested right shall be terminated.

(i) A municipality has no authority to adopt a resolution or petition itself under this Part for annexation of property it does not own or have any legal interest in. For the purpose of this subsection, a municipality has no legal interest in a State-maintained street unless it owns the underlying fee and not just an easement.

(j) Using the procedures under this section, the governing board of any municipality may annex by ordinance any distressed area contiguous to its boundaries upon presentation to the governing board of a petition signed by at least one adult resident of at least two-thirds of the resident households located within such area. For purposes of this subsection, a "distressed area" is defined as an area in which at least fifty-one percent (51%) of the households in the area petitioning to be annexed have incomes that are two hundred percent (200%) or less than the most recently published United States Census Bureau poverty thresholds. The municipality may require reasonable proof that the petitioner in fact resides at the address indicated.

(k) The petition under subsection (j) of this section shall be prepared in substantially the following form:

DATE:

To the _____ (name of governing board) of the (City or Town) of _____

1. We the undersigned residents of real property believe that the area described in paragraph 2 below meets the requirements of G.S. 160A-31(j) and respectfully request that the area described in paragraph 2 below be annexed to the (City or Town) of _____.

2. The area to be annexed is contiguous to the (City or Town) of _____, and the boundaries of such territory are as follows:

(l) For purposes of determining whether the percentage of households in the area petitioning for annexation meets the poverty thresholds under subsections (b1) and (j) of this section, the petitioners shall submit to the municipal governing board any reasonable evidence that demonstrates the area in fact meets the income requirements of that subsection. The evidence presented may include data from the most recent federal decennial census, other official census documents, signed affidavits by at least one adult resident of the household attesting to the household size and income level, or any other documentation verifying the incomes for a majority of the households within the petitioning area. Petitioners may select to submit name, address, and social security number to the clerk, who shall in turn submit the information to the Department of Revenue. Such information shall be kept confidential and is not a public record. The Department shall provide the municipality with a summary report of income for households in the petitioning area. Information for the report shall be gleaned from income tax returns, but the report submitted to the municipality shall not identify individuals or households. (1947, c. 725, s. 8; 1959, c. 713; 1973, c. 426, s. 74; 1975, c. 576, s. 2; 1977, c. 517, s. 4; 1987, c. 562, s. 1; 1989 (Reg. Sess., 1990), c. 996, s. 3; 2011-57, s. 3; 2011-396, s. 10.)

§ 160A-31.1. Assumption of debt.

(a)   If the city has annexed under this Part any area which is served by a rural fire department and which is in:

(1)   An insurance district defined under G.S. 153A-233;

(2)   A rural fire protection district under Article 3A of Chapter 69 of the General Statutes; or

(3)   A fire service district under Article 16 of Chapter 153A of the General Statutes,

then beginning with the effective date of annexation the city shall pay annually a proportionate share of any payments due on any debt (including principal and interest) relating to facilities or equipment of the rural fire department, if the debt was existing at the time of submission of the petition for annexation to the city under this Part. The rural fire department shall make available to the city not later than 30 days following a written request from the city, information concerning such debt. The rural fire department forfeits its rights under this section if it fails to make a good faith response within 45 days following receipt of the written request for information from the city, provided that the city's written request so states by specific reference to this section.

(b)   The annual payments from the city to the rural fire department on such shared debt service shall be calculated as follows:

(1)   The rural fire department shall certify to the city each year the amount that will be expended for debt service subject to be shared by the city as provided by subsection (a) of this section; and

(2)   The amount determined under subdivision (1) of this subsection shall be multiplied by the percentage determined by dividing the assessed valuation of the area of the district annexed by the assessed valuation of the entire district,

each such valuation to be fixed as of the date the annexation ordinance becomes effective.

(c)   This section does not apply in any year as to any annexed area(s) for which the payment calculated under this section as to all annexation ordinances adopted under this Part by a city during a particular calendar year does not exceed one hundred dollars ($100.00).

(d)   The city and rural fire department shall jointly present a payment schedule to the Local Government Commission for approval and no payment may be made until such schedule is approved. The Local Government Commission shall approve a payment schedule agreed upon between the city and the rural fire department in cases where the assessed valuation of the district may not readily be determined, if there is a reasonable basis for the agreement. (1989, c. 598, s. 2.)

§ 160A-32. Repealed by Session Laws 1983, c. 636, s. 26.1, effective June 29, 1983.

Part 2. Annexation by Cities of Less Than 5,000.

§ 160A-33: Repealed by Session Laws 2011-396, s. 1, effective July 1, 2011. For applicability, see editor's note.

§ 160A-34: Repealed by Session Laws 2011-396, s. 1, effective July 1, 2011. For applicability, see editor's note.

§ 160A-35: Repealed by Session Laws 2011-396, s. 1, effective July 1, 2011. For applicability, see editor's note.

§ 160A-35.1: Repealed by Session Laws 2011-396, s. 1, effective July 1, 2011. For applicability, see editor's note.

§ 160A-36: Repealed by Session Laws 2011-396, s. 1, effective July 1, 2011. For applicability, see editor's note.

§ 160A-37: Repealed by Session Laws 2011-396, s. 1, effective July 1, 2011. For applicability, see editor's note.

§ 160A-37.1: Repealed by Session Laws 2011-396, s. 1, effective July 1, 2011. For applicability, see editor's note.

§ 160A-37.2: Repealed by Session Laws 2011-396, s. 1, effective July 1, 2011. For applicability, see editor's note.

§ 160A-37.3: Repealed by Session Laws 2011-396, s. 1, effective July 1, 2011. For applicability, see editor's note.

§ 160A-38: Repealed by Session Laws 2011-396, s. 1, effective July 1, 2011. For applicability, see editor's note.

§ 160A-39: Repealed by Session Laws 2011-396, s. 1, effective July 1, 2011. For applicability, see editor's note.

§ 160A-40: Repealed by Session Laws 2011-396, s. 1, effective July 1, 2011. For applicability, see editor's note.

§ 160A-41: Repealed by Session Laws 2011-396, s. 1, effective July 1, 2011. For applicability, see editor's note.

§ 160A-42: Repealed by Session Laws 2011-396, s. 1, effective July 1, 2011. For applicability, see editor's note.

§§ 160A-43 through 160A-44. Repealed by Session Laws 1983, c. 636, s. 27, effective June 29, 1983.

§ 160A-45: Repealed by Session Laws 2011-396, s. 7, effective July 1, 2011. For applicability, see editor's note.

§ 160A-46: Repealed by Session Laws 2011-396, s. 7, effective July 1, 2011. For applicability, see editor's note.

§ 160A-47: Repealed by Session Laws 2011-396, s. 7, effective July 1, 2011. For applicability, see editor's note.

§ 160A-47.1: Repealed by Session Laws 2011-396, s. 7, effective July 1, 2011. For applicability, see editor's note.

§ 160A-48: Repealed by Session Laws 2011-396, s. 7, effective July 1, 2011. For applicability, see editor's note.

§ 160A-49: Repealed by Session Laws 2011-396, s. 7, effective July 1, 2011. For applicability, see editor's note.

§ 160A-49.1: Recodified to G.S. 160A-58.57 by Session Laws 2011-396, s. 2, effective July 1, 2011.

§ 160A-49.2: Recodified to G.S. 160A-58.58 by Session Laws 2011-396, s. 3, effective July 1, 2011.

§ 160A-49.3: Recodified to G.S. 160A-58.59 by Session Laws 2011-396, s. 4, effective July 1, 2011.

§ 160A-50: Repealed by Session Laws 2011-396, s. 7, effective July 1, 2011. For applicability, see editor's note.

§ 160A-51: Recodified to G.S. 160A-58.61 by Session Laws 2011-396, s. 5, effective July 1, 2011.

§ 160A-52: Recodified to G.S. 160A-58.62 by Session Laws 2011-396, s. 6, effective July 1, 2011.

§ 160A-53: Repealed by Session Laws 2011-396, s. 7, effective July 1, 2011. For applicability, see editor's note.

§ 160A-54: Repealed by Session Laws 2011-396, s. 7, effective July 1, 2011. For applicability, see editor's note.

§§ 160A-55 through 160A-56. Repealed by Session Laws 1983, c. 636, s. 27, effective June 29, 1983.

§ 160A-57. Reserved for future codification purposes.

Part 4. Annexation of Noncontiguous Areas.

§ 160A-58. Definitions.

The words and phrases defined in this section have the meanings indicated when used in this Part unless the context clearly requires another meaning:

(1)   "City" means any city, town, or village without regard to population, except cities not qualified to receive gasoline tax allocations under G.S. 136-41.2.

(2)   "Primary corporate limits" means the corporate limits of a city as defined in its charter, enlarged or diminished by subsequent annexations or exclusions of contiguous territory pursuant to Parts 1, 2, and 3 of this Article or local acts of the General Assembly.

(3)   "Satellite corporate limits" means the corporate limits of a noncontiguous area annexed pursuant to this Part or a local act authorizing or effecting noncontiguous annexations. (1973, c. 1173, s. 2.)

§ 160A-58.1. Petition for annexation; standards.

(a)   Upon receipt of a valid petition signed by all of the owners of real property in the area described therein, a city may annex an area not contiguous to its primary corporate limits when the area meets the standards set out in subsection (b) of this section. The petition need not be signed by the owners of real property that is wholly exempt from property taxation under the Constitution and laws of North Carolina, nor by railroad companies, public utilities as defined in G.S. 62-3(23), or electric or telephone membership corporations. A petition is not valid in any of the following circumstances:

(1)   It is unsigned.

(2)   It is signed by the city for the annexation of property the city does not own or have a legal interest in. For the purpose of this subdivision, a city has no legal interest in a State-maintained street unless it owns the underlying fee and not just an easement.

(3) It is for the annexation of property for which a signature is not required and the property owner objects to the annexation.

(b) A noncontiguous area proposed for annexation must meet all of the following standards:

(1) The nearest point on the proposed satellite corporate limits must be not more than three miles from the primary corporate limits of the annexing city.

(2) No point on the proposed satellite corporate limits may be closer to the primary corporate limits of another city than to the primary corporate limits of the annexing city, except as set forth in subsection (b2) of this section.

(3) The area must be so situated that the annexing city will be able to provide the same services within the proposed satellite corporate limits that it provides within its primary corporate limits.

(4) If the area proposed for annexation, or any portion thereof, is a subdivision as defined in G.S. 160A-376, all of the subdivision must be included.

(5) The area within the proposed satellite corporate limits, when added to the area within all other satellite corporate limits, may not exceed ten percent (10%) of the area within the primary corporate limits of the annexing city.

This subdivision does not apply to the Cities of Belmont, Claremont, Concord, Conover, Durham, Elizabeth City, Gastonia, Greenville, Hickory, Kannapolis, Locust, Marion, Mount Airy, Mount Holly, New Bern, Newton, Oxford, Randleman, Roanoke Rapids, Rockingham, Sanford, Salisbury, Southport, Statesville, and Washington and the Towns of Ahoskie, Angier, Apex, Ayden, Benson, Bladenboro, Bridgeton, Burgaw, Calabash, Catawba, Clayton, Columbia, Columbus, Cramerton, Creswell, Dallas, Dobson, Four Oaks, Fuquay-Varina, Garner, Godwin, Granite Quarry, Green Level, Grimesland, Holly Ridge, Holly Springs, Hookerton, Huntersville, Jamestown, Kenansville, Kenly, Knightdale, Landis, Leland, Lillington, Louisburg, Maggie Valley, Maiden, Mayodan, Maysville, Middlesex, Midland, Mocksville, Morrisville, Mount Pleasant, Nashville, Oak Island, Ocean Isle Beach, Pembroke, Pine Level, Princeton, Ranlo, Richlands, Rolesville, Rutherfordton, Shallotte, Smithfield, Spencer, Stem, Stovall, Surf City, Swansboro, Taylorsville, Troutman, Troy, Wallace, Warsaw, Watha, Waynesville, Weldon, Wendell, Windsor, Yadkinville, and Zebulon.

(b1) Repealed by Session Laws 2004-203, ss. 13(a) and 13(d), effective August 17, 2004.

(b2) A city may annex a noncontiguous area that does not meet the standard set out in subdivision (b)(2) of this section if the city has entered into an annexation agreement pursuant to Part 6 of this Article with the city to which a point on the proposed satellite corporate limits is closer and the agreement states that the other city will not annex the area but does not say that the annexing city will not annex the area. The annexing city shall comply with all other requirements of this section.

(c) The petition shall contain the names, addresses, and signatures of all owners of real property within the proposed satellite corporate limits (except owners not required to sign by subsection (a)), shall describe the area proposed for annexation by metes and bounds, and shall have attached thereto a map showing the area proposed for annexation with relation to the primary corporate limits of the annexing city. When there is any substantial question as to whether the area may be closer to another city than to the annexing city, the map shall also show the area proposed for annexation with relation to the primary corporate limits of the other city. The city council may prescribe the form of the petition.

(d) A city council which receives a petition for annexation under this section may by ordinance require that the petitioners file a signed statement declaring whether or not vested rights with respect to the properties subject to the petition have been established under G.S. 160A-385.1 or G.S. 153A-344.1. If the statement declares that such rights have been established, the city may require petitioners to provide proof of such rights. A statement which declares that no vested rights have been established under G.S. 160A-385.1 or G.S. 153A-344.1 shall be binding on the landowner and any such vested rights shall be terminated. (1973, c. 1173, s. 2; 1989 (Reg. Sess., 1990), c. 996, s. 4; 1997-2, s. 1; 2001-37, s. 1; 2001-72, s. 1; 2001-438, s. 1; 2002-121, s. 1; 2003-30, s. 1; 2004-203, s. 13(a), (c); 2004-57, s. 1; 2004-99, s. 1; 2004-203, ss. 13(a)-(d); 2005-52, s. 1; 2005-71, s. 1; 2005-79, s. 1; 2005-173, s. 1; 2005-433, s. 9; 2006-62, s. 1; 2006-122, s. 1; 2006-130, s. 1; 2007-17, s. 1; 2007-26, ss. 1, 2(a); 2007-62, s. 1; 2007-225, s. 1; 2007-311, s. 1; 2007-342, s. 1; 2008-24, s. 1; 2008-30, s. 1; 2009-40, s. 2; 2009-53, s. 1; 2009-111, s. 1; 2009-156, s. 1; 2009-298, s. 1; 2009-323, s. 1; 2011-57, s. 1; 2012-96, s. 1; 2013-248, s. 1.)

§ 160A-58.2. Public hearing.

Upon receipt of a petition for annexation under this Part, the city council shall cause the city clerk to investigate the petition, and to certify the results of his investigation. If the clerk certifies that upon investigation the petition appears to be valid, the council shall fix a date for a public hearing on the annexation. Notice of the hearing shall be published once at least 10 days before the date of hearing.

At the hearing, any person residing in or owning property in the area proposed for annexation and any resident of the annexing city may appear and be heard on the questions of the sufficiency of the petition and the desirability of the annexation. If the council then finds and determines that (i) the area described in the petition meets all of the standards set out in G.S. 160A-58.1(b), (ii) the petition bears the signatures of all of the owners of real property within the area proposed for annexation (except those not required to sign by G.S. 160A-58.1(a)), (iii) the petition is otherwise valid, and (iv) the public health, safety and welfare of the inhabitants of the city and of the area proposed for annexation will be best served by the annexation, the council may adopt an ordinance annexing the area described in the petition. The ordinance may be made effective immediately or on any specified date within six months from the date of passage. (1973, c. 1173, s. 2.)

§ 160A-58.2A. Assumption of debt.

(a) If the city has annexed under this Part any area which is served by a rural fire department and which is in:

(1) An insurance district defined under G.S. 153A-233;

(2) A rural fire protection district under Article 3A of Chapter 69 of the General Statutes; or

(3) A fire service district under Article 16 of Chapter 153A of the General Statutes,

then beginning with the effective date of annexation the city shall pay annually a proportionate share of any payments due on any debt (including principal and interest) relating to facilities or equipment of the rural fire department, if the debt was existing at the time of submission of the petition for annexation to the city under this Part. The rural fire department shall make available to the city not later than 30 days following a written request from the city, information concerning such debt. The rural fire department forfeits its rights under this section if it fails to make a good faith response within 45 days following receipt of the written request for information from the city, provided that the city's written request so states by specific reference to this section.

(b) The annual payments from the city to the rural fire department on such shared debt service shall be calculated as follows:

(1) The rural fire department shall certify to the city each year the amount that will be expended for debt service subject to be shared by the city as provided by subsection (a) of this section; and

(2) The amount determined under subdivision (1) of this subsection shall be multiplied by the percentage determined by dividing the assessed valuation of the area of the district annexed by the assessed valuation of the entire district, each such valuation to be fixed as of the date the annexation ordinance becomes effective.

(c) This section does not apply in any year as to any annexed area(s) for which the payment calculated under this section as to all annexation ordinances adopted under this Part by a city during a particular calendar year does not exceed one hundred dollars ($100.00).

(d) The city and rural fire department shall jointly present a payment schedule to the Local Government Commission for approval and no payment may be made until such schedule is approved. The Local Government Commission shall approve a payment schedule agreed upon between the city and the rural fire department in cases where the assessed valuation of the district may not readily be determined, if there is a reasonable basis for the agreement. (1989, c. 598, s. 3.)

§ 160A-58.3. Annexed area subject to city taxes and debts.

From and after the effective date of the annexation ordinance, the annexed area and its citizens and property are subject to all debts, laws, ordinances and regulations of the annexing city, and are entitled to the same privileges and benefits as other parts of the city. Real and personal property in the newly annexed territory on the January 1 immediately preceding the beginning of the fiscal year in which the annexation becomes effective is subject to municipal taxes as provided in G.S. 160A-58.10. If the effective date of annexation falls between June 1 and June 30, and the privilege licenses of the annexing city are due on June 1, then businesses in the annexed area are liable for privilege license taxes at the full-year rate. (1973, c. 1173, s. 2; 1975, c. 576, s. 5; 1977, c. 517, s. 7.)

§ 160A-58.4. Extraterritorial powers.

Satellite corporate limits shall not be considered a part of the city's corporate limits for the purposes of extraterritorial land-use regulation pursuant to G.S. 160A-360, or abatement of public health nuisances pursuant to G.S. 160A-193. However, a city's power to regulate land use pursuant to Chapter 160A, Article 19, or to abate public health nuisances pursuant to G.S. 160A-193, shall be the same within satellite corporate limits as within its primary corporate limits. (1973, c. 1173, s. 2.)

§ 160A-58.5. Special rates for water, sewer and other enterprises.

For the purposes of G.S. 160A-314, provision of public enterprise services within satellite corporate limits shall be considered provision of service for special classes of service distinct from the classes of service provided within the primary corporate limits of the city, and the city may fix and enforce schedules of rents, rates, fees, charges and penalties in excess of those fixed and enforced within the primary corporate limits. A city providing enterprise services within satellite corporate limits shall annually review the cost thereof, and shall take such steps as may be necessary to insure that the current operating costs of such services, excluding debt service on bonds issued to finance services within satellite corporate limits, does not exceed revenues realized therefrom. (1973, c. 1173, s. 2.)

§ 160A-58.6. Transition from satellite to primary corporate limits.

An area annexed pursuant to this Part ceases to constitute satellite corporate limits and becomes a part of the primary corporate limits of a city when, through annexation of intervening territory, the two boundaries touch. (1973, c. 1173, s. 2.)

§ 160A-58.7. Annexation of municipal property.

(a) The city council may initiate annexation of property not contiguous to the primary corporate limits and owned by the city by adopting a resolution stating its intent to annex the property, in lieu of filing a petition. The property must satisfy the requirements of G.S. 160A-58.1. The resolution shall contain an adequate description of the property and fix a date for a public hearing on the question of annexation. Notice of the public hearing shall be published once at least 10 days before the date of the hearing. At the hearing, any resident of the city may appear and be heard on the question of the desirability of the annexation. If the council finds that annexation is in the public interest, it may adopt an ordinance annexing the property. The ordinance may be made effective immediately or on any specified date within six months from the date of passage.

(b) A city has no authority to adopt a resolution or petition itself under this Part for annexation of property it does not own or have any legal interest in. For the purpose of this subsection, a city has no legal interest in a State-maintained street unless it owns the underlying fee and not just an easement. (1987, c. 562, s. 2; 2011-57, s. 2.)

§ 160A-58.8. Recording and Reporting.

Annexations made under this part shall be recorded and reported in the same manner as under G.S. 160A-29. (1987, c. 879, s. 4.)

Part 4A. Effective Dates of Certain Annexation Ordinances.

§ 160A-58.9. Effective date of certain annexation ordinances adopted from January 1, 1987, to August 3, 1987.

(a) In the case of any annexation ordinance adopted during the period beginning January 1, 1987, and ending on August 3, 1987, if the effective date of the annexation under the ordinance is during 1988, the governing board of the municipality may, notwithstanding G.S. 160A-37(j) or G.S. 160A-49(j), amend the ordinance to provide for an effective date of December 31, 1987. The board must give notice by publication of its intent to consider adoption of such ordinance, such notice to be published at least 10 days before the meeting at which the ordinance is adopted. Copies of the adopted ordinance shall be recorded in accordance with the provisions of G.S. 160A-39 or G.S. 160A-51, as applicable.

(b) This section applies only to territory located in counties with a population of 55,000 or over, according to the 1980 decennial federal census. (1987, c. 715, s. 2.)

§ 160A-58.9A. Effective date of certain annexation ordinances adopted under Article 4A of Chapter 160A.

(a) No annexation ordinance adopted under Article 4A of Chapter 160A of the General Statutes may become effective during the period beginning November 1, 1989, and ending January 1, 1990. If because of the operation of G.S. 160A-37.1(h), G.S. 160A-37.3(g), G.S. 160A-38, G.S. 160A-58.57(h), G.S. 160A-58.59(g), G.S. 160A-50, the order of any court, or the operation of Section 5 of the Voting Rights Act of 1965, an annexation ordinance is to become effective during the period beginning November 1, 1989, and ending January 1, 1990, it shall instead become effective on a date during the period beginning January 2, 1990, and ending December 31, 1990, set by ordinance of the governing board of the city.

(b) If the final date upon which an annexation ordinance adopted under Article 4A of Chapter 160A of the General Statutes, may be made effective occurs during the period beginning November 1, 1989, and ending January 1, 1990, the effective date of the annexation may be set in the annexation ordinance as any date during the period beginning January 2, 1990, and ending December 31, 1990, in addition to any date permitted by law before November 1, 1989.

(c) This section applies to territory located in counties with a population of 55,000 or over, according to the 1980 decennial federal census, and to territory located in all other counties subject to Article 12A of Chapter 163 of the General Statutes, pursuant to G.S. 163-132.6. (1987, c. 715, s. 3; 1989, c. 440, s. 6.)

Part 5. Property Tax Liability of Newly Annexed Territory.

§ 160A-58.10. Tax of newly annexed territory.

(a) Applicability of Section. - Real and personal property in territory annexed pursuant to this Article is subject to municipal taxes as provided in this section.

(b) Prorated Taxes. - Real and personal property in the newly annexed territory on the January 1 immediately preceding the beginning of the fiscal year in which the annexation becomes effective is subject to prorated municipal taxes levied for that fiscal year as provided in this subsection. The amount of municipal taxes that would have been due on the property had it been within the municipality for the full fiscal year shall be multiplied by the following fraction: the denominator shall be 12 and the numerator shall be the number of full calendar months remaining in the fiscal year, following the day on which the annexation becomes effective. The product of the multiplication is the amount of prorated taxes due. The lien for prorated taxes levied on a parcel of real property shall attach to the parcel taxed on the listing date, as provided in G.S. 105-285, immediately preceding the fiscal year in which the annexation becomes effective. The lien for prorated taxes levied on personal property shall attach on the same date to all real property of the taxpayer in the taxing unit, including the newly annexed territory. If the annexation becomes effective after June 30 and before September 2, the prorated taxes shall be due and payable on the first day of September of the fiscal year for which the taxes are levied. If the annexation becomes effective after September 1 and before the following July 1, the prorated taxes shall be due and payable on the first day of September of the next succeeding fiscal year. The prorated taxes are subject to collection and foreclosure in the same manner as other taxes levied for the fiscal year in which the prorated taxes become due.

(c) Taxes in Subsequent Fiscal Years. - In fiscal years subsequent to the fiscal year in which an annexation becomes effective, real and personal property in the newly annexed territory is subject to municipal taxes on the same basis as is the preexisting territory of the municipality.

(d) Transfer of Tax Records. - For purposes of levying prorated taxes the municipality shall obtain from the county a record of property in the area being annexed that was listed for taxation on the January 1 immediately preceding the fiscal year for which the prorated taxes are levied. In addition, if the effective date of annexation falls between January 1 and June 30, the municipality shall, for purposes of levying taxes for the fiscal year beginning July 1 following the date of annexation, obtain from the county a record of property in the area being annexed that was listed for taxation as of said January 1. (1977, c. 517, s. 9.)

§§ 160A-58.11 through 160A-58.20. Reserved for future codification purposes.

Part 6. Annexation Agreements.

§ 160A-58.21. Purpose.

It is the purpose of this Part to authorize cities to enter into binding agreements concerning future annexation in order to enhance orderly planning by such cities as well as residents and property owners in areas adjacent to such cities. (1989, c. 143, s. 1.)

§ 160A-58.22. Definitions.

The words defined in this section shall have the meanings indicated when used in this Part:

(1)   "Agreement" means any written agreement authorized by this Part.

(2)   "Annexation" means any extension of a city's corporate limits as authorized by this Article, the charter of the city, or any local act applicable to the city, as such statutory authority exists now or is hereafter amended.

(3)   "Participating city" means any city which is a party to an agreement. (1989, c. 143, s. 1.)

§ 160A-58.23. Annexation agreements authorized.

Two or more cities may enter into agreements in order to designate one or more areas which are not subject to annexation by one or more of the participating cities. The agreements shall be of reasonable duration, not to exceed 20 years, and shall be approved by ordinance of the governing board and executed by the mayor of each city and spread upon its minutes. (1989, c. 143, s. 1.)

§ 160A-58.24. Contents of agreements; procedure.

(a)   The agreement shall:

(1) State the duration of the agreement.

(2) Describe clearly the area or areas subject to the agreement. The boundaries of such area or areas may be established at such locations as the participating cities shall agree. Thereafter, any participating city may follow such boundaries in annexing any property, whether or not such boundaries follow roads or natural topographical features.

(3) Specify one or more participating cities which may not annex the area or areas described in the agreement.

(4) State the effective date of the agreement.

(5) Require each participating city which proposes any annexation to give written notice to the other participating city or cities of the annexation at least 60 days before the adoption of any annexation ordinance; provided, however, that the agreement may provide for a waiver of this time period by the notified city.

(6) Include any other necessary or proper matter.

(b) The written notice required by subdivision (a)(5) of this section shall describe the area to be annexed by a legible map, clearly and accurately showing the boundaries of the area to be annexed in relation to: the area or areas described pursuant to subdivision (a)(2) of this section, roads, streams and any other prominent geographical features. Such notice shall not be effective for more than 180 days.

(c) No agreement may be entered into under this Part unless each participating city has held a public hearing on the agreement prior to adopting the ordinance approving the agreement. The governing boards of the participating cities may hold a joint public hearing if desired. Notice of the public hearing or hearings shall be given as provided in G.S. 160A-31(c).

(d) Any agreement entered into under this Part may be modified or terminated by a subsequent agreement entered into by all the participating cities to that agreement. The subsequent agreement shall be approved by ordinance after a public hearing or hearings as provided in subsection (c).

(e) No agreement entered into under this Part shall be binding beyond three miles of the primary corporate limits of a participating city which is permitted to annex the area under the agreement, unless approved by the board of county commissioners with jurisdiction over the area. Provided however, that an area where the agreement is not binding because of failure of the board of county commissioners to approve it, shall become subject to the agreement if subsequent annexation brings it within three miles. The approval of a board of county commissioners shall be evidenced by a resolution adopted after a public hearing as provided in subsection (c).

(f) A participating city may terminate an annexation agreement unilaterally or withdraw itself from the agreement, by repealing the ordinance by which it approved the agreement and providing five years' written notice to the other participating cities. Upon the expiration of the five-year period, an agreement originally involving only two cities shall terminate, and an agreement originally involving more than two cities shall terminate unless each of the other participating cities shall have adopted an ordinance reaffirming the agreement. (1989, c. 143, s. 1.)

§ 160A-58.25. Effect of agreement.

From and after the effective date of an agreement, no participating city may adopt an annexation ordinance as to all or any portion of an area in violation of the agreement. (1989, c. 143, s. 1.)

§ 160A-58.26. Part grants no annexation authority.

Nothing in this Part shall be construed to authorize the annexation of any area which is not otherwise subject to annexation under applicable law. (1989, c. 143, s. 1.)

§ 160A-58.27. Relief.

(a) Each provision of an agreement shall be binding upon the respective parties. Not later than 30 days following the passage of an annexation ordinance concerning territory subject to an agreement, a participating city which believes that another participating city has violated this Part or the agreement may file a petition in the superior court of the county where any of the territory proposed to be annexed is located, seeking review of the action of the city alleged to have violated this Part or the agreement.

(b) Within five days after the petition is filed with the court, the petitioning city shall serve copies of the petition by certified mail, return receipt requested, upon the respondent city.

(c) Within 15 days after receipt of the copy of the petition for review, or within such additional time as the court may allow, the respondent city shall transmit to the reviewing court:

(1) A transcript of the portions of the ordinance or minute book in which the procedure for annexation has been set forth;

(2) A copy of resolutions, ordinances, and any other document received or approved by the respondent city's governing board as part of the annexation proceeding.

(d) The court shall fix the date for review of the petition so that review shall be expeditious and without unnecessary delays. The review shall be conducted by the court without a jury. The court may hear oral arguments and receive written briefs, and may take evidence intended to show either:

(1) That the provisions of this Part were not met; or

(2) That the provisions of the agreement were not met.

(e) At any time before or during the review proceeding, any petitioner may apply to the reviewing court for an order staying the operation of the annexation ordinance pending the outcome of the review. The court may grant or deny the stay in its discretion upon such terms as it deems proper, and it may permit annexation of any part of the area described in the ordinance concerning which no question for review has been raised.

(f) Upon a finding that the respondent city has not violated this Part or the agreement, the court may affirm the action of the respondent city without change. Upon a finding that the respondent city has violated this Part or the agreement, the court may:

(1) Remand to the respondent city's governing board any ordinance adopted pursuant to Parts 2 or 3 of this Article, as the same exists now or is hereafter amended, for amendment of the boundaries, or for such other action as is necessary, to conform to the provisions of this Part and the agreement.

(2) Declare any annexation begun pursuant to any other applicable law to be void. If the respondent city shall fail to take action in accordance with the court's instructions upon remand under subdivision (d)(1) of this section within three months from receipt of such instructions, the annexation proceeding shall be void.

(g) Any participating city which is a party to the review proceedings may appeal from the final judgment of the superior court under rules of procedure applicable in other civil cases. The appealing party may apply to superior court for a stay in its final determination, or a stay of the annexation ordinance, whichever shall be appropriate, pending the outcome of the appeal to the appellate division; provided, that the superior court may, with the agreement of the parties, permit annexation to be effective with respect to any part of the area concerning which no appeal is being made and which can be incorporated into the respondent city without regard to any part of the area concerning which an appeal is being made.

(h) If part or all of the area annexed under the terms of a challenged annexation ordinance is the subject of an appeal to the superior court or appellate division on the effective date of the ordinance, then the ordinance shall be deemed amended to make the effective date with respect to such area the date of the final judgment of the superior court or appellate division, whichever is appropriate, or the date the respondent city's governing board completes action to make the ordinance conform to the court's instructions in the event of remand.

(i) A participating city which is prohibited from annexing into an area under a binding agreement may file a petition in the superior court where any of the territory proposed to be annexed is located, or a response in a proceeding initiated by another participating city, seeking permission to annex territory in the area notwithstanding the agreement. If the territory qualifies for annexation by the city seeking to annex it, the court may enter an order allowing the annexation to proceed with respect to all or a portion of the territory upon a finding that there is an imminent threat to public health or safety that can be remedied only by the city seeking annexation. The procedural provisions of this section shall apply to proceedings under this subsection, so far as applicable. (1989, c. 143, s. 1.)

§ 160A-58.28. Effect on prior local acts.

This Part does not affect Chapter 953, Session Laws of 1983, Chapter 847, Session Laws of 1985 (1986 Regular Session), or Chapters 204, 233, or 1009, Session Laws of 1987, authorizing annexation agreements, but any city which is authorized to enter into agreements by one of those acts may enter into future agreements either under such act or this Part. (1989, c. 143, s. 1; 1991 (Reg. Sess., 1992), c. 1030, s. 48.)

§ 160A-58.29: Reserved for future codification purposes.

§ 160A-58.30: Reserved for future codification purposes.

§ 160A-58.31: Reserved for future codification purposes.

§ 160A-58.32: Reserved for future codification purposes.

§ 160A-58.33: Reserved for future codification purposes.

§ 160A-58.34: Reserved for future codification purposes.

§ 160A-58.35: Reserved for future codification purposes.

§ 160A-58.36: Reserved for future codification purposes.

§ 160A-58.37: Reserved for future codification purposes.

§ 160A-58.38: Reserved for future codification purposes.

§ 160A-58.39: Reserved for future codification purposes.

§ 160A-58.40: Reserved for future codification purposes.

§ 160A-58.41: Reserved for future codification purposes.

§ 160A-58.42: Reserved for future codification purposes.

§ 160A-58.43: Reserved for future codification purposes.

§ 160A-58.44: Reserved for future codification purposes.

§ 160A-58.45: Reserved for future codification purposes.

§ 160A-58.46: Reserved for future codification purposes.

§ 160A-58.47: Reserved for future codification purposes.

§ 160A-58.48: Reserved for future codification purposes.

§ 160A-58.49: Reserved for future codification purposes.

Part 7. Annexations Initiated by Municipalities.

§ 160A-58.50. Declaration of policy.

It is hereby declared as a matter of State policy:

(1)   That sound urban development is essential to the continued economic development of North Carolina.

(2)   That municipalities are created to provide the governmental services essential for sound urban development and for the protection of health, safety, and welfare in areas being intensively used for residential, commercial, industrial, institutional, and governmental purposes or in areas undergoing such development.

(3)   That municipal boundaries should be extended in accordance with legislative standards applicable throughout the State to include such areas and to provide the high quality of governmental services needed therein for the public health, safety, and welfare.

(4)   That areas annexed to municipalities in accordance with such uniform legislative standards should receive the services provided by the annexing municipality.

(5)   That the provision of services to protect the health, safety, and welfare is a public purpose.

(6)   That it is essential for citizens to have an effective voice in annexations initiated by municipalities. (2011-396, s. 9.)

§ 160A-58.51. Definitions.

As used in this Part, the following definitions apply:

(1) Contiguous area. - Any area which, at the time annexation procedures are initiated, either abuts directly on the municipal boundary or is separated from the municipal boundary by a street or street right-of-way, a creek or river, the right-of-way of a railroad or other public service corporation, lands owned by the municipality or some other political subdivision, or lands owned by the State of North Carolina. A connecting corridor consisting solely of the length of a street or street right-of-way may not be used to establish contiguity.

(2) Eligible property owner. - A property owner who is eligible to be notified of the opportunity to have water lines and sewer lines and connections installed at no cost to the property owner. A property owner is eligible to be notified of the opportunity to have water lines and sewer lines and connections installed at no cost to the property owner if that property owner held a freehold interest in the real property to be annexed as of the date of the combined notice of public informational meeting and public hearing.

(3) Necessary land connection. - An area that does not exceed twenty-five percent (25%) of the total area to be annexed.

(4) Property owner. - Any person having a freehold interest in real property.

(5) Used for residential purposes. - Any lot or tract five acres or less in size on which is constructed a habitable dwelling unit. The term also includes any lot or tract that is used in common for social or recreational purposes by either owners of lots with habitable dwelling units or owners of lots intended for occupation by dwelling units and the lot owners have a real property interest in the commonly used property that attaches to or is appurtenant to the owners' lots. (2011-396, s. 9; 2012-11, s. 4.)

§ 160A-58.52. Authority to annex.

The governing board of any municipality may extend the corporate limits of such municipality under the procedure set forth in this Part. (2011-396, s. 9.)

§ 160A-58.53. Prerequisites to annexation.

A municipality exercising authority under this Part shall make plans for the extension of services to the area proposed to be annexed and shall, prior to the public hearing provided for in G.S. 160A-58.55, prepare a report setting forth such plans to provide services to the area proposed to be annexed. The report shall include the following:

(1) A map or maps of the municipality and adjacent territory to show the following information:

a. The present and proposed boundaries of the municipality.

b. The present major trunk water mains and sewer interceptors and outfalls, and the proposed extensions of such mains, outfalls, and lines as required in subdivision (3) of this section. The water and sewer map shall bear the seal of a registered professional engineer.

c. The general land use pattern in the area proposed to be annexed.

(2) A statement showing that the area proposed to be annexed meets the requirements of G.S. 160A-58.54.

(3) A statement setting forth the plans for extending to the area proposed to be annexed each major municipal service on substantially the same basis and in the same manner as such services are provided within the rest of the municipality prior to annexation and the method to finance the extension of major municipal services into the area proposed to be annexed as follows:

a. Provision of police protection, fire protection, solid waste collection, and street maintenance services on the effective date of annexation. A contract with a rural fire department to provide fire protection shall be an acceptable method of providing fire protection. A contract with a private firm to provide solid waste collection services shall be an acceptable method of providing solid waste collection services.

b. Extension of water and sewer services to each lot or parcel, if an installation easement is provided by the affected property owner, with a proposed timetable for construction of such mains, outfalls, and lines within three and one-half years of the effective date of annexation, in accordance with G.S. 160A-58.56.

(4) A statement of the impact of the annexation on any rural fire department providing service in the area proposed to be annexed and a statement of the impact of the annexation on fire protection and fire insurance rates in the area proposed to be annexed, if the area where service is provided is in an insurance district designated under G.S. 153A-233, a rural fire protection district under Article 3A of Chapter 69 of the General Statutes, or a fire service district under Article 16 of Chapter 153A of the General Statutes. The rural fire department shall make available to the municipality not later than 30 days following a written request from the municipality all information in its possession or control, including operational, financial, and budgetary information, necessary for preparation of a statement of impact. The municipality shall, in a timely fashion, supply the rural fire department with information requested by the rural fire department to respond to the written request. The rural fire department forfeits its rights under G.S. 160A-58.57 if it fails to make a good faith response within 45 days following receipt of the written request for information from the municipality, provided that the municipality's written request so states by specific reference to this subdivision.

(5) A statement showing how the proposed annexation will affect the municipality's finances and services, including municipal revenue change estimates. This statement shall be delivered to the clerk of the board of county commissioners at least 30 days before the date of the public informational meeting on any annexation under this Part. (2011-396, s. 9.)

§ 160A-58.54. Character of area to be annexed.

(a) A municipal governing board may extend the municipal corporate limits to include any area that meets all of the following criteria:

(1) It shall be adjacent or contiguous to the municipality's boundaries at the time the annexation proceeding is begun, except if the entire territory of a county water and sewer district created under G.S. 162A-86(b1) is being annexed, the annexation shall also include any noncontiguous pieces of the district as long as the part of the district with the greatest land area is adjacent or contiguous to the municipality's boundaries at the time the annexation proceeding is begun.

(2) At least one-eighth of the aggregate external boundaries of the area shall coincide with the municipal boundary.

(3) No part of the area shall be included within the boundary of another incorporated municipality.

(4) The total area to be annexed shall meet the requirements of any of the following:

a. Part or all of the area to be annexed must be developed for urban purposes at the time of approval of the report provided for in G.S. 160A-58.53. The area of streets and street rights-of-way shall not be used to determine total acreage under this subdivision. An area developed for urban purposes is defined as any area which meets any one of the following standards:

1. Has a total resident population equal to at least two and three-tenths persons for each acre of land included within its boundaries.

2. Has a total resident population equal to at least one person for each acre of land included within its boundaries, and is subdivided into lots and tracts such that at least sixty percent (60%) of the total acreage consists of lots and tracts three acres or less in size and such that at least sixty-five percent (65%) of the total number of lots and tracts are one acre or less in size.

3. Is so developed that at least sixty percent (60%) of the total number of lots and tracts in the area at the time of annexation are used for residential, commercial, industrial, institutional, or governmental purposes, and is subdivided into lots and tracts such that at least sixty percent (60%) of the total acreage, not counting the acreage used at the time of annexation for commercial, industrial, governmental, or institutional purposes, consists of lots and tracts three acres or less in size.

4. Is the entire area of any county water and sewer district created under G.S. 162A-86(b1), if all of the following apply:

I. The municipality has provided in a contract with that district that the area is developed for urban purposes.

II. The contract provides for the municipality to operate the sewer system of that county water and sewer district.

III. The municipality is annexing in one ordinance the entire territory of the district not already within the corporate limits of a municipality.

5. Is so developed that, at the time of the approval of the annexation report, all tracts in the area to be annexed are used for commercial, industrial, governmental, or institutional purposes.

b. Part or all of the area to be annexed meets either of the following:

1. Lies between the municipal boundary and an area developed for urban purposes so that the area developed for urban purposes is either not adjacent to the municipal boundary or cannot be served by the municipality without extending major municipal services, including water or sewer lines, through such sparsely developed area.

2. Is adjacent, on at least sixty percent (60%) of its external boundary, to any combination of the municipal boundary and the boundary of an area or areas developed for urban purposes as defined in sub-subdivision a. of this subsection.

The purpose of paragraphs 1. and 2. of this sub-subdivision is to permit municipal governing boards to extend corporate limits to include all nearby areas developed for urban purposes and where necessary to include areas which at the time of annexation are not yet developed for urban purposes but which constitute necessary land connections between the municipality and areas developed for urban purposes or between two or more areas developed for urban purposes.

c. The total area to be annexed is completely surrounded by the municipality's primary corporate limits.

(b) In fixing new municipal boundaries and determining whether an area is developed for urban purposes, a municipal governing board shall comply with all the following:

(1) Use recorded property lines and streets as boundaries. Some or all of the boundaries of a county water and sewer district may also be used when the entire district is not already within the corporate limits of the municipality.

(2) Use whole parcels of property in that if any portion of that parcel is included, the entire parcel of real property as recorded in the deed transferring title shall be included.

(3) Not use a connecting corridor consisting solely of the length of a street or street right-of-way to establish contiguity.

(4) Not consider property in use for a commercial, industrial, institutional, or governmental purpose if the lot or tract is used only temporarily, occasionally, or on an incidental or insubstantial basis in relation to the size and character of the lot or tract.

(5) Include acreage actually occupied by buildings or other man-made structures together with all areas that are reasonably necessary and appurtenant to such facilities for purposes of parking, storage, ingress and egress, utilities, buffering, and other ancillary services and facilities when determining acreage in use for commercial, industrial, institutional, or governmental purposes.

(6) Consider the area of an abolished water and sewer district to be a water and sewer district for the purpose of this section even after its abolition under G.S. 162A-87.2(b).

(c) As used in this subsection, "bona fide farm purposes" is as described in G.S. 153A-340. As used in this subsection, "property" means a single tract of property or an identifiable portion of a single tract. Property that is being used for bona fide farm purposes on the date of the resolution of intent to consider annexation may not be annexed without the written consent of the owner or owners of the property. (2011-396, s. 9; 2011-363, s. 3.1.)

§ 160A-58.55. Procedure for annexation.

(a) Resolution of Consideration. - Any municipal governing board desiring to annex territory under the provisions of this Part shall first pass a resolution of consideration identifying the area under consideration for annexation by either a metes and bounds description or a map. The resolution of consideration shall remain effective for two years after adoption and be filed with the municipal clerk. A new resolution of consideration adopted before expiration of the two-year period for a previously adopted resolution covering the same area shall relate back to the date of the previous resolution. Adoption of a resolution of consideration shall not confer prior jurisdiction over the area as to any other municipality.

(b) Notice of Resolution of Consideration. - A notice of the adoption of the resolution of consideration shall be published once a week for two successive weeks, with each publication being on the same day of the week, in a newspaper having general circulation in the municipality. The second publication shall be no more than 30 days following adoption of the resolution of consideration. The resolution of consideration shall contain a map or description of the area under consideration and a summary of the annexation process and time lines. A copy of the resolution of consideration shall be mailed within 30 days after the adoption of the resolution of consideration by first class mail to the property owners of real property located within the area under consideration for annexation as shown by the tax records of the county. If a proposed annexation extends across a county border into a county other that the county where the majority of the area of the existing municipality is located, a copy of the resolution of consideration shall be mailed within 30 days after the adoption of the resolution of consideration by first class mail to the clerk of the board of county commissioners of that county.

(c) Resolution of Intent. - At least one year after adoption of the resolution of consideration, the municipal governing body may adopt a resolution of intent of the municipality to proceed with the annexation of some or all of the area described in the resolution of consideration. The resolution of intent shall describe the boundaries of the area proposed for annexation, fix a date for a public informational meeting, fix a date for a public hearing on the question of annexation, and fix a date for the referendum on annexation. The date for the public informational meeting shall be not less than 45 days and not more than 55 days following passage of the resolution of intent. The date for the public hearing shall be not less than 130 days and not more than 150 days following passage of the resolution of intent. The date of the referendum on annexation shall be set for the next municipal general election that is more than 45 days from the date of the resolution of intent.

(d) Notice of Public Informational Meeting, Public Hearing, and Opportunity for Water and Sewer. - A combined notice of public informational meeting and public hearing shall be issued as provided for in this subsection as follows:

(1) The notice shall be a combined notice that includes at least all of the following:

a. The date, hour, and place of the public informational meeting.

b. The date, hour, and place of the public hearing.

c. A clear description of the boundaries of the area under consideration, including a legible map of the area.

d. A statement that the report required by G.S. 160A-58.53 will be available at the office of the municipal clerk.

e. An explanation of a property owner's rights under this section.

f. A summary of the annexation process with time lines.

g. A summary of the opportunity to vote in the referendum and available statutory remedies appealing the annexation and the failure to provide services.

h. Information on how to request to become a customer of the water and sewer service, all forms to request that service, and the consequences of opting in or opting out, as provided in G.S. 160A-58.56.

i. A clear description of the distinction between the public informational meeting and the public hearing.

(2) The combined notice shall be given by publication of the information required by sub-subdivisions (1)a., b., and c. of this subsection and a statement regarding the availability of the information required by the remaining sub-subdivisions of subdivision (1) of this subsection in a newspaper having general circulation in the municipality once a week for at least two successive weeks prior to the date of the public informational meeting, with each publication being on the same day of the week. The date of the last publication shall be not more than 10 days preceding the date of the public informational meeting. In addition thereto, if the area proposed to be annexed lies in a county containing less than fifty percent (50%) of the land area of the municipality, the same publication shall be given in a newspaper having general circulation in the area of proposed annexation. If there is no such newspaper, the municipality shall post the notice in at least five public places within the municipality and at least five public places in the area to be annexed for 30 days prior to the date of public informational meeting.

(3) The combined notice, together with the information about requesting water and sewer service, shall be mailed within five business days of the passage of the resolution of intent by first class mail to the property owners of real property located within the area to be annexed as shown by the tax records of the county. The person or persons mailing such notices shall certify to the

governing board that fact, and such certificate shall become a part of the public record of the annexation proceeding and shall be deemed conclusive in the absence of fraud. If a notice is returned to the municipality by the postal service by the tenth day before the informational meeting, a copy of the notice shall be sent by certified mail, return receipt requested, at least seven days before the informational meeting. Failure to comply with the mailing requirement of this subsection shall not invalidate the annexation unless it is shown that the requirements were not substantially complied with.

(4)   If the governing board by resolution finds that the tax records are not adequate to identify the property owners within the area to be annexed after exercising reasonable efforts to locate the property owners, it may, in lieu of the mail procedure required by subdivision (3) of this subsection, post the notice at least 30 days prior to the date of the public informational meeting on all buildings, on such parcels, and in at least five other places within the area to be annexed as to those parcels where the property owner could not be so identified. In any case where notices are placed on property, the person placing the notice shall certify that fact to the governing board.

(e)   Action Prior to Informational Meeting. - At least 30 days before the date of the public informational meeting, the municipal governing board shall do all of the following:

(1)   Approve the report provided for in G.S. 160A-58.53.

(2)   Prepare a summary of the approved report for public distribution.

(3)   Post in the office of the clerk all of the following:

a.   The approved report provided for in G.S. 160A-58.53.

b.   The summary of the approved report.

c.   A legible map of the area to be annexed.

d.   The list of the property owners, and associated mailing addresses, in the area to be annexed that the municipality has identified and mailed notice.

e.   Information for property owners on how to request to become a customer of the water service or sewer service and all forms to request that service.

(4) If the municipality has a Web site, post on that Web site all of the information under this section together with any forms to apply for water and sewer service.

(5) Prepare a summary of the opportunity to vote in the referendum and available statutory remedies for appealing the annexation for public distribution.

(f) Public Informational Meeting. - At the public informational meeting, a representative of the municipality shall first make an explanation of the report required in G.S. 160A-58.53 and an explanation of the provision of major municipal services. The explanation of the provision of services shall include how to request water service or sewer service to individual lots, the average cost of a residential connection to the water and sewer system, and the opportunity for installation of a residential connection under G.S. 160A-58.56. A summary of the annexation process with time lines, a summary of opportunity to vote in the referendum and available statutory remedies for appealing the annexation, an explanation of the provision of services, and information for requesting water service or sewer service to individual lots and any forms to so request shall also be distributed at the public informational meeting. Following such explanation, all property owners and residents of the area proposed to be annexed as described in the notice of public informational meeting and hearing, and all residents of the municipality shall be given the opportunity to ask questions and receive answers regarding the proposed annexation.

(g) Public Hearing. - At the public hearing, a representative of the municipality shall first make an explanation of the report required in G.S. 160A-58.53. Following such explanation, all property owners and residents of the area proposed to be annexed as described in the notice of public informational meeting and hearing, and all residents of the municipality, shall be given an opportunity to be heard.

(h) The municipal governing board shall take into consideration facts presented at the public hearing and shall have authority to amend the report required by G.S. 160A-58.53 to make changes in the plans for serving the area proposed to be annexed so long as such changes meet the requirements of G.S. 160A-58.53. At any regular or special meeting held no sooner than the tenth day following the certification of the election held under G.S. 160A-58.64, the governing board shall have authority to adopt an ordinance, subject to subsection (i) of this section, extending the corporate limits of the municipality to include all, or part, of the area described in the notice of public hearing which the governing board has concluded should be annexed. The annexation ordinance shall:

(1)   Contain specific findings showing that the area to be annexed meets the requirements of G.S. 160A-58.54.

(2)   Describe the external boundaries of the area to be annexed by metes and bounds.

(3)   Include a statement of the intent of the municipality to provide services to the area being annexed as set forth in the report required by G.S. 160A-58.53 and a time line for the provision of those services.

(4)   Contain a specific finding that on the effective date of annexation, the municipality will have funds appropriated in sufficient amount to finance construction of any water and sewer lines stated in the report required by G.S. 160A-58.53 to extend the water and sewer services into the area to be annexed, or that on the effective date of annexation the municipality will have authority to issue bonds in an amount sufficient to finance such construction. If authority to issue such bonds shall be secured from the electorate of the municipality prior to the effective date of annexation, then the effective date of annexation shall be no earlier than the day following the statement of the successful result of the bond election.

(5)   Fix the effective date for annexation as June 30 next following the adoption of the ordinance or the second June 30 following adoption of the ordinance, but not before the completion of the water and sewer request appeal periods are complete.

(6)   Together, with the list of the property owners of parcels within the area described in the annexation ordinance to which a notice was mailed under subsection (d) of this section, be delivered within five business days to the tax assessor and the board of elections of the county in which a majority of the municipality lies.

(7)   Repealed by Session Laws 2012-11, s. 2, effective July 1, 2012.

(8)   If a public body has a Web site, conspicuously post notice of the referendum until after the certification of the election.

(i) Referendum Vote on Annexation Ordinance. - The procedures in G.S. 160A-58.64 shall apply to any annexation under this Part. The municipality shall reimburse the board or boards of elections the costs of the referendum required under G.S. 160A-58.64.

(j) Effect of Annexation Ordinance. - From and after the effective date of the annexation ordinance, the territory and its citizens and property shall be subject to all debts, laws, ordinances, and regulations in force in such municipality and shall be entitled to the same privileges and benefits as other parts of such municipality.

(k) Reserved.

(l) Reserved.

(m) Simultaneous Annexation Proceedings. - If a municipality is considering the annexation of two or more areas which are all adjacent to the municipal boundary but are not adjacent to one another, it may undertake simultaneous proceedings under authority of this Part for the annexation of such areas.

(n) Remedies for Failure to Provide Services. - If, not earlier than 30 days after the effective date of annexation and not later than 15 months from the effective date of annexation, any property owner in the annexed territory shall believe that the municipality has not followed through providing services as set forth in the report adopted under G.S. 160A-58.53 and subsection (e) of this section, the property owner may apply for a writ of mandamus. Relief may be granted by the judge of superior court if the municipality has not provided the services set forth in its plan submitted under the provisions of G.S. 160A-58.53(3)a. on substantially the same basis and in the same manner as such services were provided within the rest of the municipality prior to the effective date of annexation and those services are still being provided on substantially the same basis and in the same manner within the original corporate limits of the municipality. If a writ is issued, costs in the action, including reasonable attorneys' fees for such aggrieved property owner, shall be charged to the municipality.

(o) Reports to the Local Government Commission. - The municipality shall report to the Local Government Commission as follows:

(1) As to whether police protection, fire protection, solid waste services, and street maintenance services were provided in accordance with G.S. 160A-

58.53(3)a., within 30 days after the effective date of the annexation. Such report shall be filed no more than 30 days following the expiration of the 30-day period. If the Local Government Commission determines that the municipality failed to deliver police protection, fire protection, solid waste services, or street maintenance services as provided for in G.S. 160A-58.53(3)a. within 30 days after the effective date of the annexation, the Local Government Commission shall notify the municipality that the municipality may not count any of the residents as part of the population of the municipality for the purpose of receiving any State, federal, or county dollars distributed based on population until all of the services are provided.

(2)   As to whether the extension of water and sewer lines was completed within the time period specified in G.S. 160A-58.53(3), within six months after the effective date of the annexation ordinance, and again within three and one-half years of the effective date of the annexation ordinance or upon the completion of the installation, whichever occurs first. If the municipality failed to deliver either water or sewer services, or both, as provided for in G.S. 160A-58.53(3)b. within three and one-half years after the effective date of the annexation, the municipality shall stop any other annexations in progress and may not begin any other annexation until the water and sewer services are provided. The municipality shall adopt a resolution of consideration to begin again any annexation that is stopped due to this subdivision. (2011-396, s. 9; 2012-11, s. 2.)

§ 160A-58.56. Provision of water and sewer service.

(a)   The municipality shall provide water and sewer service to the annexed area as required by plans for extension under G.S. 160A-58.53(3) within three and one-half years of the effective date of the annexation ordinance except as provided in subdivision (b)(4) of this section. If (i) the residents in the existing city boundaries are served by a public water or sewer system, or by a combination of a public water or sewer system and one or more nonprofit entities providing service by contract with the public system, (ii) the annexing municipality does not provide that service within the existing city boundaries, (iii) the area to be annexed is in an area served by the public water or sewer system, and (iv) the municipality has no responsibility through an agreement with the public water or sewer system to pay for the extension of lines to areas annexed to the city, the city shall have no financial responsibility for the extension of water and sewer lines under this section. For purposes of this provision, "public water or sewer system" means a water or sewer authority formed under Article 1 of Chapter 162A of the General Statutes; a metropolitan water or sewerage district formed under Article 4 or Article 5 of Chapter 162A of the General Statutes; a county water or sewer district formed under Article 6 of Chapter 162A of the General Statutes; a sanitary district formed under Article 2 of Chapter 130A of the General Statutes; a county-owned water or sewer system; a municipal-owned water or sewer system; a water or sewer utility created by an act of the General Assembly; or a joint agency providing a water or sewer system by interlocal agreement under Article 20 of Chapter 160A of the General Statutes.

(b) Prior to the adoption of the annexation ordinance, the municipality shall offer to each eligible property owner of real property located within the area proposed to be annexed an opportunity to obtain water or sewer service, or both, at no cost other than periodic user fees based upon usage as follows:

(1) After passage of the resolution of intent, the property owner of real property located within the area proposed to be annexed shall be notified in writing, as provided in G.S. 160A-58.55(d), within five business days of the passage of the resolution of intent, of the opportunity to have water and sewer lines and connections installed at no cost to the property owner. The notice shall state that a request for extending water and sewer lines does not waive the right to contest the annexation. The property owners of real property located within the area proposed to be annexed shall be allowed 65 days from the date of the passage of the resolution of intent to respond yes or no to the opportunity. Any property owner of a parcel that is an existing customer of the municipality's water or sewer, whether provided by the municipality or by a third party under contract with the municipality, shall be deemed to respond yes to the opportunity, whether or not the property owner returns the notification.

(2) At the close of the 65-day period, the municipality shall determine if the eligible property owners of a majority of the parcels to be annexed have responded favorably. A majority of the property owners of a single parcel of real property must respond favorably before the municipality may count that parcel of real property as responding favorably.

(3) If the property owners of a majority of the parcels located within the area proposed to be annexed respond favorably, the municipality shall do all of the following:

a. Provide water and sewer lines, service lines, and connections at no cost other than periodic user fees to all real property for which an owner responded favorably if the annexation ordinance is adopted. The right to receive water and sewer lines shall run with the land.

b. Notify, within five days of the close of the 65-day period under subdivision (2) of this subsection, those property owners of real property located within the area proposed to be annexed who failed to respond or responded negatively that the property owners of a majority of the parcels located within the area proposed to be annexed responded favorably and offer a second opportunity for that property owner to respond favorably within 30 days.

(4) If the property owners of a majority of the parcels located within the area proposed to be annexed fail to respond favorably to the offer to obtain water and sewer services made under this section, the municipality may nevertheless proceed with the annexation. If the municipality proceeds with the annexation when the property owners of a majority of the parcels located within the area proposed to be annexed fail to respond favorably to the offer to obtain water and sewer services, the municipality is not required to provide water and sewer services to any property owners in the area that is annexed. If the municipality does provide water and sewer services, and if a property owner requests those services, the municipality may charge the property owner for the connection to a residential lot as provided in subsection (d) of this section during the first five years following the effective date of the annexation. After five years, and only if connection is requested by a property owner in accordance with subsection (e) of this section, the municipality may charge for the connection according to the municipality's policy.

(c) The process required by subsection (b) of this section shall be completed by the municipality at least 30 days prior to the public hearing. The report required by G.S. 160A-58.53 shall include the results of the process required by subsection (b) of this section.

(d) Any property owner of the real property located within the area described in the annexation ordinance may apply to participate in the water and sewer system after the completion of the process required by subsection (b) of this section. For a property owner of real property located within the area described in the annexation ordinance applying within the first year, that property owner may be charged an amount not to exceed fifty percent (50%) of average cost of the installation of the water and sewer for a residential lot. For a property owner of real property located within the area described in the annexation ordinance applying within the second year, that property owner may be charged an amount not to exceed sixty percent (60%) of average cost of the installation of the water and sewer for a residential lot. For a property owner of real property located within the area described in the annexation ordinance applying within the third year, that property owner may be charged an amount not to exceed seventy percent (70%) of average cost of the installation of the water and sewer for a residential lot. For a property owner of real property located within the area described in the annexation ordinance applying within the fourth year, that property owner may be charged an amount not to exceed eighty percent (80%) of average cost of the installation of the water and sewer for a residential lot. For a property owner of real property located within the area described in the annexation ordinance applying within the fifth year, that property owner may be charged an amount not to exceed ninety percent (90%) of average cost of the installation of the water and sewer for a residential lot. Charges pursuant to this section shall be made when the water and sewer connection is operable.

(e) Notwithstanding Article 16 of this Chapter, the municipality may not charge, for any reason, any property owner within the area described in the annexation ordinance, for the installation or use of the water or sewer system unless that property owner is, or has requested to become, a customer of the water or sewer system.

(f) The initial installation of water or sewer connection lines to property shall be completed without charge to the property owner. Title to water or sewer connection lines shall vest in the property owner following completion of the initial installation. The property owner shall be responsible for maintenance and repair of water and sewer connection lines on the owner's property following the initial installation.

(g) If the municipality is unable to provide water or sewer service within three and one-half years, as required by this section, due to permitting delays that are caused through no fault of the municipality, the municipality may petition the Local Government Commission for a reasonable time extension.

(h) For purposes of this section, the following definitions apply:

(1) "At no cost other than periodic user fees." - The municipality may not charge the property owner who responded favorably under subdivision (b)(3) of this section for any costs associated with the installation of the water or sewer system. The municipality may not charge a property owner who applies to

participate in the water and sewer system under subsection (d) of this section prior to the first periodic user fee charge, and on that bill the owner may be charged no more then as provided in subsection (d) of this section.

(2) "Average installation of a connection for a residential lot." - The average of the cost for residential installations from curb to residence, including connection and tap fees, in the area described in the annexation ordinance. (2011-396, s. 9.)

§ 160A-58.57. Contract with rural fire department.

(a) If the area to be annexed described in a resolution of intent passed under G.S. 160A-58.55(c) includes an area in an insurance district defined under G.S. 153A-233, a rural fire protection district under Article 3A of Chapter 69 of the General Statutes, or a fire service district under Article 16 of Chapter 153A of the General Statutes, and a rural fire department was on the date of adoption of the resolution of intent providing fire protection in the area to be annexed, then the city (if the rural fire department makes a written request for a good faith offer, and the request is signed by the chief officer of the fire department and delivered to the city clerk no later than 15 days before the public hearing) is required to make a good faith effort to negotiate a five-year contract with the rural fire department to provide fire protection in the area to be annexed.

(b) If the area is a rural fire protection district or a fire service district, then an offer to pay annually for the term of the contract the amount of money that the tax rate in the district in effect on the date of adoption of the resolution of intent would generate based on property values on January 1 of each year in the area to be annexed which is in such a district is deemed to be a good faith offer of consideration for the contract.

(c) If the area is an insurance district but not a rural fire protection district or fire service district, then an offer to pay annually over the term of the contract the amount of money which is determined to be the equivalent of the amount which would be generated by multiplying the fraction of the city's general fund budget in that current fiscal year which is proposed to be expended for fire protection times the tax rate for the city in the current year, and multiplying that result by the property valuation in the area to be annexed which is served by the rural fire department is deemed to be a good faith offer of consideration for the contract; Provided that the payment shall not exceed the equivalent of fifteen cents (15¢) on one hundred dollars ($100.00) valuation of annexed property in the district according to county valuations for the current fiscal year.

(d)   Any offer by a city to a rural fire department which would compensate the rural fire department for revenue loss directly attributable to the annexation by paying such amount annually for five years, is deemed to be a good faith offer of consideration for the contract.

(e)   Under subsections (b), (c), or (d) of this section, if the good faith offer is for first responder service, an offer of one-half the calculated amount under those subsections is deemed to be a good faith offer.

(f)   This section does not obligate the city or rural fire department to enter into any contract.

(g)   The rural fire department may, if it feels that no good faith offer has been made, appeal to the Local Government Commission within 30 days following the passage of an annexation ordinance. The rural fire department may apply to the Local Government Commission for an order staying the operation of the annexation ordinance pending the outcome of the review. The Commission may grant or deny the stay in its discretion upon such terms as it deems proper, and it may permit annexation of any part of the area described in the ordinance concerning which no question for review has been raised, provided that no other appeal under G.S. 160A-58.60 is pending.

(h)   The Local Government Commission may affirm the ordinance, or if the Local Government Commission finds that no good faith offer has been made, it shall remand the ordinance to the municipal governing board for further proceedings, and the ordinance shall then not become effective unless the Local Government Commission finds that a good faith offer has been made.

(i)   Any party to the review under subsection (h) may obtain judicial review in accordance with Chapter 150B of the General Statutes. (1983, c. 636, s. 21; 1987, c. 827, s. 1; 2011-396, ss. 2, 9.)

§ 160A-58.58. Assumption of debt.

(a)   If the city has annexed any area which is served by a rural fire department and which is in an insurance district defined under G.S. 153A-233, a rural fire protection district under Article 3A of Chapter 69 of the General Statutes or a fire service district under Article 16 of Chapter 153A of the General Statutes, then upon the effective date of annexation if the city has not contracted with the rural fire department for fire protection, or when the rural fire department ceases to provide fire protection under contract, then the city shall pay annually a proportionate share of any payments due on any debt (including principal and interest) relating to facilities or equipment of the rural fire department, if the debt was existing at the time of adoption of the resolution of intent, with the payments in the same proportion that the assessed valuation of the area of the district annexed bears to the assessed valuation of the entire district on the date the annexation ordinance becomes effective or another date for valuation mutually agreed upon by the city and the fire department.

(b)   The city and rural fire department shall jointly present a payment schedule to the Local Government Commission for approval and no payment may be made until such schedule is approved. (1983, c. 636, s. 23; 1998-150, s. 16; 2011-396, s. 3.)

§ 160A-58.59. Contract with private solid waste collection firms.

(a)   If the area to be annexed described in a resolution of intent passed under G.S. 160A-58.55(c) includes an area where a firm (i) meets the requirements of subsection (b) of this section, (ii) on the ninetieth day preceding the date of adoption of the resolution of intent or resolution of consideration was providing solid waste collection services in the area to be annexed, (iii) on the date of adoption of the resolution of intent is still providing such services, and (iv) by reason of the annexation the firm's franchise with a county or arrangements with third parties for solid waste collection will be terminated, the city shall do one of the following:

(1)   Contract with the firm for a period of two years after the effective date of the annexation ordinance to allow the firm to provide collection services to the city in the area to be annexed for sums determined under subsection (f) of this section.

(2)   Pay the firm for the firm's economic loss, with one-third of the economic loss to be paid within 30 days of the termination and the balance paid in 12 equal monthly installments during the next succeeding 12 months. Any remaining economic loss payment is forfeited if the firm terminates service to customers in the annexation area prior to the effective date of the annexation.

(3) Make other arrangements satisfactory to the parties.

(b) To qualify for the options set forth in subsection (a) of this section, a firm must have done one of the following:

(1) Subsequent to receiving notice of the annexation in accordance with subsection (d) of this section, filed with the city clerk at least 10 days prior to the public hearing a written request to contract with the city to provide solid waste collection services containing a certification, signed by an officer or owner of the firm, that the firm serves at least 50 customers within the county at that time.

(2) Contacted the city clerk pursuant to public notice published by the city, pursuant to G.S. 160A-58.55(d), at least 10 days before the hearing and provided to the city clerk a written request to contract with the city to provide solid waste collection services. The request must contain a certification signed by an officer or owner of the firm that the firm serves at least 50 customers within the county at that time.

(c) Firms shall file notice of provision of solid waste collection service with the city clerk of all cities located in the firm's collection area or within five miles thereof.

(d) At least four weeks prior to the date of the informational meeting, the city shall provide written notice of the resolution of intent to all firms serving the area to be annexed. The notice shall be sent to all firms that filed notice in accordance with subsection (c) of this section by certified mail, return receipt requested, to the address provided by the firm under subsection (c) of this section.

(e) The city may require that the contract contain:

(1) A requirement that the firm post a performance bond and maintain public liability insurance coverage;

(2) A requirement that the firm agree to service customers in the annexed area that were not served by that firm on the effective date of annexation;

(3) A provision that divides the annexed area into service areas if there were more than one firm being contracted within the area, such that the entire area is served by the firms, or by the city as to customers not served by the firms;

(4) A provision that the city may serve customers not served by the firm on the effective date of annexation;

(5) A provision that the contract can be cancelled in writing, delivered by certified mail to the firm in question with 30 days to cure substantial violations of the contract, but no contract may be cancelled on these grounds unless the Local Government Commission finds that substantial violations have occurred, except that the city may suspend the contract for up to 30 days if it finds substantial violation of health laws;

(6) Performance standards, not exceeding city standards existing at the time of notice published pursuant to G.S. 160A-49(b) [160A-58.55(d)] with provision that the contract may be cancelled for substantial violations of those standards, but no contract may be cancelled on those grounds unless the Local Government Commission finds that substantial violations have occurred;

(7) A provision for monetary damages if there are violations of the contract or of performance standards.

(f) If the services to be provided to the city by reason of the annexation are substantially the same as rendered under the franchise with the county or arrangements with the parties, the amount paid by the city shall be at least ninety percent (90%) of the amount paid or required under the existing franchise or arrangements. If such services are required to be adjusted to conform to city standards or as a result of changes in the number of customers and as a result there are changes in disposal costs (including mileage and landfill charges), requirements for storage capacity (dumpsters and/or residential carts), and/or frequency of collection, the amount paid by the city for the service shall be increased or decreased to reflect the value of such adjusted services as if computed under the existing franchise or arrangements. In the event agreement cannot be reached between the city and the firm under this subsection, the matters shall be determined by the Local Government Commission.

(g) The firm may, if it contends that no contract has been offered, appeal to the Local Government Commission within 30 days following passage of an annexation ordinance. The firm may appeal to the Local Government Commission for an order staying the operation of the annexation ordinance pending the outcome of the review. The Commission may grant or deny the stay upon such terms as it deems proper. If the Local Government Commission finds that the city has not made an offer which complies with this section, it shall remand the ordinance to the municipal governing board for further proceedings, and the ordinance shall not become effective until the Local Government Commission finds that such an offer has been made. Either the firm or the city may obtain judicial review in accordance with Chapter 150B of the General Statutes.

(h)   A firm which has given notice under subsection (a) of this section that it desires to contract, and any firm that the city believes is eligible to give such notice, shall make available to the city not later than 30 days following a written request of the city, sent by certified mail return receipt requested, all information in its possession or control, including but not limited to operational, financial and budgetary information, necessary for the city to determine if the firm qualifies for the benefits of this section and to determine the nature and scope of the potential contract and/or economic loss. The firm forfeits its rights under this section if it fails to make a good faith response within 30 days following receipt of the written request for information from the city, provided that the city's written request so states by specific reference to this section.

(i)   As used in this section, the following terms mean:

(1)   Economic loss. - A sum equal to 15 times the average gross monthly revenue for the three months prior to the passage of the resolution of intent or resolution of consideration, as applicable under subsection (a) of this section, collected or due the firm for residential, commercial, and industrial collection service in the area annexed or to be annexed; provided that revenues shall be included in calculations under this subdivision only if policies of the city will provide solid waste collection to those customers such that arrangements between the firm and the customers will be terminated.

(2)   Firm. - A private solid waste collection firm. (1985, c. 610, s. 4; 1987, c. 827, s. 1; 1989, c. 598, s. 9; 1998-150, s. 17; 2006-193, s. 2; 2006-259, s. 53; 2011-396, ss. 4, 9.)

§ 160A-58.60. Appeal.

(a)   Within 60 days following the adoption of the annexation ordinance, any property owner of real property located within the area described in the annexation ordinance who believes that property owner will suffer material injury by reason of the failure of the municipal governing board to comply with the procedure or to meet the requirements set forth in this Part as they apply to the annexation may file a petition in the superior court of the county in which the municipality is located seeking review of the action of the governing board.

(b) Such petition shall explicitly state what exceptions are taken to the action of the governing board and what relief the petitioner seeks. Within 10 days after the petition is filed with the court, the person seeking review shall serve copies of the petition by registered mail, return receipt requested, upon the municipality.

(c) Within 15 days after receipt of the copy of the petition for review or within such additional time as the court may allow, the municipality shall transmit to the reviewing court both of the following:

(1) A transcript of the portions of the municipal journal or minute book in which the procedure for annexation has been set forth.

(2) A copy of the report setting forth the plans for extending services to the annexed area as required in G.S. 160A-58.53.

(d) If two or more petitions for review are submitted to the court, the court may consolidate all such petitions for review at a single hearing, and the municipality shall be required to submit only one set of minutes and one report as required in subsection (c) of this section.

(e) At any time before or during the review proceeding, any petitioner or petitioners may apply to the reviewing court for an order staying the operation of the annexation ordinance pending the outcome of the review. The court may grant or deny the stay in its discretion upon such terms as it deems proper, and it may permit annexation of any part of the area described in the ordinance concerning which no question for review has been raised.

(f) The court shall fix the date for review of annexation proceedings under this Part, which review date shall be expeditious and without unnecessary delays. The review shall be conducted by the court without a jury. The court may hear oral arguments and receive written briefs and may take evidence intended to show one or more of the following:

(1) That the statutory procedure was not followed.

(2) That the provisions of G.S. 160A-58.53 were not met.

(3) That the provisions of G.S. 160A-58.54 have not been met.

(4) That the provisions of G.S. 160A-58.50 have not been met.

(g) The court may affirm the action of the governing board without change, or it may order any of the following:

(1) Remand the ordinance to the municipal governing board for further proceedings if procedural irregularities are found to have materially prejudiced the substantive rights of any of the petitioners.

(2) Remand the ordinance to the municipal governing board for amendment of the boundaries to conform to the provisions of G.S. 160A-58.54 if it finds that the provisions of G.S. 160A-58.54 have not been met; provided, that the court cannot remand the ordinance to the municipal governing board with directions to add area to the municipality which was not included in the notice of public hearing and not provided for in plans for service.

(3) Remand the report to the municipal governing board for amendment of the plans for providing services to the end that the provisions of G.S. 160A-58.53 are satisfied or to correct errors in [the] municipal governing board's estimates that fall below the standards in G.S. 160A-58.63.

(4) Declare the ordinance null and void, if the court finds that the ordinance cannot be corrected by remand as provided in subdivisions (1), (2), or (3) of this subsection.

If any municipality shall fail to take action in accordance with the court's instructions upon remand within 90 days following entry of the order embodying the court's instructions, the annexation proceeding shall be deemed null and void.

(h) Any party to the review proceedings, including the municipality, may appeal to the Court of Appeals from the final judgment of the superior court under rules of procedure applicable in other civil cases. The superior court may, with the agreement of the municipality, permit annexation to be effective with respect to any part of the area concerning which no appeal is being made and which can be incorporated into the municipality without regard to any part of the area concerning which an appeal is being made.

(i)   If part or all of the area annexed under the terms of an annexation ordinance is the subject of an appeal to the superior court, Court of Appeals, or Supreme Court on the effective date of the ordinance, then the ordinance shall be deemed amended to make the effective date with respect to such area the first June 30th at least six months following the date of the final judgment of the superior court or appellate division, or the first June 30th at least six months from the date the municipal governing board completes action to make the ordinance conform to the court's instructions in the event of remand. For the purposes of this subsection, a denial of a petition for rehearing or for discretionary review shall be treated as a final judgment.

(j)   If a petition for review is filed under subsection (a) of this section or an appeal is filed under G.S. 160A-58.57(g) or G.S. 160A-58.59(g) and a stay is granted, then the time periods of three and one-half years or G.S. 160A-58.55(n) are each extended by the lesser of the length of the stay or one year for that annexation.

(k)   The provisions of subsection (i) of this section shall apply to any judicial review authorized in whole or in part by G.S. 160A-58.57(i) or G.S. 160A-58.57(g).

(l)   In any proceeding related to an annexation ordinance appeal under this section, a municipality shall not state a claim for lost property tax revenue caused by the appeal. Nothing in this Article shall be construed to mean that as a result of an appeal a municipality may assert a claim for property tax revenue lost during the pendency of the appeal.

(m)   Any settlement reached by all parties in an appeal under this section may be presented to the superior court in the county in which the municipality is located. If the superior court, in its discretion, approves the settlement, it shall be binding on all parties without the need for approval by the General Assembly.

(n)   If a final court order is issued against the annexing municipality, costs in the action, including reasonable attorneys' fees for such aggrieved person having a freehold interest in the real property located within the area described in the annexation ordinance, may be charged to the municipality. (2011-396, s. 9 2012-11, s. 5; 2013-410, s. 15.)

§ 160A-58.61. Annexation recorded.

Whenever the limits of a municipality are enlarged in accordance with the provisions of this Part, it shall be the duty of the mayor of the municipality to cause an accurate map of such annexed territory, together with a copy of the ordinance duly certified, to be recorded in the office of the register of deeds of the county or counties in which such territory is situated and in the office of the Secretary of State. The documents required to be filed with the Secretary of State under this section shall be filed not later than 30 days following the effective date of the annexation ordinance. All documents shall have an identifying number affixed thereto and shall conform in size in accordance with rules prescribed by the Secretary. Failure to file within 30 days shall not affect the validity of the annexation. Any annexation shall be reported as part of the Boundary and Annexation Survey of the United States Bureau of the Census. (1959, c. 1009, s. 7; 1973, c. 426, s. 74; 1987, c. 715, s. 8; c. 879, s. 3; 1989, c. 440, s. 9; 1991, c. 586, s. 3; 2011-396, s. 5.)

§ 160A-58.62. Authorized expenditures.

Municipalities initiating annexations under the provisions of this Part are authorized to make expenditures for surveys required to describe the property under consideration or for any other purpose necessary to plan for the study and/or annexation of unincorporated territory adjacent to the municipality. In addition, following final passage of the annexation ordinance, the annexing municipality shall have authority to proceed with expenditures for construction of water and sewer lines and other capital facilities and for any other purpose calculated to bring services into the annexed area in a more effective and expeditious manner prior to the effective date of annexation. (1959, c. 1009, s. 8; 1973, c. 426, s. 74; 2011-396, s. 6.)

§ 160A-58.63. Population and land estimates.

In determining population and degree of land subdivision for purposes of meeting the requirements of G.S. 160A-58.54, the municipality shall use methods calculated to provide reasonably accurate results. In determining whether the standards set forth in G.S. 160A-58.54 have been met on appeal to the superior court under G.S. 160A-58.60, the reviewing court shall accept the estimates of the municipality unless the actual population, total area, or degree of land subdivision falls below the standards in G.S. 160A-58.54:

(1) As to population, if the estimate is based on the number of dwelling units in the area multiplied by the average family size in such area, or in the township or townships of which such area is a part, as determined by the last preceding federal decennial census; or if it is based on a new enumeration carried out under reasonable rules and regulations by the annexing municipality; provided, that the court shall not accept such estimates if the petitioners demonstrate that such estimates are in error in the amount of ten percent (10%) or more.

(2) As to total area, if the estimate is based on an actual survey, or on county tax maps or records, or on aerial photographs, or on some other reasonably reliable map used for official purposes by a governmental agency, unless the petitioners on appeal demonstrate that such estimates are in error in the amount of five percent (5%) or more.

(3) As to degree of land subdivision, if the estimates are based on an actual survey, or on county tax maps or records, or on aerial photographs, or on some other reasonably reliable source, unless the petitioners on appeal show that such estimates are in error in the amount of five percent (5%) or more. (2011-396, s. 9.)

§ 160A-58.64. Referendum prior to involuntary annexation ordinance.

(a) After the adoption of the resolution of intent under this Part, the municipality shall place the question of annexation on the ballot. The municipal governing board shall notify the appropriate county board or boards of elections of the adoption of the resolution of intent and provide a legible map and clear written description of the proposed annexation area.

(b) In accordance with G.S. 163-58.55, the municipal governing board shall adopt a resolution setting the date for the referendum and so notify the appropriate county board or boards of elections.

(c) The county board or boards of elections shall cause legal notice of the election to be published. That notice shall include the general statement of the referendum. The referendum shall be conducted, returned, and the results declared as in other municipal elections in the municipality. Only registered voters of the proposed annexation area shall be allowed to vote on the referendum.

(d) The referendum of any number of proposed involuntary annexations may be submitted at the same election; but as to each proposed involuntary annexation, there shall be an entirely separate ballot question.

(e) The ballots used in a referendum shall submit the following proposition:

"[ ] FOR   [ ] AGAINST

The annexation of (clear description of the proposed annexation area)."

(f) If less than a majority of the votes cast on the referendum are for annexation, the municipal governing body may not proceed with the adoption of the annexation ordinance or begin a separate involuntary annexation process with respect to that proposed annexation area for at least 36 months from the date of the referendum. If a majority of the votes cast on the referendum are for annexation, the municipal governing body may proceed with the adoption of the annexation ordinance under G.S. 160A-58.55. (2012-11, s. 1.)

§ 160A-58.65: Reserved for future codification purposes.

§ 160A-58.66: Reserved for future codification purposes.

§ 160A-58.67: Reserved for future codification purposes.

§ 160A-58.68: Reserved for future codification purposes.

§ 160A-58.69: Reserved for future codification purposes.

§ 160A-58.70: Reserved for future codification purposes.

§ 160A-58.71: Reserved for future codification purposes.

§ 160A-58.72: Reserved for future codification purposes.

§ 160A-58.73: Reserved for future codification purposes.

§ 160A-58.74: Reserved for future codification purposes.

§ 160A-58.75: Reserved for future codification purposes.

§ 160A-58.76: Reserved for future codification purposes.

§ 160A-58.77: Reserved for future codification purposes.

§ 160A-58.78: Reserved for future codification purposes.

§ 160A-58.79: Reserved for future codification purposes.

§ 160A-58.80: Reserved for future codification purposes.

§ 160A-58.81: Reserved for future codification purposes.

§ 160A-58.82: Reserved for future codification purposes.

§ 160A-58.83: Reserved for future codification purposes.

§ 160A-58.84: Reserved for future codification purposes.

§ 160A-58.85: Reserved for future codification purposes.

§ 160A-58.86: Reserved for future codification purposes.

§ 160A-58.87: Reserved for future codification purposes.

§ 160A-58.88: Reserved for future codification purposes.

§ 160A-58.89: Reserved for future codification purposes.

Part 8. Recording and Reporting.

§ 160A-58.90. Recording and Reporting.

(a)   Annexations made under this Article shall be recorded and reported in the same manner as under G.S. 160A-29.

(b)   To be enforceable, any written agreement with a person having a freehold interest in real property regarding annexation shall be recorded in the county register of deeds office in which the real property lies. (2011-396, s. 11.)

Article 5.

Form of Government.

Part 1. General Provisions.

§ 160A-59. Qualifications for elective office.

All city officers elected by the people shall possess the qualifications set out in Article VI of the Constitution. In addition, when the city is divided into electoral districts for the purpose of electing members of the council, council members shall reside in the district they represent. When any elected city officer ceases to meet all of the qualifications for holding office pursuant to the Constitution, or when a council member ceases to reside in an electoral district that he was elected to represent, the office is ipso facto vacant. (1973, c. 609.)

§ 160A-60. Qualifications for appointive office.

Residence within a city shall not be a qualification for or prerequisite to appointment to any city office not filled by election of the people, unless the charter or an ordinance provides otherwise. City councils shall have authority to fix qualifications for appointive offices, but shall have no authority to waive qualifications for appointive offices fixed by charters or general laws. (1870-1, c. 24, s. 3; Code, s. 3796; Rev., s. 2941; C.S., s. 2646; 1951, c. 24; 1969, c. 134, s. 1; 1971, c. 698, s. 1.)

§ 160A-61. Oath of office.

Every person elected by the people or appointed to any city office shall, before entering upon the duties of the office, take and subscribe the oath of office prescribed in Article VI, § 7 of the Constitution. Oaths of office shall be administered by some person authorized by law to administer oaths, and shall be filed with the city clerk. (R.C., c. 111, s. 12; Code, s. 3799; Rev., s. 2920; C.S., s. 2628; 1971, c. 698, s. 1.)

§ 160A-62. Officers to hold over until successors qualified.

All city officers, whether elected or appointed, shall continue to hold office until their successors are chosen and qualified. This section shall not apply when an office or position has been abolished, when an appointed officer or employee has been discharged, or when an elected officer has been removed from office. (R.C., c. 111, s. 8; Code, s. 3792; Rev., s. 2943; C.S., s. 2648; 1971, c. 698, s. 1.)

§ 160A-63. Vacancies.

A vacancy that occurs in an elective office of a city shall be filled by appointment of the city council. If the term of the office expires immediately following the next regular city election, or if the next regular city election will be held within 90 days after the vacancy occurs, the person appointed to fill the vacancy shall serve the remainder of the unexpired term. Otherwise, a successor shall be elected at the next regularly scheduled city election that is held more than 90 days after the vacancy occurs, and the person appointed to fill the vacancy shall serve only until the elected successor takes office. The elected successor shall then serve the remainder of the unexpired term. If the number of vacancies on the council is such that a quorum of the council cannot be obtained, the mayor shall appoint enough members to make up a quorum, and the council shall then proceed to fill the remaining vacancies. If the number of vacancies on the council is such that a quorum of the council cannot be obtained and the office of mayor is vacant, the Governor may fill the vacancies upon the request of any remaining member of the council, or upon the petition of any five registered voters of the city. Vacancies in appointive offices shall be filled by the same authority that makes the initial appointment. This section shall not apply to vacancies in cities that have not held a city election, levied any taxes, or engaged in any municipal functions for a period of five years or more.

In cities whose elections are conducted on a partisan basis, a person appointed to fill a vacancy in an elective office shall be a member of the same political party as the person whom he replaces if that person was elected as the nominee of a political party. (R.C., c. 111, ss. 9, 10; Code, ss. 3793, 3794; Rev., ss. 2921, 2931; C.S., ss. 2629, 2631; 1971, c. 698, s. 1; 1973, c. 426, s. 11; c. 827, s. 1; 1983, c. 827, s. 1.)

§ 160A-64. Compensation of mayor and council.

(a) The council may fix its own compensation and the compensation of the mayor and any other elected officers of the city by adoption of the annual budget ordinance, but the salary of an elected officer other than a member of the council may not be reduced during the then-current term of office unless he agrees thereto. The mayor, councilmen, and other elected officers are entitled to reimbursement for actual expenses incurred in the course of performing their official duties at rates not in excess of those allowed to other city officers and employees, or to a fixed allowance, the amount of which shall be established by the council, for travel and other personal expenses of office; provided, any fixed allowance so established during a term of office shall not be increased during such term of office.

(b)   All charter provisions in effect as of January 1, 1972, fixing the compensation or allowances of any city officer or employee are repealed, but persons holding office or employment on January 1, 1972, shall continue to receive the compensation and allowances then prescribed by law until the council provides otherwise in accordance with this section or G.S. 160A-162. (1969, c. 181, s. 1; 1971, c. 698, s. 1; 1973, c. 426, s. 12; c. 1145; 1979, 2nd Sess., c. 1247, s. 1.)

§ 160A-65. Repealed by Session Laws 1975, c. 514, s. 17.)

Part 2. Mayor and Council.

§ 160A-66. Composition of council.

Unless otherwise provided by its charter, each city shall be governed by a mayor and a council of three members, who shall be elected from the city at large for terms of two years. (1971, c. 698, s. 1.)

§ 160A-67. General powers of mayor and council.

Except as otherwise provided by law, the government and general management of the city shall be vested in the council. The powers and duties of the mayor shall be such as are conferred upon him by law, together with such other powers and duties as may be conferred upon him by the council pursuant to law. The mayor shall be recognized as the official head of the city for the purpose of service of civil process, and for all ceremonial purposes. (1971, c. 698, s. 1.)

Part 3. Organization and Procedures of the Council.

§ 160A-68. Organizational meeting of council.

(a)   The council may fix the date and time of its organizational meeting. The organizational meeting may be held at any time after the results of the municipal election have been officially determined and published pursuant to Subchapter IX of Chapter 163 of the General Statutes but not later than the date and time of the first regular meeting of the council in December after the results of the municipal election have been certified pursuant to that Subchapter. If the council fails to fix the date and time of its organizational meeting, then the meeting shall be held on the date and at the time of the first regular meeting in December after the results of the municipal election have been certified pursuant to Subchapter IX of Chapter 163 of the General Statutes.

(b)   At the organizational meeting, the newly elected mayor and councilmen shall qualify by taking the oath of office prescribed in Article VI, Section 7 of the Constitution. The organization of the council shall take place notwithstanding the absence, death, refusal to serve, failure to qualify, or nonelection of one or more members, but at least a quorum of the members must be present.

(c)   All local acts or provisions of city charters which prescribe a particular meeting day or date for the organizational meeting of a council are hereby repealed. (1971, c. 698, s. 1; 1973, c. 426, s. 13; c. 607; 1979, c. 168; 1979, 2nd Sess., c. 1247, s. 2.)

§ 160A-69. Mayor to preside over council.

The mayor shall preside at all council meetings, but shall have the right to vote only when there are equal numbers of votes in the affirmative and in the negative. In a city where the mayor is elected by the council from among its membership, and the city charter makes no provision as to the right of the mayor to vote, he shall have the right to vote as a council member on all matters before the council, but shall have no right to break a tie vote in which he participated. (1971, c. 698, s. 1; 1979, 2nd Sess., c. 1247, s. 3.)

§ 160A-70. Mayor pro tempore; disability of mayor.

At the organizational meeting, the council shall elect from among its members a mayor pro tempore to serve at the pleasure of the council. A councilman serving as mayor pro tempore shall be entitled to vote on all matters and shall be considered a councilman for all purposes, including the determination of whether a quorum is present. During the absence of the mayor, the council may confer upon the mayor pro tempore any of the powers and duties of the mayor. If the mayor should become physically or mentally incapable of performing the duties of his office, the council may by unanimous vote declare that he is incapacitated and confer any of his powers and duties on the mayor pro tempore. Upon the mayor's declaration that he is no longer incapacitated, and with the concurrence of a majority of the council, the mayor shall resume the exercise of his powers and duties. In the event both the mayor and the mayor pro tempore are absent from a meeting, the council may elect from its members a temporary chairman to preside in such absence. (1971, c. 698, s. 1; 1979, 2nd Sess., c. 1247, s. 4.)

§ 160A-71. Regular and special meetings; recessed and adjourned meetings; procedure.

(a)   The council shall fix the time and place for its regular meetings. If no action has been taken fixing the time and place for regular meetings, a regular meeting shall be held at least once a month at 10:00 A.M. on the first Monday of the month.

(b)   (1)   The mayor, the mayor pro tempore, or any two members of the council may at any time call a special council meeting by signing a written notice stating the time and place of the meeting and the subjects to be considered. The notice shall be delivered to the mayor and each councilman or left at his usual dwelling place at least six hours before the meeting. Only those items of business specified in the notice may be transacted at a special meeting, unless all members are present or have signed a written waiver of notice. In addition to the procedures set out in this subsection or any city charter, a person or persons calling a special meeting of a city council shall comply with the notice requirements of Article 33C of General Statutes Chapter 143.

(2)   Special meetings may be held at any time when the mayor and all members of the council are present and consent thereto, or when those not present have signed a written waiver of notice.

(3) During any regular meeting, or any duly called special meeting, the council may call or schedule a special meeting, provided that the motion or resolution calling or scheduling any such special meeting shall specify the time, place and purpose or purposes of such meeting and shall be adopted during an open session.

(b1) Any regular or duly called special meeting may be recessed to reconvene at a time and place certain, or may be adjourned to reconvene at a time and place certain, by the council.

(c) The council may adopt its own rules of procedure, not inconsistent with the city charter, general law, or generally accepted principles of parliamentary procedure. (1917, c. 136, subch. 13, s. 1; C.S., s. 2822; 1971, c. 698, s. 1; 1973, c. 426, s. 14; 1977, 2nd Sess., c. 1191, s. 7; 1979, 2nd Sess., c. 1247, s. 5; 1989, c. 770, s. 37.)

§ 160A-72. Minutes to be kept; ayes and noes.

Full and accurate minutes of the council proceedings shall be kept, and shall be open to the inspection of the public. The results of each vote shall be recorded in the minutes, and upon the request of any member of the council, the ayes and noes upon any question shall be taken. (1917, c. 136, subch. 13, s. 1; C.S., s. 2822; 1971, c. 698, s. 1; 1973, c. 426, s. 15.)

§ 160A-73. Repealed by Session Laws 1971, c. 896, s. 16.

§ 160A-74. Quorum.

A majority of the actual membership of the council plus the mayor, excluding vacant seats, shall constitute a quorum. A member who has withdrawn from a meeting without being excused by majority vote of the remaining members present shall be counted as present for purposes of determining whether or not a quorum is present. (1917, c. 136, subch. 13, s. 1; C.S., s. 2821; 1971, c. 698, s. 1; 1975, c. 664, s. 5; 1979, 2nd Sess., c. 1247, s. 6.)

§ 160A-75. Voting.

No member shall be excused from voting except upon matters involving the consideration of the member's own financial interest or official conduct or on matters on which the member is prohibited from voting under G.S. 14-234, 160A-381(d), or 160A-388(e)(2). In all other cases, a failure to vote by a member who is physically present in the council chamber, or who has withdrawn without being excused by a majority vote of the remaining members present, shall be recorded as an affirmative vote. The question of the compensation and allowances of members of the council is not a matter involving a member's own financial interest or official conduct.

An affirmative vote equal to a majority of all the members of the council not excused from voting on the question in issue, including the mayor's vote in case of an equal division, shall be required to adopt an ordinance, take any action having the effect of an ordinance, authorize or commit the expenditure of public funds, or make, ratify, or authorize any contract on behalf of the city. In addition, no ordinance nor any action having the effect of any ordinance may be finally adopted on the date on which it is introduced except by an affirmative vote equal to or greater than two thirds of all the actual membership of the council, excluding vacant seats and not including the mayor unless the mayor has the right to vote on all questions before the council. For purposes of this section, an ordinance shall be deemed to have been introduced on the date the subject matter is first voted on by the council. (1917, c. 136, subch. 13, s. 1; C.S., s. 2821; 1971, c. 698, s. 1; 1973, c. 426, s. 16; 1979, 2nd Sess., c. 1247, s. 7; 1983, c. 696; 2001-409, s. 9; 2005-426, s. 5.1(a); 2013-126, s. 11.)

§ 160A-76. Franchises; technical ordinances.

(a) No ordinance making a grant, renewal, extension, or amendment of any franchise shall be finally adopted until it has been passed at two regular meetings of the council, and no such grant, renewal, extension, or amendment shall be made otherwise than by ordinance.

(b) Any published technical code or any standards or regulations promulgated by any public agency may be adopted in an ordinance by reference subject to G.S. 143-138(e). A technical code or set of standards or regulations adopted by reference in a city ordinance shall have the force of law within the city. Official copies of all technical codes, standards, and regulations adopted by reference shall be maintained for public inspection in the office of the city clerk. (1917, c. 136, subch. 13; C.S., s. 2823; 1963, c. 790; 1971, c. 698, s. 1; 1973, c. 426, s. 17.)

§ 160A-77. Code of ordinances.

(a)   Not later than July 1, 1974, each city having a population of 5,000 or more shall adopt and issue a code of its ordinances. The code may be reproduced by any method that gives legible and permanent copies, and may be issued as a securely bound book or books with periodic separately bound supplements, or as a loose-leaf book maintained by replacement pages. Supplements or replacement pages should be adopted and issued annually at least, unless no additions to or modifications of the code have been adopted by the council during the year. The code may consist of two separate parts, the "General Ordinances" and the "Technical Ordinances." The technical ordinances may be published as separate books or pamphlets, and may include ordinances regarding the construction of buildings, the installation of plumbing and electric wiring, the installation of cooling and heating equipment, the use of public utilities, buildings, or facilities operated by the city, the zoning ordinance, the subdivision control ordinance, the privilege license tax ordinance, and other similar technical ordinances designated as such by the council. The council may omit from the code designated classes of ordinances of limited interest or transitory nature, but the code should clearly describe the classes of ordinances omitted therefrom.

(b)   The council may provide that one or more of the following classes of ordinances shall be codified by appropriate entries upon official map books to be retained permanently in the office of the city clerk or some other city office generally accessible to the public:

(1)   Establishing or amending the boundaries of zoning districts;

(2)   Designating the location of traffic control devices;

(3)   Designating areas or zones where regulations are applied to parking, loading, bus stops, or taxicab stands;

(4)   Establishing speed limits;

(4a) Restricting or regulating traffic at certain times on certain streets, or to certain types, weights or sizes of vehicles;

(5) Designating the location of through streets, stop intersections, yield-right-of-way intersections, waiting lanes, one-way streets, or truck traffic routes; and

(6) Establishing regulations upon vehicle turns at designated locations.

(b1) The council may provide that the classes of ordinances described in paragraphs (2) through (6) of subsection (b) above, and ordinances establishing rates for utility or other public enterprise services, or ordinances establishing fees of any nature, shall be codified by entry upon official lists or schedules of the regulations established by such ordinances, or schedules of such rates or fees, to be maintained in the office of the city clerk.

(c) It is the intent of this section to make uniform the law concerning the adoption of city codes. To this end, all charter provisions in conflict with this section in effect as of January 1, 1972, are expressly repealed, except to the extent that the charter makes adoption of a code mandatory, and no local act taking effect on or after January 1, 1972, shall be construed to repeal or amend this section in whole or in part unless it shall expressly so provide by specific reference. (1971, c. 698, s. 1; 1979, 2nd Sess., c. 1247, ss. 8, 9.)

§ 160A-78. Ordinance book.

Effective January 1, 1972, each city shall file a true copy of each ordinance adopted on or after January 1, 1972, in an ordinance book separate and apart from the council's minute book. The ordinance book shall be appropriately indexed and maintained for public inspection in the office of the city clerk. Effective July 1, 1973, true copies of all ordinances that were adopted before January 1, 1972, and are still in effect shall be filed and indexed in the ordinance book. If the city has adopted and issued a code of ordinances in compliance with G.S. 160A-77, its ordinances shall be filed and indexed in the ordinance book until they are codified. (1971, c. 698, s. 1.)

§ 160A-79. Pleading and proving city ordinances.

(a) In all civil and criminal cases a city ordinance that has been codified in a code of ordinances adopted and issued in compliance with G.S. 160A-77 must be pleaded by both section number and caption. In all civil and criminal cases a city ordinance that has not been codified in a code of ordinances adopted and issued in compliance with G.S. 160A-77 must be pleaded by its caption. In both instances, it is not necessary to plead or allege the substance or effect of the ordinance unless the ordinance has no caption and has not been codified.

(b) Any of the following shall be admitted in evidence in all actions or proceedings before courts or administrative bodies and shall have the same force and effect as would an original ordinance:

(1) A city code adopted and issued in compliance with G.S. 160A-77, containing a statement that the code is published by order of the council.

(2) Copies of any part of an official map book maintained in accordance with G.S. 160A-77 and certified under seal by the city clerk as having been adopted by the council and maintained in accordance with its directions (the clerk's certificate need not be authenticated).

(3) A copy of an ordinance as set out in the minutes, code, or ordinance book of the council, certified under seal by the city clerk as a true copy (the clerk's certificate need not be authenticated).

(4) Copies of any official lists or schedules maintained in accordance with G.S. 160A-77 and certified under seal by the city clerk as having been adopted by the council and maintained in accordance with its directions (the clerk's certificate need not be authenticated).

(c) The burden of pleading and proving the existence of any modification or repeal of an ordinance, map, or code, a copy of which has been duly pleaded or admitted in evidence in accordance with this section, shall be upon the party asserting such modification or repeal. It shall be presumed that any portion of a city code that is admitted in evidence in accordance with this section has been codified in compliance with G.S. 160A-77, and the burden of pleading and proving to the contrary shall be upon the party seeking to obtain an advantage thereby.

(d) From and after the respective effective dates of G.S. 160A-77 and 160A-78, no city ordinance shall be enforced or admitted into evidence in any court unless it has been codified or filed and indexed in accordance with G.S.

160A-77 or 160A-78. It shall be presumed that an ordinance which has been properly pleaded and proved in accordance with this section has been codified or filed and indexed in accordance with G.S. 160A-77 or 160A-78, and the burden of pleading and proving to the contrary shall be upon the party seeking to obtain an advantage thereby.

(e) It is the intent of this section to make uniform the law concerning the pleading and proving of city ordinances. To this end, all charter provisions in conflict with this section in effect as of January 1, 1972, are expressly repealed, and no local act taking effect on or after January 1, 1972, shall be construed to repeal or amend this section in whole or in part unless it shall expressly so provide by specific reference. (1917, c. 136, subch. 13, s. 14; C.S., s. 2825; 1959, c. 631; 1971, c. 698, s. 1; 1973, c. 426, s. 18; 1979, 2nd Sess., c. 1247, s. 10.)

§ 160A-80. Power of investigation; subpoena power.

(a) The council shall have power to investigate the affairs of the city, and for that purpose may subpoena witnesses, administer oaths, and compel the production of evidence.

(b) If a person fails or refuses to obey a subpoena issued pursuant to this section, the council may apply to the General Court of Justice for an order requiring that its order be obeyed, and the court shall have jurisdiction to issue these orders after notice to all proper parties. No testimony of any witness before the council pursuant to a subpoena issued in exercise of the power conferred by this section may be used against him on the trial of any civil or criminal action other than a prosecution for false swearing committed on the examination. If any person, while under oath at an investigation by the council, willfully swears falsely, he is guilty of a Class 1 misdemeanor.

(c) Repealed by Session Laws 1991, c. 512, s. 1. (1971, c. 698, s. 1; 1991, c. 512, s. 1; 1993, c. 539, s. 1083; 1994, Ex. Sess., c. 24, s. 14(c).)

§ 160A-81. Conduct of public hearings.

Public hearings may be held at any place within the city or within the county in which the city is located. The council may adopt reasonable rules governing the conduct of public hearings, including but not limited to rules (i) fixing the maximum time allotted to each speaker, (ii) providing for the designation of spokesmen for groups of persons supporting or opposing the same positions, (iii) providing for the selection of delegates from groups of persons supporting or opposing the same positions when the number of persons wishing to attend the hearing exceeds the capacity of the hall, and (iv) providing for the maintenance of order and decorum in the conduct of the hearing.

The council may continue any public hearing without further advertisement. If a public hearing is set for a given date and a quorum of the council is not then present, the hearing shall be continued until the next regular council meeting without further advertisement. (1971, c. 698, s. 1.)

§ 160A-81.1. Public comment period during regular meetings.

The council shall provide at least one period for public comment per month at a regular meeting of the council. The council may adopt reasonable rules governing the conduct of the public comment period, including, but not limited to, rules (i) fixing the maximum time allotted to each speaker, (ii) providing for the designation of spokesmen for groups of persons supporting or opposing the same positions, (iii) providing for the selection of delegates from groups of persons supporting or opposing the same positions when the number of persons wishing to attend the hearing exceeds the capacity of the hall, and (iv) providing for the maintenance of order and decorum in the conduct of the hearing. The council is not required to provide a public comment period under this section if no regular meeting is held during the month. (2005-170, s. 3.)

§ 160A-82. Applicability of Part.

Nothing in this Part, except G.S. 160A-77, 160A-78 and 160A-79, shall be construed to repeal any portion of any city charter inconsistent with anything contained herein. (1971, c. 698, s. 1.)

§ 160A-83. Reserved for future codification purposes.

§ 160A-84. Reserved for future codification purposes.

§ 160A-85. Reserved for future codification purposes.

Part 3A. Ethics Codes and Education Programs.

§ 160A-86. Local governing boards' code of ethics.

(a) Governing boards of cities, counties, local boards of education, unified governments, sanitary districts, and consolidated city-counties shall adopt a resolution or policy containing a code of ethics to guide actions by the governing board members in the performance of the member's official duties as a member of that governing board.

(b) The resolution or policy required by subsection (a) of this section shall address at least all of the following:

(1) The need to obey all applicable laws regarding official actions taken as a board member.

(2) The need to uphold the integrity and independence of the board member's office.

(3) The need to avoid impropriety in the exercise of the board member's official duties.

(4) The need to faithfully perform the duties of the office.

(5) The need to conduct the affairs of the governing board in an open and public manner, including complying with all applicable laws governing open meetings and public records. (2009-403, s. 1.)

§ 160A-87. Ethics education program required.

(a) All members of governing boards of cities, counties, local boards of education, unified governments, sanitary districts, and consolidated city-counties shall receive a minimum of two clock hours of ethics education within 12 months after initial election or appointment to the office and again within 12 months after each subsequent election or appointment to the office.

(b) The ethics education shall cover laws and principles that govern conflicts of interest and ethical standards of conduct at the local government level.

(c) The ethics education may be provided by the North Carolina League of Municipalities, North Carolina Association of County Commissioners, North Carolina School Boards Association, the School of Government at the University of North Carolina at Chapel Hill, or other qualified sources at the choice of the governing board.

(d) The clerk to the governing board shall maintain a record verifying receipt of the ethics education by each member of the governing board. (2009-403, s. 1.)

§ 160A-88. Reserved for future codification purposes.

§ 160A-89. Reserved for future codification purposes.

§ 160A-90. Reserved for future codification purposes.

§ 160A-91. Reserved for future codification purposes.

§ 160A-92. Reserved for future codification purposes.

§ 160A-93. Reserved for future codification purposes.

§ 160A-94. Reserved for future codification purposes.

§ 160A-95. Reserved for future codification purposes.

§ 160A-96. Reserved for future codification purposes.

§ 160A-97. Reserved for future codification purposes.

§ 160A-98. Reserved for future codification purposes.

§ 160A-99. Reserved for future codification purposes.

§ 160A-100. Reserved for future codification purposes.

Part 4. Modification of Form of Government.

§ 160A-101. Optional forms.

Any city may change its name or alter its form of government by adopting any one or combination of the options prescribed by this section:

(1)   Name of the corporation:

The name of the corporation may be changed to any name not deceptively similar to that of another city in this State.

(2)   Style of the corporation:

The city may be styled a city, town, or village.

(3)   Style of the governing board:

The governing board may be styled the board of commissioners, the board of aldermen, or the council.

(4)   Terms of office of members of the council:

Members of the council shall serve terms of office of either two or four years. All of the terms need not be of the same length, and all of the terms need not expire in the same year.

(5)   Number of members of the council:

The council shall consist of any number of members not less than three nor more than 12.

(6)   Mode of election of the council:

a.   All candidates shall be nominated and elected by all the qualified voters of the city.

b.   The city shall be divided into single-member electoral districts; council members shall be apportioned to the districts so that each member represents the same number of persons as nearly as possible, except for members apportioned to the city at large, if any; the qualified voters of each district shall nominate and elect candidates who reside in the district for seats apportioned to that district; and all the qualified voters of the city shall nominate and elect candidates apportioned to the city at large, if any.

c. The city shall be divided into single-member electoral districts; council members shall be apportioned to the districts so that each member represents the same number of persons as nearly as possible, except for members apportioned to the city at large; and candidates shall reside in and represent the districts according to the apportionment plan adopted, but all candidates shall be nominated and elected by all the qualified voters of the city.

d. The city shall be divided into electoral districts equal in number to one half the number of council seats; the council seats shall be divided equally into "ward seats" and "at-large seats," one each of which shall be apportioned to each district, so that each council member represents the same number of persons as nearly as possible; the qualified voters of each district shall nominate and elect candidates to the "ward seats"; candidates for the "at-large seats" shall reside in and represent the districts according to the apportionment plan adopted, but all candidates for "at-large" seats shall be nominated and elected by all the qualified voters of the city.

e. The city shall be divided into single-member electoral districts; council members shall be apportioned to the districts so that each member represents the same number of persons as nearly as possible, except for members apportioned to the city at large, if any; in a nonpartisan primary, the qualified voters of each district shall nominate two candidates who reside in the district, and the qualified voters of the entire city shall nominate two candidates for each seat apportioned to the city at large, if any; and all candidates shall be elected by all the qualified voters of the city.

If either of options b, c, d or e is adopted, the council shall divide the city into the requisite number of single-member electoral districts according to the apportionment plan adopted, and shall cause a map of the districts so laid out to be drawn up and filed as provided by G.S. 160A-22 and 160A-23. No more than one half of the council may be apportioned to the city at large. An initiative petition may specify the number of single-member electoral districts to be laid out, but the drawing of district boundaries and apportionment of members to the districts shall be done in all cases by the council.

(7) Elections:

a. Partisan. - Municipal primaries and elections shall be conducted on a partisan basis as provided in G.S. 163-291.

b. Nonpartisan Plurality. - Municipal elections shall be conducted as provided in G.S. 163-292.

c. Nonpartisan Election and Runoff Election. - Municipal elections and runoff elections shall be conducted as provided in G.S. 163-293.

d. Nonpartisan Primary and Election. - Municipal primaries and elections shall be conducted as provided in G.S. 163-294.

(8) Selection of mayor:

a. The mayor shall be elected by all the qualified voters of the city for a term of not less than two years nor more than four years.

b. The mayor shall be selected by the council from among its membership to serve at its pleasure.

Under option a, the mayor may be given the right to vote on all matters before the council, or he may be limited to voting only to break a tie. Under option b, the mayor has the right to vote on all matters before the council. In both cases the mayor has no right to break a tie vote in which he participated.

(9) Form of government:

a. The city shall operate under the mayor-council form of government in accordance with Part 3 of Article 7 of this Chapter.

b. The city shall operate under the council-manager form of government in accordance with Part 2 of Article 7 of this Chapter and any charter provisions not in conflict therewith. (1969, c. 629, s. 2; 1971, c. 698, s. 1; c. 1076, s. 1; 1973, c. 426, s. 19; c. 1001, ss. 1, 2; 1975, c. 19, s. 64; c. 664, s. 6.)

§ 160A-102. Amendment by ordinance.

By following the procedure set out in this section, the council may amend the city charter by ordinance to implement any of the optional forms set out in G.S. 160A-101. The council shall first adopt a resolution of intent to consider an ordinance amending the charter. The resolution of intent shall describe the proposed charter amendments briefly but completely and with reference to the pertinent provisions of G.S. 160A-101, but it need not contain the precise text of the charter amendments necessary to implement the proposed changes. At the same time that a resolution of intent is adopted, the council shall also call a public hearing on the proposed charter amendments, the date of the hearing to be not more than 45 days after adoption of the resolution. A notice of the hearing shall be published at least once not less than 10 days prior to the date fixed for the public hearing, and shall contain a summary of the proposed amendments. Following the public hearing, but not earlier than the next regular meeting of the council and not later than 60 days from the date of the hearing, the council may adopt an ordinance amending the charter to implement the amendments proposed in the resolution of intent.

The council may, but shall not be required to unless a referendum petition is received pursuant to G.S. 160A-103, make any ordinance adopted pursuant to this section effective only if approved by a vote of the people, and may by resolution adopted at the same time call a special election for the purpose of submitting the ordinance to a vote. The date fixed for the special election shall be not more than 90 days after adoption of the ordinance.

Within 10 days after an ordinance is adopted under this section, the council shall publish a notice stating that an ordinance amending the charter has been adopted and summarizing its contents and effect. If the ordinance is made effective subject to a vote of the people, the council shall publish a notice of the election in accordance with G.S. 163-287, and need not publish a separate notice of adoption of the ordinance.

The council may not commence proceedings under this section between the time of the filing of a valid initiative petition pursuant to G.S. 160A-104 and the date of any election called pursuant to such petition. (1969, c. 629, s. 2; 1971, c. 698, s. 1; 1973, c. 426, s. 20; 1979, 2nd Sess., c. 1247, s. 11.)

§ 160A-103. Referendum on charter amendments by ordinance.

An ordinance adopted under G.S. 160A-102 that is not made effective upon approval by a vote of the people shall be subject to a referendum petition. Upon receipt of a referendum petition bearing the signatures and residence addresses of a number of qualified voters of the city equal to at least 10 percent of the whole number of voters who are registered to vote in city elections according to the most recent figures certified by the State Board of Elections or 5,000, whichever is less, the council shall submit an ordinance adopted under G.S. 160A-102 to a vote of the people. The date of the special election shall be fixed on a date permitted by G.S. 163-287. A referendum petition shall be addressed to the council and shall identify the ordinance to be submitted to a vote. A referendum petition must be filed with the city clerk not later than 30 days after publication of the notice of adoption of the ordinance. (1969, c. 629, s. 2; 1971, c. 698, s. 1; 1979, 2nd Sess., c. 1247, ss. 13, 15; 2013-381, s. 10.27.)

§ 160A-104. Initiative petitions for charter amendments.

The people may initiate a referendum on proposed charter amendments. An initiative petition shall bear the signatures and resident addresses of a number of qualified voters of the city equal to at least ten percent (10%) of the whole number of voters who are registered to vote in city elections according to the most recent figures certified by the State Board of Elections or 5,000, whichever is less. The petition shall set forth the proposed amendments by describing them briefly but completely and with reference to the pertinent provisions of G.S. 160A-101, but it need not contain the precise text of the charter amendments necessary to implement the proposed changes. The petition may not propose changes in the alternative, or more than one integrated set of charter amendments. Upon receipt of a valid initiative petition, the council shall call a special election on the question of adopting the charter amendments proposed therein, and shall give public notice thereof in accordance with G.S. 163-287. The date of the special election shall be fixed on a date permitted by G.S. 163-287. If a majority of the votes cast in the special election shall be in favor of the proposed changes, the council shall adopt an ordinance amending the charter to put them into effect. Such an ordinance shall not be subject to a referendum petition. No initiative petition may be filed (i) between the time the council initiates proceedings under G.S. 160A-102 by publishing a notice of hearing on proposed charter amendments and the time proceeding under that section have been carried to a conclusion either through adoption or rejection of a proposed ordinance or lapse of time, nor (ii) within one year and six months following the effective date of an ordinance amending the city charter pursuant to this Article, nor (iii) within one year and six months following the date of any election on charter amendments that were defeated by the voters.

The restrictions imposed by this section on filing initiative petitions shall apply only to petitions concerning the same subject matter. For example, pendency of council action on amendments concerning the method of electing the council shall not preclude an initiative petition on adoption of the council-manager form of government.

Nothing in this section shall be construed to prohibit the submission of more than one proposition for charter amendments on the same ballot so long as no proposition offers a different plan under the same option as another proposition on the same ballot. (1969, c. 629, s. 2; 1971, c. 698, s. 1; 1973, c. 426, s. 21; 1979, 2nd Sess., c. 1247, ss. 12, 14; 2013-381, s. 10.28.)

§ 160A-105. Submission of propositions to voters; form of ballot.

A proposition to approve an ordinance or petition shall be printed on the ballot in substantially the following form:

"Shall the ordinance (describe the effect of the ordinance) be approved?

( )   YES

( )   NO"

The ballot shall be separate from all other ballots used at the election.

If a majority of the votes cast on a proposition shall be in the affirmative, the plan contained therein shall be put into effect as provided in this Article. If a majority of the votes cast shall be against the proposition, the ordinance or petition proposing the amendments shall be void and of no effect. (1969, c. 629, s. 2; 1971, c. 698, s. 1.)

§ 160A-106. Amendment of charter provisions dependent on form of government.

The authority conferred by this Article to amend charter provisions within the options set out in G.S. 160A-101 also includes authority to amend other charter provisions dependent on the form of city government to conform them to the form of government amendments. By way of illustration and not limitation, if a charter providing for a five-member council is amended to increase the size of the council to seven members, a charter provision defining a quorum of the council as three members shall be amended to define a quorum as four members. (1971, c. 698, s. 1.)

§ 160A-107. Plan to continue for two years.

Charter amendments adopted as provided in this Article shall continue in force for at least two years after the beginning of the term of office of the officers elected thereunder. (1969, c. 629, s. 2; 1971, c. 698, s. 1.)

§ 160A-108. Municipal officers to carry out plan.

It shall be the duty of the mayor, the council, the city clerk, and other city officials in office, and all boards of election and election officials, when any plan of government is adopted as provided by this Article or is proposed for adoption, to comply with all requirements of this Article, to the end that all things may be done which are necessary for the nomination and election of the officers first to be elected under the new plan so adopted. (1969, c. 629, s. 2; 1971, c. 698, s. 1.)

§ 160A-109. Effective date.

The council may submit new charter amendments proposed under this Article at any regular or special municipal election, or at a special election called for that sole purpose. Any amendment affecting the election of city officers shall be finally adopted and approved at least 90 days before the first election for mayor or council members held thereunder. (1969, c. 629, s. 2; 1971, c. 698, s. 1.)

§ 160A-110. Charters to remain in force.

The charter of any city that adopts a new form of government as provided in this Article shall continue in full force and effect notwithstanding adoption of a new form of government, except to the extent modified by an ordinance adopted under the authority conferred and pursuant to the procedures prescribed by this Article. (1969, c. 629, s. 2; 1971, c. 698, s. 1.)

§ 160A-111. Filing certified true copies of charter amendments.

The city clerk shall file a certified true copy of any charter amendment adopted under this Part with the Secretary of State and the Legislative Library. (1985 (Reg. Sess., 1986), c. 935, s. 2; 1989, c. 191, s. 2.)

§§ 160A-112 through 160A-115. Reserved for future codification purposes.

Article 6.

Elections.

§§ 160A-116 through 160A-127. Repealed by Session Laws 1971, c. 1076, s. 2.

§§ 160A-128 through 160A-145. Reserved for future codification purposes.

Article 7.

Administrative Offices.

Part 1. Organization and Reorganization of City Government.

§ 160A-146. Council to organize city government.

The council may create, change, abolish, and consolidate offices, positions, departments, boards, commissions, and agencies of the city government and generally organize and reorganize the city government in order to promote orderly and efficient administration of city affairs, subject to the following limitations:

(1) The council may not abolish any office, position, department, board, commission, or agency established and required by law;

(2) The council may not combine offices or confer certain duties on the same officer when such action is specifically forbidden by law;

(3) The council may not discontinue or assign elsewhere any functions or duties assigned by law to a particular office, position, department, or agency. (1971, c. 698, s. 1.)

Part 2. Administration of Council-Manager Cities.

§ 160A-147. Appointment of city manager; dual office holding.

(a) In cities whose charters provide for the council-manager form of government, the council shall appoint a city manager to serve at its pleasure. The manager shall be appointed solely on the basis of the manager's executive and administrative qualifications. The manager need not be a resident of the city or State at the time of appointment. The office of city manager is hereby declared to be an office that may be held concurrently with other appointive (but not elective) offices pursuant to Article VI, Sec. 9, of the Constitution.

(b) Notwithstanding the provisions of subsection (a), a city manager may serve on a county board of education that is elected on a non-partisan basis if the following criteria are met:

(1) The population of the city by which the city manager is employed does not exceed 10,000;

(2) The city is located in two counties; and

(3) The population of the county in which the city manager resides does not exceed 40,000.

(b1) Notwithstanding the provisions of subsection (a) of this section, a city manager may serve on a county board of education that is elected on a nonpartisan basis if the population of the city by which the city manager is employed does not exceed 3,000.

(c) Notwithstanding the provisions of subsection (a), a city manager may hold elective office if the following criteria are met:

(1) The population of the city by which the city manager is employed does not exceed 3,000.

(2) The city manager is an elected official of a city other than the city by which the city manager is employed.

(d) For the purposes of this section, population figures shall be according to the latest United States decennial figures issued at the time the second office is assumed. If census figures issued after the second office is assumed increase the city or county population beyond the limits of this section, the city manager may complete the term of elected office that the city manager is then serving.

(1969, c. 629, s. 2; 1971, c. 698, s. 1; 1989, c. 49; 1997-25, s. 1; 2009-321, s. 1.)

§ 160A-148. Powers and duties of manager.

The manager shall be the chief administrator of the city. He shall be responsible to the council for administering all municipal affairs placed in his charge by them, and shall have the following powers and duties:

(1)   He shall appoint and suspend or remove all city officers and employees not elected by the people, and whose appointment or removal is not otherwise provided for by law, except the city attorney, in accordance with such general personnel rules, regulations, policies, or ordinances as the council may adopt.

(2)   He shall direct and supervise the administration of all departments, offices, and agencies of the city, subject to the general direction and control of the council, except as otherwise provided by law.

(3)   He shall attend all meetings of the council and recommend any measures that he deems expedient.

(4)   He shall see that all laws of the State, the city charter, and the ordinances, resolutions, and regulations of the council are faithfully executed within the city.

(5)   He shall prepare and submit the annual budget and capital program to the council.

(6)   He shall annually submit to the council and make available to the public a complete report on the finances and administrative activities of the city as of the end of the fiscal year.

(7)   He shall make any other reports that the council may require concerning the operations of city departments, offices, and agencies subject to his direction and control.

(8)   He shall perform any other duties that may be required or authorized by the council. (1969, c. 629, s. 2; 1971, c. 698, s. 1; 1973, c. 426, s. 22.)

§ 160A-149. Acting city manager.

By letter filed with the city clerk, the manager may designate, subject to the approval of the council, a qualified person to exercise the powers and perform the duties of manager during his temporary absence or disability. During this absence or disability, the council may revoke that designation at any time and appoint another to serve until the manager returns or his disability ceases. (1971, c. 698, s. 1.)

§ 160A-150. Interim city manager.

When the position of city manager is vacant, the council shall designate a qualified person to exercise the powers and perform the duties of manager until the vacancy is filled. (1971, c. 698, s. 1.)

§ 160A-151. Mayor and councilmen ineligible to serve or act as manager.

Neither the mayor nor any member of the council shall be eligible for appointment as manager or acting or interim manager. (1971, c. 698, s. 1.)

§ 160A-152. Applicability of Part.

This Part shall apply only to those cities having the council-manager form of government. If the powers and duties of a city manager set out in any city charter shall differ materially from those set out in G.S. 160A-148, the council may by ordinance confer or impose on the manager any of the powers or duties set out in G.S. 160A-148 but not contained in the charter. (1971, c. 698, s. 1.)

§§ 160A-153 through 160A-154. Reserved for future codification purposes.

Part 3. Administration of Mayor-Council Cities.

§ 160A-155. Council to provide for administration in mayor-council cities.

The council shall appoint, suspend, and remove the heads of all city departments, and all other city employees; provided, the council may delegate to any administrative official or department head the power to appoint, suspend, and remove city employees assigned to his department. The head of each department shall see that all laws of the State, the city charter, and the ordinances, resolutions, and regulations of the council concerning his department are faithfully executed within the city. Otherwise, the administration of the city shall be performed as provided by law or direction of the council. (1971, c. 698, s. 1; 1979, 2nd Sess., c. 1247, s. 16.)

§ 160A-156. Acting department heads.

By letter filed with the city clerk, the head of any department may designate, subject to the approval of the council, a qualified person to exercise the powers and perform the duties of head of that department during his temporary absence or disability. During his absence or disability, the council may revoke that designation at any time and appoint another officer to serve until the department head returns or his disability ceases. (1971, c. 698, s. 1.)

§ 160A-157. Interim department heads.

When the position of head of any department is vacant, the council may designate a qualified person to exercise the powers and perform the duties of head of the department until the vacancy is filled. (1971, c. 698, s. 1.)

§ 160A-158. Mayor and councilmen ineligible to serve or act as heads of departments.

Neither the mayor nor any member of the council shall be eligible for appointment as head of any city department or as acting or interim head of a department; provided, that in cities having a population of less than 5,000 according to the most recent official federal census, the mayor and any member of the council shall be eligible for appointment by the council as department head or other employee, and may receive reasonable compensation for such employment, notwithstanding any other provision of law. (1971, c. 698, s. 1; 1979, 2nd Sess., c. 1247, s. 17.)

§ 160A-159. Applicability of Part.

This Part shall apply only to those cities having the mayor-council form of government. (1971, c. 698, s. 1.)

§§ 160A-160 through 160A-161. Reserved for future codification purposes.

Part 4. Personnel.

§ 160A-162. Compensation.

(a) The council shall fix or approve the schedule of pay, expense allowances, and other compensation of all city employees, and may adopt position classification plans; any compensation or pay plan may include provisions for payments to employees on account of sickness or disability. In cities with the council-manager form of government, the manager shall be responsible for preparing position classification and pay plans for submission to the council and, after any such plans have been adopted by the council, shall administer them. In cities with the mayor-council form of government, the council shall appoint a personnel officer (or confer the duties of personnel officer on some city administrative officer); the personnel officer shall then be responsible for administering the pay plan and any position classification plan in accordance with general policies and directives adopted by the council.

(b) The council may purchase life, health, and any other forms of insurance for the benefit of all or any class of city employees and their dependents, and may provide other fringe benefits for city employees. In providing health insurance to city employees, the council shall not provide abortion coverage greater than that provided by the State Health Plan for Teachers and State Employees under Article 3B of Chapter 135 of the General Statutes. (1923, c. 20; 1949, c. 103; 1969, c. 845; 1971, c. 698, s. 1; 1979, 2nd Sess., c. 1247, ss. 18, 19; 2013-366, s. 2(c).)

§ 160A-163. Retirement benefits.

(a) The council may provide for enrolling city employees in the Local Governmental Employees' Retirement System, the Law-Enforcement Officers' Benefit and Relief Fund, the Firemen's Pension Fund, or a retirement plan certified to be actuarially sound by a qualified actuary as defined in subsection (d) of this section, and may make payments into any such retirement system or plan on behalf of its employees. The city may also supplement from local funds benefits provided by the Local Governmental Employees' Retirement System, the Law-Enforcement Officers' Benefit and Relief Fund, or the Firemen's Pension Fund.

(b) The council may create and administer a special fund for the relief of members of the police and fire departments who have been retired for age, or for disability or injury incurred in the line of duty, but any such funds established on or after January 1, 1972, shall be subject to the provisions of subsection (c) of this section. The council may receive donations and devises in aid of any such fund, shall provide for its permanence and increase, and shall prescribe and regulate the conditions under which benefits may be paid.

(c) No city shall make payments into any retirement system or plan established or authorized by local act of the General Assembly unless the plan is certified to be actuarially sound by a qualified actuary as defined in subsection (d) of this section.

(d) A qualified actuary means an individual certified as qualified by the Commissioner of Insurance, or any member of the American Academy of Actuaries.

(e) A city which is providing health insurance under G.S. 160A-162(b) may provide health insurance for all or any class of former employees of the city who are receiving benefits under subsection (a) of this section or who are 65 years of age or older. Such health insurance may be paid entirely by the city, partly by the city and former employee, or entirely by the former employee, at the option of the city.

(f) The council may provide a deferred compensation plan. Where the council provides a deferred compensation plan, the investment of funds for the plan shall be exempt from the provisions of G.S 159-30 and G.S. 159-31. Cities may invest deferred compensation plan funds in life insurance, fixed or variable annuities and retirement income contracts, regulated investment trusts, or other forms of investments approved by the Board of Trustees of the North Carolina Public Employee Deferred Compensation Plan.

(g) Should the council provide for a retirement plan, a plan which supplements a State-administered plan, or a special fund, any benefits payable from such plan or fund on account of the disability of city employees may be restricted with regard to the amount which may be earned by the disabled former employee in any other employment, but only to the extent that the earnings of disability beneficiaries in the Local Governmental Employees' Retirement System are restricted in accordance with G.S. 128-27(e)(1). (1917, c. 136, subch. 5, s. 1; 1919, cc. 136, 237; C.S., s. 2787; 1965, c. 931; 1971, c. 698, s. 1; 1981, c. 347, s. 2; 1991, c. 277, s. 2; 1995, c. 259, s. 3; 2011-284, s. 111.)

§ 160A-164. Personnel rules.

The council may adopt or provide for rules and regulations or ordinances concerning but not limited to annual leave, sick leave, special leave with full pay or with partial pay supplementing workers' compensation payments for employees injured in accidents arising out of and in the course of employment, hours of employment, holidays, working conditions, service award and incentive award programs, other personnel policies, and any other measures that promote the hiring and retention of capable, diligent, and honest career employees. (1917, c. 136, subch. 5, s. 1; 1919, cc. 136, 237; C.S., s. 2787; 1965, c. 931; 1971, c. 698, s. 1; 1979, c. 714, s. 2.)

§ 160A-164.1. Smallpox vaccination policy (see editor's note on condition precedent).

All municipalities that employ firefighters, police officers, paramedics, or other first responders shall, not later than 90 days after this section becomes law, enact a policy regarding sick leave and salary continuation for those employees for absence from work due to an adverse medical reaction resulting from the employee receiving in employment vaccination against smallpox incident to the Administration of Smallpox Countermeasures by Health Professionals, section 304 of the Homeland Security Act, Pub. L. No. 107-296 (Nov. 25, 2002) (to be codified at 42 U.S.C. § 233(p)). (2003-169, s. 5.)

§ 160A-164.2. Criminal history record check of employees permitted.

The council may adopt or provide for rules and regulations or ordinances concerning a requirement that any applicant for employment be subject to a criminal history record check of State and National Repositories of Criminal Histories conducted by the Department of Justice in accordance with G.S. 114-19.14. The city may consider the results of these criminal history record checks in its hiring decisions. (2003-214, s. 5.)

§ 160A-165. Personnel board.

The council may establish a personnel board with authority to administer tests designed to determine the merit and fitness of candidates for appointment or promotion, to conduct hearings upon the appeal of employees who have been suspended, demoted, or discharged, and hear employee grievances. (1917, c. 136, subch. 5, s. 1; 1919, cc. 136, 237; C.S., s. 2787; 1965, c. 931; 1971, c. 698, s. 1.)

§ 160A-166. Participation in Social Security Act.

The council may take any action necessary to allow city employees to participate fully in benefits provided by the federal Social Security Act. (1949, c. 103; 1969, c. 845; 1971, c. 698, s. 1.)

§ 160A-167. Defense of employees and officers; payment of judgments.

(a) Upon request made by or in behalf of any member or former member of the governing body of any authority, or any city, county, or authority employee or officer, or former employee or officer, any soil and water conservation supervisor or any local soil and water conservation employee, whether the employee is a district or county employee, or any member of a volunteer fire department or rescue squad which receives public funds, any city, authority, county, soil and water conservation district, or county alcoholic beverage control board may provide for the defense of any civil or criminal action or proceeding brought against him either in his official or in his individual capacity, or both, on account of any act done or omission made, or any act allegedly done or omission allegedly made, in the scope and course of his employment or duty as an employee or officer of the city, authority, county or county alcoholic beverage control board. The defense may be provided by the city, authority, county or county alcoholic beverage control board by its own counsel, or by employing other counsel, or by purchasing insurance which requires that the insurer provide the defense. Providing for a defense pursuant to this section is hereby declared to be for a public purpose, and the expenditure of funds therefor is hereby declared to be a necessary expense. Nothing in this section shall be deemed to require any city, authority, county or county alcoholic beverage control board to provide for the defense of any action or proceeding of any nature.

(b)   Any city council or board of county commissioners may appropriate funds for the purpose of paying all or part of a claim made or any civil judgment entered against any of its members or former members of the governing body of any authority, or any city, county, or authority employees or officers, or former employees or officers, or any soil and water conservation supervisor or any local soil and water conservation employee, whether the employee is a district or county employee, when such claim is made or such judgment is rendered as damages on account of any act done or omission made, or any act allegedly done or omission allegedly made, in the scope and course of his employment or duty as a member or former member of the governing body of any authority, or any city, county, district, or authority employee or officer of the city, authority, district, or county; provided, however, that nothing in this section shall authorize any city, authority, district, or county to appropriate funds for the purpose of paying any claim made or civil judgment entered against any of its members or former members of the governing body of any authority, or any city, county, district, or authority employees or officers or former employees or officers if the city council or board of county commissioners finds that such members or former members of the governing body of any authority, or any city, county, or authority employee or officer acted or failed to act because of actual fraud, corruption or actual malice on his part. Any city, authority, or county may purchase insurance coverage for payment of claims or judgments pursuant to this section. Nothing in this section shall be deemed to require any city, authority, or county to pay any claim or judgment referred to herein, and the purchase of insurance coverage for payment of any such claim or judgment shall not be deemed an assumption of any liability not covered by such insurance contract, and shall not be deemed an assumption of liability for payment of any claim or judgment in excess of the limits of coverage in such insurance contract.

(c)   Subsection (b) shall not authorize any city, authority, or county to pay all or part of a claim made or civil judgment entered unless (1) notice of the claim or litigation is given to the city council, authority governing board, or board of county commissioners as the case may be prior to the time that the claim is settled or civil judgment is entered, and (2) the city council, authority governing board, or board of county commissioners as the case may be shall have adopted, and made available for public inspection, uniform standards under which claims made or civil judgments entered against members or former members of the governing body of any authority, or any city, county, or authority employees or officers, or former employees or officers, shall be paid.

(d)   For the purposes of this section, "authority" means an authority organized under Article 1 of Chapter 162A of the General Statutes, the North Carolina Water and Sewer Authorities Act. "District" means a soil and water conservation district organized under Chapter 139 of the General Statutes. (1967, c. 1093; 1971, c. 698, s. 1; 1973, c. 426, s. 23; c. 1450; 1977, c. 307, s. 2; c. 834, s. 1; 1983, c. 525, ss. 1-4; 2001-300, s. 2.)

§ 160A-168. Privacy of employee personnel records.

(a)   Notwithstanding the provisions of G.S. 132-6 or any other general law or local act concerning access to public records, personnel files of employees, former employees, or applicants for employment maintained by a city are subject to inspection and may be disclosed only as provided by this section. For purposes of this section, an employee's personnel file consists of any information in any form gathered by the city with respect to that employee and, by way of illustration but not limitation, relating to his application, selection or nonselection, performance, promotions, demotions, transfers, suspension and other disciplinary actions, evaluation forms, leave, salary, and termination of employment. As used in this section, "employee" includes former employees of the city.

(b)   The following information with respect to each city employee is a matter of public record:

(1)   Name.

(2)   Age.

(3)   Date of original employment or appointment to the service.

(4)   The terms of any contract by which the employee is employed whether written or oral, past and current, to the extent that the city has the written contract or a record of the oral contract in its possession.

(5)   Current position.

(6) Title.

(7) Current salary.

(8) Date and amount of each increase or decrease in salary with that municipality.

(9) Date and type of each promotion, demotion, transfer, suspension, separation, or other change in position classification with that municipality.

(10) Date and general description of the reasons for each promotion with that municipality.

(11) Date and type of each dismissal, suspension, or demotion for disciplinary reasons taken by the municipality. If the disciplinary action was a dismissal, a copy of the written notice of the final decision of the municipality setting forth the specific acts or omissions that are the basis of the dismissal.

(12) The office to which the employee is currently assigned.

(b1) For the purposes of this subsection, the term "salary" includes pay, benefits, incentives, bonuses, and deferred and all other forms of compensation paid by the employing entity.

(b2) The city council shall determine in what form and by whom this information will be maintained. Any person may have access to this information for the purpose of inspection, examination, and copying, during regular business hours, subject only to such rules and regulations for the safekeeping of public records as the city council may have adopted. Any person denied access to this information may apply to the appropriate division of the General Court of Justice for an order compelling disclosure, and the court shall have jurisdiction to issue such orders.

(c) All information contained in a city employee's personnel file, other than the information made public by subsection (b) of this section, is confidential and shall be open to inspection only in the following instances:

(1) The employee or his duly authorized agent may examine all portions of his personnel file except (i) letters of reference solicited prior to employment, and (ii) information concerning a medical disability, mental or physical, that a prudent physician would not divulge to his patient.

(2) A licensed physician designated in writing by the employee may examine the employee's medical record.

(3) A city employee having supervisory authority over the employee may examine all material in the employee's personnel file.

(4) By order of a court of competent jurisdiction, any person may examine such portion of an employee's personnel file as may be ordered by the court.

(5) An official of an agency of the State or federal government, or any political subdivision of the State, may inspect any portion of a personnel file when such inspection is deemed by the official having custody of such records to be inspected to be necessary and essential to the pursuance of a proper function of the inspecting agency, but no information shall be divulged for the purpose of assisting in a criminal prosecution (of the employee), or for the purpose of assisting in an investigation of (the employee's) tax liability. However, the official having custody of such records may release the name, address, and telephone number from a personnel file for the purpose of assisting in a criminal investigation.

(6) An employee may sign a written release, to be placed with his personnel file, that permits the person with custody of the file to provide, either in person, by telephone, or by mail, information specified in the release to prospective employers, educational institutions, or other persons specified in the release.

(7) The city manager, with concurrence of the council, or, in cities not having a manager, the council may inform any person of the employment or nonemployment, promotion, demotion, suspension or other disciplinary action, reinstatement, transfer, or termination of a city employee and the reasons for that personnel action. Before releasing the information, the manager or council shall determine in writing that the release is essential to maintaining public confidence in the administration of city services or to maintaining the level and quality of city services. This written determination shall be retained in the office of the manager or the city clerk, and is a record available for public inspection and shall become part of the employee's personnel file.

(c1) Even if considered part of an employee's personnel file, the following information need not be disclosed to an employee nor to any other person:

(1) Testing or examination material used solely to determine individual qualifications for appointment, employment, or promotion in the city's service, when disclosure would compromise the objectivity or the fairness of the testing or examination process.

(2) Investigative reports or memoranda and other information concerning the investigation of possible criminal actions of an employee, until the investigation is completed and no criminal action taken, or until the criminal action is concluded.

(3) Information that might identify an undercover law enforcement officer or a law enforcement informer.

(4) Notes, preliminary drafts and internal communications concerning an employee. In the event such materials are used for any official personnel decision, then the employee or his duly authorized agent shall have a right to inspect such materials.

(c2) The city council may permit access, subject to limitations they may impose, to selected personnel files by a professional representative of a training, research, or academic institution if that person certifies that he will not release information identifying the employees whose files are opened and that the information will be used solely for statistical, research, or teaching purposes. This certification shall be retained by the city as long as each personnel file examined is retained.

(c3) Notwithstanding any provision of this section to the contrary, the Retirement Systems Division of the Department of State Treasurer may disclose the name and mailing address of former local governmental employees to domiciled, nonprofit organizations representing 2,000 or more active or retired State government, local government, or public school employees.

(d) The city council of a city that maintains personnel files containing information other than the information mentioned in subsection (b) of this section shall establish procedures whereby an employee who objects to material in his file on grounds that it is inaccurate or misleading may seek to have the material removed from the file or may place in the file a statement relating to the material.

(e) A public official or employee who knowingly, willfully, and with malice permits any person to have access to information contained in a personnel file, except as is permitted by this section, is guilty of a Class 3 misdemeanor and upon conviction shall only be fined an amount not more than five hundred dollars ($500.00).

(f) Any person, not specifically authorized by this section to have access to a personnel file designated as confidential, who shall knowingly and willfully examine in its official filing place, remove or copy any portion of a confidential personnel file shall be guilty of a Class 3 misdemeanor and upon conviction shall only be fined in the discretion of the court but not in excess of five hundred dollars ($500.00). (1975, c. 701, s. 2; 1981, c. 926, ss. 1-4; 1993, c. 539, ss. 1084, 1085; 1994, Ex. Sess., c. 24, s. 14(c); 2007-508, s. 7; 2008-194, s. 11(e); 2010-169, s. 18(f).)

§ 160A-169. City employee political activity.

(a) Purpose. The purpose of this section is to ensure that city employees are not subjected to political or partisan coercion while performing their job duties, to ensure that employees are not restricted from political activities while off duty, and to ensure that public funds are not used for political or partisan activities.

It is not the purpose of this section to allow infringement upon the rights of employees to engage in free speech and free association. Every city employee has a civic responsibility to support good government by every available means and in every appropriate manner. Employees shall not be restricted from affiliating with civic organizations of a partisan or political nature, nor shall employees, while off duty, be restricted from attending political meetings, or advocating and supporting the principles or policies of civic or political organizations, or supporting partisan or nonpartisan candidates of their choice in accordance with the Constitution and laws of the State and the Constitution and laws of the United States of America.

(b) Definitions. For the purposes of this section:

(1) "City employee" or ""employee" means any person employed by a city or any department or program thereof that is supported, in whole or in part, by city funds;

(2) "On duty" means that time period when an employee is engaged in the duties of his or her employment; and

(3) "Workplace" means any place where an employee engages in his or her job duties.

(c) No employee while on duty or in the workplace may:

(1) Use his or her official authority or influence for the purpose of interfering with or affecting the result of an election or nomination for political office; or

(2) Coerce, solicit, or compel contributions for political or partisan purposes by another employee.

(d) No employee may be required as a duty or condition of employment, promotion, or tenure of office to contribute funds for political or partisan purposes.

(e) No employee may use city funds, supplies, or equipment for partisan purposes, or for political purposes except where such political uses are otherwise permitted by law.

(f) To the extent that this section conflicts with the provisions of any local act, city charter, local ordinance, resolution, or policy, this section prevails to the extent of the conflict. (1991, c. 619, s. 2; 1993, c. 298, s. 2.)

§ 160A-169.1. Municipality verification of employee work authorization.

(a) Municipalities Must Use E-Verify. - Each municipality shall register and participate in E-Verify to verify the work authorization of new employees hired to work in the United States.

(b) E-Verify Defined. - As used in this section, the term "E-Verify" means the federal E-Verify program operated by the United States Department of Homeland Security and other federal agencies, or any successor or equivalent program used to verify the work authorization of newly hired employees pursuant to federal law.

(c) Nondiscrimination. - This section shall be enforced without regard to race, religion, gender, ethnicity, or national origin. (2011-263, s. 5.)

§ 160A-170. Reserved for future codification purposes.

Part 5. City Clerk.

§ 160A-171. City clerk; duties.

There shall be a city clerk who shall give notice of meetings of the council, keep a journal of the proceedings of the council, be the custodian of all city records, and shall perform any other duties that may be required by law or the council. (1917, c. 136, subch. 13, s. 1; C.S., s. 2826; 1941, c. 103; 1949, c. 14; 1971, c. 698, s. 1.)

§ 160A-172. Deputy clerk.

The council may provide for a deputy city clerk who shall have full authority to exercise and perform any of the powers and duties of the city clerk that may be specified by the council. (1917, c. 136, subch. 13, s. 1; C.S., s. 2826; 1941, c. 103; 1949, c. 14; 1971, c. 698, s. 1.)

Part 6. City Attorney.

§ 160A-173. City attorney; appointment and duties.

The council shall appoint a city attorney to serve at its pleasure and to be its legal adviser. (1971, c. 698, s. 1.)

Article 8.

Delegation and Exercise of the General Police Power.

§ 160A-174. General ordinance-making power.

(a) A city may by ordinance define, prohibit, regulate, or abate acts, omissions, or conditions, detrimental to the health, safety, or welfare of its citizens and the peace and dignity of the city, and may define and abate nuisances.

(b) A city ordinance shall be consistent with the Constitution and laws of North Carolina and of the United States. An ordinance is not consistent with State or federal law when:

(1) The ordinance infringes a liberty guaranteed to the people by the State or federal Constitution;

(2) The ordinance makes unlawful an act, omission or condition which is expressly made lawful by State or federal law;

(3) The ordinance makes lawful an act, omission, or condition which is expressly made unlawful by State or federal law;

(4) The ordinance purports to regulate a subject that cities are expressly forbidden to regulate by State or federal law;

(5) The ordinance purports to regulate a field for which a State or federal statute clearly shows a legislative intent to provide a complete and integrated regulatory scheme to the exclusion of local regulation;

(6) The elements of an offense defined by a city ordinance are identical to the elements of an offense defined by State or federal law.

The fact that a State or federal law, standing alone, makes a given act, omission, or condition unlawful shall not preclude city ordinances requiring a higher standard of conduct or condition. (1971, c. 698, s. 1.)

§ 160A-175. Enforcement of ordinances.

(a) A city shall have power to impose fines and penalties for violation of its ordinances, and may secure injunctions and abatement orders to further insure compliance with its ordinances as provided by this section.

(b) Unless the Council shall otherwise provide, violation of a city ordinance is a misdemeanor or infraction as provided by G.S. 14-4. An ordinance may provide by express statement that the maximum fine, term of imprisonment, or infraction penalty to be imposed for a violation is some amount of money or number of days less than the maximum imposed by G.S. 14-4.

(c) An ordinance may provide that violation shall subject the offender to a civil penalty to be recovered by the city in a civil action in the nature of debt if the offender does not pay the penalty within a prescribed period of time after he has been cited for violation of the ordinance.

(c1) An ordinance may provide for the recovery of a civil penalty by the city for violation of the fire prevention code of the State Building Code as authorized under G.S. 143-139.

(d) An ordinance may provide that it may be enforced by an appropriate equitable remedy issuing from a court of competent jurisdiction. In such case, the General Court of Justice shall have jurisdiction to issue such orders as may be appropriate, and it shall not be a defense to the application of the city for equitable relief that there is an adequate remedy at law.

(e) An ordinance that makes unlawful a condition existing upon or use made of real property may be enforced by injunction and order of abatement, and the General Court of Justice shall have jurisdiction to issue such orders. When a violation of such an ordinance occurs the city may apply to the appropriate division of the General Court of Justice for a mandatory or prohibitory injunction and order of abatement commanding the defendant to correct the unlawful condition upon or cease the unlawful use of the property. The action shall be governed in all respects by the laws and rules governing civil proceedings, including the Rules of Civil Procedure in general and Rule 65 in particular.

In addition to an injunction, the court may enter an order of abatement as a part of the judgment in the cause. An order of abatement may direct that buildings or other structures on the property be closed, demolished, or removed; that fixtures, furniture, or other movable property be removed from buildings on the property; that grass and weeds be cut; that improvements or repairs be made; or that any other action be taken that is necessary to bring the property into compliance with the ordinance. If the defendant fails or refuses to comply with an injunction or with an order of abatement within the time allowed by the court, he may be cited for contempt, and the city may execute the order of abatement. The city shall have a lien on the property for the cost of executing an order of abatement in the nature of a mechanic's and materialman's lien. The defendant may secure cancellation of an order of abatement by paying all costs of the proceedings and posting a bond for compliance with the order. The bond shall be given with sureties approved by the clerk of superior court in an amount approved by the judge before whom the matter is heard and shall be conditioned on the defendant's full compliance with the terms of the order of abatement within a time fixed by the judge. Cancellation of an order of abatement shall not suspend or cancel an injunction issued in conjunction therewith.

(f) Subject to the express terms of the ordinance, a city ordinance may be enforced by any one, all, or a combination of the remedies authorized and prescribed by this section.

(g) A city ordinance may provide, when appropriate, that each day's continuing violation shall be a separate and distinct offense.

(h) Notwithstanding any authority under this Article or any local act of the General Assembly, no ordinance regulating trees may be enforced on land owned or operated by a public airport authority. (1971, c. 698, s. 1; 1985, c. 764, s. 35; 1993, c. 329, s. 4; 2013-331, s. 2.)

§ 160A-176. Ordinances effective on city property outside limits.

Any city ordinance may be made effective on and to property and rights-of-way belonging to the city and located outside the corporate limits. (1917, c. 136, subch. 5, s. 2; C.S., s. 2790; 1971, c. 698, s. 1; 1973, c. 426, s. 24.)

§ 160A-176.1. Ordinances effective in Atlantic Ocean.

(a) A city may adopt ordinances to regulate and control swimming, surfing and littering in the Atlantic Ocean adjacent to that portion of the city within its boundaries or within its extraterritorial jurisdiction; provided, however, nothing contained herein shall be construed to permit any city to prohibit altogether swimming and surfing or to make these activities unlawful.

(b) This section shall apply only to cities in the counties of Brunswick, Carteret, Currituck, Dare, Hyde, New Hanover, Onslow, and Pender. (1973, c. 539, ss. 1, 2.)

§ 160A-176.2. Ordinances effective in Atlantic Ocean.

(a) A city may adopt ordinances to regulate and control swimming, personal watercraft operation, surfing and littering in the Atlantic Ocean and other waterways adjacent to that portion of the city within its boundaries or within its extraterritorial jurisdiction; provided, however, nothing contained herein shall be construed to permit any city to prohibit altogether swimming or surfing or to make these activities unlawful.

(b) Subsection (a) of this section applies to the Towns of Atlantic Beach, Calabash, Cape Carteret, Carolina Beach, Caswell Beach, Duck, Emerald Isle, Holden Beach, Kill Devil Hills, Kitty Hawk, Manteo, Nags Head, Oak Island, Ocean Isle Beach, Southern Shores, Sunset Beach, Topsail Beach, and Wrightsville Beach, and the City of Southport only. (1991, c. 494, ss. 1, 2; 1991 (Reg. Sess., 1992), c. 801; 1993, c. 67, s. 5; c. 125, s. 2; 1993 (Reg. Sess., 1994), c. 625, s. 1; 1997-48, s. 1; 2002-141, s. 1; 2004-203, s. 55.)

§ 160A-177. Enumeration not exclusive.

The enumeration in this Article or other portions of this Chapter of specific powers to regulate, restrict or prohibit acts, omissions, and conditions shall not be deemed to be exclusive or a limiting factor upon the general authority to adopt ordinances conferred on cities by G.S. 160A-174. (1971, c. 698, s. 1.)

§ 160A-178. Regulation of solicitation campaigns, flea markets and itinerant merchants.

A city may by ordinance regulate, restrict or prohibit the solicitation of contributions from the public for any charitable or eleemosynary purpose, and also the business activities of itinerant merchants, salesmen, promoters, drummers, peddlers, flea market operators and flea market vendors or hawkers. These ordinances may include, but shall not be limited to, requirements that an application be made and a permit issued, that an investigation be made, that activities be reasonably limited as to time and place, that proper credentials and proof of financial stability be submitted, that not more than a stated percentage of contributions to solicitation campaigns be retained for administrative expenses, and that an adequate bond be posted to protect the public from fraud. (1963, c. 789; 1971, c. 698, s. 1; 1987, c. 708, s. 8.)

§ 160A-179. Regulation of begging.

A city may by ordinance prohibit or regulate begging or otherwise canvassing the public for contributions for the private benefit of the solicitor or any other person. (1971, c. 698, s. 1.)

§ 160A-180. Regulation of aircraft overflights.

A city may by ordinance regulate the operation of aircraft over the city. (1971, c. 698, s. 1.)

§ 160A-181. Regulation of places of amusement.

A city may by ordinance regulate places of amusement and entertainment, and may regulate, restrict or prohibit the operation of pool and billiard halls, dance halls, carnivals, circuses, or any itinerant show or exhibition of any kind. Places of amusement and entertainment shall include coffee houses, cocktail lounges, night clubs, beer halls, and similar establishments, but any regulations thereof shall be consistent with any permits or licenses issued by the North Carolina Alcoholic Beverage Control Commission. (1917, c. 136, subch. 5, s. 1; 1919, cc. 136, 237; C.S., s. 2787; 1971, c. 698, s. 1; 1981, c. 412, ss. 4, 5.)

§ 160A-181.1. Regulation of sexually oriented businesses.

(a)   The General Assembly finds and determines that sexually oriented businesses can and do cause adverse secondary impacts on neighboring properties. Numerous studies that are relevant to North Carolina have found increases in crime rates and decreases in neighboring property values as a result of the location of sexually oriented businesses in inappropriate locations or from the operation of such businesses in an inappropriate manner. Reasonable local government regulation of sexually oriented businesses in order to prevent or ameliorate adverse secondary impacts is consistent with the federal constitutional protection afforded to nonobscene but sexually explicit speech.

(b)   In addition to State laws on obscenity, indecent exposure, and adult establishments, local government regulation of the location and operation of sexually oriented businesses is necessary to prevent undue adverse secondary impacts that would otherwise result from these businesses.

(c) A city or county may regulate sexually oriented businesses through zoning regulations, licensing requirements, or other appropriate local ordinances. The city or county may require a fee for the initial license and any annual renewal. Such local regulations may include, but are not limited to:

(1) Restrictions on location of sexually oriented businesses, such as limitation to specified zoning districts and minimum separation from sensitive land uses and other sexually oriented businesses;

(2) Regulations on operation of sexually oriented businesses, such as limits on hours of operation, open booth requirements, limitations on exterior advertising and noise, age of patrons and employees, required separation of patrons and performers, clothing restrictions for masseuses, and clothing restrictions for servers of alcoholic beverages;

(3) Clothing restrictions for entertainers; and

(4) Registration and disclosure requirements for owners and employees with a criminal record other than minor traffic offenses, and restrictions on ownership by or employment of a person with a criminal record that includes offenses reasonably related to the legal operation of sexually oriented businesses.

(d) In order to preserve the status quo while appropriate studies are conducted and the scope of potential regulations is deliberated, cities and counties may enact moratoria of reasonable duration on either the opening of any new businesses authorized to be regulated under this section or the expansion of any such existing business. Businesses existing at the time of the effective date of regulations adopted under this section may be required to come into compliance with newly adopted regulations within an appropriate and reasonable period of time.

(e) Cities and counties may enter into cooperative agreements regarding coordinated regulation of sexually oriented businesses, including provision of adequate alternative sites for the location of constitutionally protected speech within an interrelated geographic area.

(f) For the purpose of this section, "sexually oriented businesses" means any businesses or enterprises that have as one of their principal business purposes or as a significant portion of their business an emphasis on matter and conduct depicting, describing, or related to anatomical areas and sexual activities specified in G.S. 14-202.10. Local governments may adopt detailed definitions of these and similar businesses in order to precisely define the scope of any local regulations. (1998-46, s. 1.)

§ 160A-182. Abuse of animals.

A city may by ordinance define and prohibit the abuse of animals. (1917, c. 136, subch. 5, s. 1; 1919, cc. 136, 237; C.S., s. 2787; 1971, c. 698, s. 1.)

§ 160A-183. Regulation of explosive, corrosive, inflammable, or radioactive substances.

A city may by ordinance restrict, regulate or prohibit the sale, possession, storage, use, or conveyance of any explosive, corrosive, inflammable, or radioactive substances, or any weapons or instrumentalities of mass death and destruction within the city. (1917, c. 136, subch. 5, s. 1; 1919, cc. 136, 237; C.S., s. 2787; 1971, c. 698, s. 1.)

§ 160A-184. Noise regulation.

A city may by ordinance regulate, restrict, or prohibit the production or emission of noises or amplified speech, music, or other sounds that tend to annoy, disturb, or frighten its citizens. (1971, c. 698, s. 1; 1973, c. 426, s. 25.)

§ 160A-185. Emission of pollutants or contaminants.

A city may by ordinance regulate, restrict, or prohibit the emission or disposal of substances or effluents that tend to pollute or contaminate land, water, or air, rendering or tending to render it injurious to human health or welfare, to animal or plant life or to property, or interfering or tending to interfere with the enjoyment of life or property. A city may by ordinance regulate the illegal disposal of solid waste, including littering on public and private property, provide for enforcement by civil penalties as well as other remedies, and provide that such regulations may be enforced by city employees specially appointed as environmental enforcement officers. Any such ordinance shall be consistent with and supplementary to State and federal laws and regulations. (1917, c. 136, subch. 5, s. 1; 1919, cc. 136, 237; C.S., s. 2787; 1949, c. 594, s. 2; 1971, c. 698, s. 1; 1973, c. 426, s. 26; 2001-512, s. 6.)

§ 160A-186. Regulation of domestic animals.

A city may by ordinance regulate, restrict, or prohibit the keeping, running, or going at large of any domestic animals, including dogs and cats. The ordinance may provide that animals allowed to run at large in violation of the ordinance may be seized and sold or destroyed after reasonable efforts to notify their owner. (1917, c. 136, subch. 5, s. 1; 1919, cc. 136, 237; C.S., s. 2787; 1971, c. 698, s. 1.)

§ 160A-187. Possession or harboring of dangerous animals.

A city may by ordinance regulate, restrict, or prohibit the possession or harboring within the city of animals which are dangerous to persons or property. No such ordinance shall have the effect of permitting any activity or condition with respect to a wild animal which is prohibited or more severely restricted by regulations of the Wildlife Resources Commission. (1971, c. 698, s. 1; 1977, c. 407, s. 2.)

§ 160A-188. Bird sanctuaries.

A city may by ordinance create and establish a bird sanctuary within the city limits. The ordinance may not protect any birds classed as a pest under Article 22A of Chapter 113 of the General Statutes and the Structural Pest Control Act of North Carolina of 1955 or the North Carolina Pesticide Law of 1971. When a bird sanctuary has been established, it shall be unlawful for any person to hunt, kill, trap, or otherwise take any protected birds within the city limits except pursuant to a permit issued by the North Carolina Wildlife Resources Commission under G.S. 113-274(c) (1a) or under any other license or permit of the Wildlife Resources Commission specifically made valid for use in taking birds within city limits. (1951, c. 411, ss. 1, 2; 1971, c. 698, s. 1; 1979, c. 830, s. 3.)

§ 160A-189. Firearms.

A city may by ordinance regulate, restrict, or prohibit the discharge of firearms at any time or place within the city except when used in defense of person or property or pursuant to lawful directions of law-enforcement officers, and may regulate the display of firearms on the streets, sidewalks, alleys, or other public property. Nothing in this section shall be construed to limit a city's authority to take action under Article 1A of Chapter 166A of the General Statutes. (1971, c. 698, s. 1; 2012-12, s. 2(zz).)

§ 160A-190. Pellet guns.

A city may by ordinance regulate, restrict, or prohibit the sale, possession or use within the city of pellet guns or any other mechanism or device designed or used to project a missile by compressed air or mechanical action with less than deadly force. (1971, c. 698, s. 1.)

§ 160A-191. Limitations on enactment of Sunday-closing ordinances.

No ordinance regulating or prohibiting business activity on Sundays shall be enacted unless the council shall hold a public hearing on the proposed ordinance. Notice of the hearing shall be published once each week for four successive weeks before the date of the hearing. The notice shall fix the date, hour and place of the public hearing, and shall contain a statement of the council's intent to consider a Sunday-closing ordinance, the purpose for such an ordinance, and one or more reasons for its enactment. No ordinance shall be held invalid for failure to observe the procedural requirements for enactment imposed by this section unless the issue is joined in an appropriate proceeding initiated within 90 days after the date of final enactment. This section shall not apply to ordinances enacted pursuant to G.S. 18B-1004(d). (1967, c. 1156, s. 1; 1971, c. 698, s. 1; 1973, c. 426, s. 27; 1983, c. 768, s. 22.)

§ 160A-192: Repealed by Session Laws 1991, c. 698, s. 1.

§ 160A-193. Abatement of public health nuisances.

(a) A city shall have authority to summarily remove, abate, or remedy everything in the city limits, or within one mile thereof, that is dangerous or prejudicial to the public health or public safety. Pursuant to this section, the governing board of a city may order the removal of a swimming pool and its appurtenances upon a finding that the swimming pool or its appurtenances is dangerous or prejudicial to public health or safety. The expense of the action shall be paid by the person in default. If the expense is not paid, it is a lien on the land or premises where the nuisance occurred. A lien established pursuant to this subsection shall have the same priority and be collected as unpaid ad valorem taxes.

(b) The expense of the action is also a lien on any other real property owned by the person in default within the city limits or within one mile of the city limits, except for the person's primary residence. A lien established pursuant to this subsection is inferior to all prior liens and shall be collected as a money judgment. This subsection shall not apply if the person in default can show that the nuisance was created solely by the actions of another. (1917, c. 136, subch. 7, s. 4; C.S., s. 2800; 1971, c. 698, s. 1; 1979, 2nd Sess., c. 1247, s. 20; 2001-448, s. 1; 2002-116, s. 3.)

§ 160A-193.1. Stream-clearing programs.

(a) A city shall have the authority to remove natural and man-made obstructions in stream channels and in the floodway of streams that may impede the passage of water during rain events.

(b) The actions of a city to clear obstructions from a stream shall not create or increase the responsibility of the city for the clearing or maintenance of the stream, or for flooding of the stream. In addition, actions by a city to clear obstructions from a stream shall not create in the city any ownership in the stream, obligation to control the stream, or affect any otherwise existing private property right, responsibility, or entitlement regarding the stream. These provisions shall not relieve a city for negligence that might be found under otherwise applicable law.

(c) Nothing in this section shall be construed to affect otherwise existing rights of the State to control or regulate streams or activities within streams. In implementing a stream-clearing program, the city shall comply with all requirements in State or federal statutes and rules. (2005-441, s. 2.)

§ 160A-194. Regulating and licensing businesses, trades, etc.

(a) A city may by ordinance, subject to the general law of the State, regulate and license occupations, businesses, trades, professions, and forms of amusement or entertainment and prohibit those that may be inimical to the public health, welfare, safety, order, or convenience. In licensing trades, occupations, and professions, the city may, consistent with the general law of the State, require applicants for licenses to be examined and charge a reasonable fee therefor. Nothing in this section shall impair the city's power to levy privilege license taxes on occupations, businesses, trades, professions, and other activities pursuant to G.S. 160A-211.

(b) Nothing in this section shall authorize a city to examine or license a person holding a license issued by an occupational licensing board of this State as to the profession or trade that he has been licensed to practice or pursue by the State.

(c) Nothing in this section shall authorize a city to regulate and license digital dispatching services for prearranged transportation services for hire. (1971, c. 698, s. 1; 2013-413, s. 12.1(a).)

§ 160A-195: Repealed by Session Laws 1998-128, s. 11.

§ 160A-196. Sewage tie-ons.

Cities that (in whole or in part) are adjacent to, adjoining, intersected by or bounded by the Atlantic Ocean and Roanoke, Albemarle, Currituck, or Pamlico Sound may by ordinance regulate the tie-ons to sewage systems within their corporate limits. (1985, c. 525, s. 1; 1987, c. 303.)

§ 160A-197: Repealed by Session Laws 1995, c. 501, s. 4.

§ 160A-198. Curfews.

A city may by an appropriate ordinance impose a curfew on persons of any age less than 18. (1997-189, s. 1.)

§ 160A-199. Regulation of outdoor advertising.

(a) As used in this section, the term "off-premises outdoor advertising" includes off-premises outdoor advertising visible from the main-traveled way of any road.

(b) A city may require the removal of an off-premises outdoor advertising sign that is nonconforming under a local ordinance and may regulate the use of off-premises outdoor advertising within the jurisdiction of the city in accordance with the applicable provisions of this Chapter.

(c) A city shall give written notice of its intent to require removal of off-premises outdoor advertising by sending a letter by certified mail to the last known address of the owner of the outdoor advertising and the owner of the property on which the outdoor advertising is located.

(d) No city may enact or amend an ordinance of general applicability to require the removal of any nonconforming, lawfully erected off-premises outdoor advertising sign without the payment of monetary compensation to the owners of the off-premises outdoor advertising, except as provided below. The payment of monetary compensation is not required if:

(1) The city and the owner of the nonconforming off-premises outdoor advertising enter into a relocation agreement pursuant to subsection (g) of this section.

(2) The city and the owner of the nonconforming off-premises outdoor advertising enter into an agreement pursuant to subsection (k) of this section.

(3) The off-premises outdoor advertising is determined to be a public nuisance or detrimental to the health or safety of the populace.

(4) The removal is required for opening, widening, extending or improving streets or sidewalks, or for establishing, extending, enlarging, or improving any of the public enterprises listed in G.S. 160A-311, and the city allows the off-premises outdoor advertising to be relocated to a comparable location.

(5) The off-premises outdoor advertising is subject to removal pursuant to statutes, ordinances, or regulations generally applicable to the demolition or removal of damaged structures.

(e) Monetary compensation is the fair market value of the off-premises outdoor advertising in place immediately prior to its removal and without consideration of the effect of the ordinance or any diminution in value caused by the ordinance requiring its removal. Monetary compensation shall be determined based on:

(1) The factors listed in G.S. 105-317.1(a); and

(2) The listed property tax value of the property and any documents regarding value submitted to the taxing authority.

(f) If the parties are unable to reach an agreement under subsection (e) of this section on monetary compensation to be paid by the city to the owner of the nonconforming off-premises outdoor advertising sign for its removal, and the city elects to proceed with the removal of the sign, the city may bring an action in superior court for a determination of the monetary compensation to be paid. In determining monetary compensation, the court shall consider the factors set forth in subsection (e) of this section. Upon payment of monetary compensation for the sign, the city shall own the sign.

(g) In lieu of paying monetary compensation, a city may enter into an agreement with the owner of a nonconforming off-premises outdoor advertising sign to relocate and reconstruct the sign. The agreement shall include the following:

(1) Provision for relocation of the sign to a site reasonably comparable to or better than the existing location. In determining whether a location is comparable or better, the following factors shall be taken into consideration:

a. The size and format of the sign.

b. The characteristics of the proposed relocation site, including visibility, traffic count, area demographics, zoning, and any uncompensated differential in the sign owner's cost to lease the replacement site.

c. The timing of the relocation.

(2) Provision for payment by the city of the reasonable costs of relocating and reconstructing the sign including:

a. The actual cost of removing the sign.

b. The actual cost of any necessary repairs to the real property for damages caused in the removal of the sign.

c. The actual cost of installing the sign at the new location.

d. An amount of money equivalent to the income received from the lease of the sign for a period of up to 30 days if income is lost during the relocation of the sign.

(h) For the purposes of relocating and reconstructing a nonconforming off-premises outdoor advertising sign pursuant to subsection (g) of this section, a city, consistent with the welfare and safety of the community as a whole, may adopt a resolution or adopt or modify its ordinances to provide for the issuance of a permit or other approval, including conditions as appropriate, or to provide for dimensional, spacing, setback, or use variances as it deems appropriate.

(i) If a city has offered to enter into an agreement to relocate a nonconforming off-premises outdoor advertising sign pursuant to subsection (g) of this section, and within 120 days after the initial notice by the city the parties have not been able to agree that the site or sites offered by the city for relocation of the sign are reasonably comparable to or better than the existing site, the parties shall enter into binding arbitration to resolve their disagreements. Unless a different method of arbitration is agreed upon by the parties, the arbitration shall be conducted by a panel of three arbitrators. Each party shall select one arbitrator and the two arbitrators chosen by the parties shall select the third member of the panel. The American Arbitration Association rules shall apply to the arbitration unless the parties agree otherwise.

(j) If the arbitration results in a determination that the site or sites offered by the city for relocation of the nonconforming sign are not comparable to or better than the existing site, and the city elects to proceed with the removal of the sign, the parties shall determine the monetary compensation under subsection (e) of this section to be paid to the owner of the sign. If the the parties are unable to reach an agreement regarding monetary compensation within 30 days of the receipt of the arbitrators' determination, and the city elects to proceed with the removal of the sign, then the city may bring an action in superior court for a determination of the monetary compensation to be paid by the city to the owner for the removal of the sign. In determining monetary compensation, the court shall consider the factors set forth in subsection (e) of this section. Upon payment of monetary compensation for the sign, the city shall own the sign.

(k) Notwithstanding the provisions of this section, a city and an off-premises outdoor advertising sign owner may enter into a voluntary agreement allowing for the removal of the sign after a set period of time in lieu of monetary compensation. A city may adopt an ordinance or resolution providing for a relocation, reconstruction, or removal agreement.

(l) A city has up to three years from the effective date of an ordinance enacted under this section to pay monetary compensation to the owner of the off-premises outdoor advertising provided the affected property remains in place until the compensation is paid.

(m) This section does not apply to any ordinance in effect on the effective date of this section. A city may amend an ordinance in effect on the effective date of this section to extend application of the ordinance to off-premises outdoor advertising located in territory acquired by annexation or located in the extraterritorial jurisdiction of the city. A city may repeal or amend an ordinance in effect on the effective date of this section so long as the amendment to the existing ordinance does not reduce the period of amortization in effect on the effective date of this section.

(n) The provisions of this section shall not be used to interpret, construe, alter or otherwise modify the exercise of the power of eminent domain by an entity pursuant to Chapter 40A or Chapter 136 of the General Statutes.

(o) Nothing in this section shall limit a city's authority to use amortization as a means of phasing out nonconforming uses other than off-premises outdoor advertising. (2004-152, s. 2.)

§ 160A-200. Annual notice to chronic violators of overgrown vegetation ordinances.

(a) A municipality may notify a chronic violator of the municipality's overgrown vegetation ordinance that, if the violator's property is found to be in violation of the ordinance, the municipality shall, without further notice in the calendar year in which notice is given, take action to remedy the violation and the expense of the action shall become a lien upon the property and shall be collected as unpaid taxes. The initial annual notice shall be served by registered or certified mail. A chronic violator is a person who owns property whereupon, in the previous calendar year, the municipality took remedial action at least three times under the overgrown vegetation ordinance.

(b) Repealed by Session Laws 2009-19, s. 1, effective April 30, 2009. (1999-58, s. 2; 2000-33, s. 1; 2000-38, s. 1; 2001-107, s. 1; 2003-77, s. 1; 2003-80, s. 1; 2005-81, s. 1; 2005-202, s. 1; 2007-31, s. 1; 2007-258, s. 1; 2008-6, s. 1; 2008-25, s. 1; 2009-3, s. 1; 2009-19, s. 1; 2009-570, s. 46.)

§ 160A-200.1. Annual notice to chronic violators of public nuisance ordinance.

A city may notify a chronic violator of the city's public nuisance ordinance that, if the violator's property is found to be in violation of the ordinance, the city shall, without further notice in the calendar year in which notice is given, take action to remedy the violation, and the expense of the action shall become a lien upon the property and shall be collected as unpaid taxes. The notice shall be sent by registered or certified mail. When service is attempted by registered or certified mail, a copy of the notice may also be sent by regular mail. Service shall be deemed sufficient if the registered or certified mail is unclaimed or refused, but the regular mail is not returned by the post office within 10 days after the mailing. If service by regular mail is used, a copy of the notice shall be posted in a conspicuous place on the premises affected. A chronic violator is a person who owns property whereupon, in the previous calendar year, the city gave notice of violation at least three times under any provision of the public nuisance ordinance. (2009-287, s. 1; 2013-151, s. 1.)

§ 160A-201. Limitations on regulating solar collectors.

(a) Except as provided in subsection (c) of this section, no city ordinance shall prohibit, or have the effect of prohibiting, the installation of a solar collector that gathers solar radiation as a substitute for traditional energy for water heating, active space heating and cooling, passive heating, or generating electricity for a residential property, and no person shall be denied permission by a city to install a solar collector that gathers solar radiation as a substitute for traditional energy for water heating, active space heating and cooling, passive heating, or generating electricity for a residential property. As used in this section, the term "residential property" means property where the predominant use is for residential purposes.

(b) This section does not prohibit an ordinance regulating the location or screening of solar collectors as described in subsection (a) of this section, provided the ordinance does not have the effect of preventing the reasonable use of a solar collector for a residential property.

(c) This section does not prohibit an ordinance that would prohibit the location of solar collectors as described in subsection (a) of this section that are visible by a person on the ground:

(1) On the facade of a structure that faces areas open to common or public access;

(2) On a roof surface that slopes downward toward the same areas open to common or public access that the facade of the structure faces; or

(3) Within the area set off by a line running across the facade of the structure extending to the property boundaries on either side of the facade, and those areas of common or public access faced by the structure.

(d) In any civil action arising under this section, the court may award costs and reasonable attorneys' fees to the prevailing party. (2007-279, s. 1; 2009-553, s. 1.)

§ 160A-202. Limitations on regulating cisterns and rain barrels.

No city ordinance may prohibit or have the effect of prohibiting the installation and maintenance of cisterns and rain barrel collection systems used to collect water for irrigation purposes. A city may regulate the installation and maintenance of those cisterns and rain barrel collection systems for the purpose of protecting the public health and safety and for the purpose of preventing them from becoming a public nuisance. (2011-394, s. 12(e).)

§ 160A-203. Limitations on regulating soft drink sizes.

No city ordinance may prohibit the sale of soft drinks above a particular size. This section does not prohibit any ordinance regulating the sanitation or other operational aspect of a device for the dispensing of soft drinks. For purposes of this section, "soft drink" shall have the meaning set forth in G.S. 105-164.3. (2013-309, s. 2.)

§ 160A-204. Transportation impact mitigation ordinances prohibited.

No city may enact or enforce an ordinance, rule, or regulation that requires an employer to assume financial, legal, or other responsibility for the mitigation of the impact of his or her employees' commute or transportation to or from the employer's workplace, which may result in the employer being subject to a fine, fee, or other monetary, legal, or negative consequences. (2013-413, s. 10.1(a).)

§ 160A-205. Cities enforce ordinances within public trust areas.

(a) Notwithstanding the provisions of G.S. 113-131 or any other provision of law, a city may, by ordinance, define, prohibit, regulate, or abate acts, omissions, or conditions upon the State's ocean beaches and prevent or abate any unreasonable restriction of the public's rights to use the State's ocean beaches. In addition, a city may, in the interest of promoting the health, safety, and welfare of the public, regulate, restrict, or prohibit the placement, maintenance, location, or use of equipment, personal property, or debris upon the State's ocean beaches. A city may enforce any ordinance adopted pursuant to this section or any other provision of law upon the State's ocean beaches located within or adjacent to the city's jurisdictional boundaries to the same extent that a city may enforce ordinances within the city's jurisdictional boundaries. A city may enforce an ordinance adopted pursuant to this section by any remedy provided for in G.S. 160A-175. For purposes of this section, the term "ocean beaches" has the same meaning as in G.S. 77-20(e).

(b) Nothing in this section shall be construed to (i) limit the authority of the State or any State agency to regulate the State's ocean beaches as authorized by G.S. 113-131, or common law as interpreted and applied by the courts of this State; (ii) limit any other authority granted to cities by the State to regulate the State's ocean beaches; (iii) deny the existence of the authority recognized in this section prior to the date this section becomes effective; (iv) impair the right of the people of this State to the customary free use and enjoyment of the State's ocean beaches, which rights remain reserved to the people of this State as provided in G.S. 77-20(d); (v) change or modify the riparian, littoral, or other ownership rights of owners of property bounded by the Atlantic Ocean; or (vi) apply to the removal of permanent residential or commercial structures and appurtenances thereto from the State's ocean beaches. (2013-384, s. 4(a).)

rticle 9.

Taxation.

§ 160A-206. (Effective July 1, 2013 until July 1, 2015 - see notes) General power to impose taxes.

A city shall have power to impose taxes only as specifically authorized by act of the General Assembly. Except when the statute authorizing a tax provides for penalties and interest, the power to impose a tax shall include the power to impose reasonable penalties for failure to declare tax liability, if required, or to impose penalties or interest for failure to pay taxes lawfully due within the time prescribed by law or ordinance. In determining the liability of any taxpayer for a tax, a city may not employ an agent who is compensated in whole or in part by the city for services rendered on a contingent basis or any other basis related to the amount of tax, interest, or penalty assessed against or collected from the taxpayer. The power to impose a tax shall also include the power to provide for its administration in a manner not inconsistent with the statute authorizing the tax. (1971, c. 698, s. 1; 2012-152, s. 5; 2012-194, s. 61.5(b).)

§ 160A-206. (Effective July 1, 2015 - see notes) General power to impose taxes.

A city shall have power to impose taxes only as specifically authorized by act of the General Assembly. Except when the statute authorizing a tax provides for penalties and interest, the power to impose a tax shall include the power to impose reasonable penalties for failure to declare tax liability, if required, or to impose penalties or interest for failure to pay taxes lawfully due within the time prescribed by law or ordinance. The power to impose a tax shall also include the power to provide for its administration in a manner not inconsistent with the statute authorizing the tax. (1971, c. 698, s. 1; 2012-152, s. 5; 2012-194, s. 61.5(b).)

§ 160A-207. Remedies for collecting taxes.

In addition to any other remedies provided by law, the remedies of levy, garnishment, and attachment shall be available for collecting any city tax under the rules and procedures prescribed by the Machinery Act for the enforcement of tax liability against personal property, except that:

(1) The remedies shall become available on the due date of the tax and not before that time;

(2) Rules dependent on the existence of a lien against real property for the same tax shall not apply; and

(3) The lien acquired by levy, garnishment, or attachment shall be inferior to any prior or simultaneous lien for property taxes acquired under the Machinery Act. (1971, c. 698, s. 1; 1973, c. 426, s. 29.)

§ 160A-208. Continuing taxes.

Except for taxes levied on property under the Machinery Act, a city may impose an authorized tax by a permanent ordinance that shall stand from year to year until amended or repealed, and it shall not be necessary to reimpose the tax in each annual budget ordinance. (1971, c. 698, s. 1; 1973, c. 426, s. 30.)

§ 160A-208.1. Disclosure of certain information prohibited.

(a) Disclosure Prohibited. - Notwithstanding Chapter 132 of the General Statutes or any other law regarding access to public records, local tax records that contain information about a taxpayer's income or receipts are not public records. A current or former officer, employee, or agent of a city who in the course of service to or employment by the city has access to information about the amount of a taxpayer's income or receipts may not disclose the information to any other person unless the disclosure is made for one of the following purposes:

(1) To comply with a court order or a law.

(2) Review by the Attorney General or a representative of the Attorney General.

(3) To sort, process, or deliver tax information on behalf of the city, as necessary to administer a tax.

(4) To include on a property tax receipt the amount of property taxes due and the amount of property taxes deferred on a residence classified under G.S. 105-277.1B, the property tax homestead circuit breaker.

(b)   Punishment. - A person who violates this section is guilty of a Class 1 misdemeanor. If the person committing the violation is an officer or employee, that person shall be dismissed from public office or public employment and may not hold any public office or public employment in this State for five years after the violation. (1993, c. 485, s. 34; 1994, Ex. Sess., c. 14, s. 67; 2008-35, s. 1.5.)

§ 160A-209. Property taxes.

(a)   Pursuant to Article V, Sec. 2(5) of the Constitution of North Carolina, the General Assembly confers upon each city in this State the power to levy, within the limitations set out in this section, taxes on property having a situs within the city under the rules and according to the procedures prescribed in the Machinery Act (Chapter 105, Subchapter II).

(b)   Each city may levy property taxes without restriction as to rate or amount for the following purposes:

(1)   Debt Service. - To pay the principal of and interest on all general obligation bonds and notes of the city.

(2)   Deficits. - To supply an unforeseen deficiency in the revenue (other than revenues of any of the enterprises listed in G.S. 160A-311), when revenues actually collected or received fall below revenue estimates made in good faith in accordance with the Local Government Budget and Fiscal Control Act.

(3)   Civil Disorders. - To meet the cost of additional law-enforcement personnel and equipment that may be required to suppress riots or other civil disorders involving an extraordinary breach of law and order within the jurisdiction of the city.

(c)   Each city may levy property taxes for one or more of the following purposes subject to the rate limitation set out in subsection (d):

(1)   Administration. - To provide for the general administration of the city through the city council, the office of the city manager, the office of the city budget officer, the office of the city finance officer, the office of the city tax collector, the city purchasing agent, the city attorney, and for all other general

administrative costs not allocated to a particular board, commission, office, agency, or activity.

(2) Air Pollution. - To maintain and administer air pollution control programs.

(3) Airports. - To establish and maintain airports and related aeronautical facilities.

(4) Ambulance Service. - To provide ambulance services, rescue squads, and other emergency medical services.

(5) Animal Protection and Control. - To provide animal protection and control programs.

(5a) Arts Programs and Museums. - To provide for arts programs and museums as authorized in G.S. 160A-488.

(6) Auditoriums, Coliseums, and Convention Centers. - To provide public auditoriums, coliseums, and convention centers.

(7) Beach Erosion and Natural Disasters. - To provide for shoreline protection, beach erosion control and flood and hurricane protection.

(8) Cemeteries. - To provide for cemeteries.

(9) Civil Defense. - To provide for civil defense programs.

(9a) Community Development. - To provide for community development as authorized by G.S. 160A-456 and 160A-457.

(10) Debts and Judgments. - To pay and discharge any valid debt of the city or any judgment lodged against it, other than debts or judgments evidenced by or based on bonds or notes.

(10a) Defense of Employees and Officers. - To provide for the defense of, and payment of civil judgments against, employees and officers or former employees and officers, as authorized by this Chapter.

(10b) (Effective until June 30, 2014) Economic Development. - To provide for economic development as authorized by G.S. 158-7.1 and G.S. 158-12.

(10b) (Effective June 30, 2014) Economic Development. - To provide for economic development as authorized by G.S. 158-7.1.

(10c) Drainage. - To provide for drainage projects or programs in accordance with Chapter 156 of the General Statutes or in accordance with this Chapter.

(11) Elections. - To provide for all city elections and referendums.

(12) Electric Power. - To provide electric power generation, transmission, and distribution services.

(12a) Energy Financing. - To provide financing for renewable energy and energy efficiency in accordance with a program established under G.S. 160A-459.1.

(13) Fire Protection. - To provide fire protection services and fire prevention programs.

(14) Gas. - To provide natural gas transmission and distribution services.

(15) Historic Preservation. - To undertake historic preservation programs and projects.

(15a) Housing. - To undertake housing projects as defined in G.S. 157-3, and urban homesteading programs under G.S. 160A-457.2.

(16) Human Relations. - To undertake human relations programs.

(17) Hospitals. - To establish, support and maintain public hospitals and clinics, and other related health programs and facilities, and to aid any private, nonprofit hospital, clinic, related facility, or other health program or facility.

(17a) Industrial Development. - To provide for industrial development as authorized by G.S. 158-7.1.

(18) Jails. - To provide for the operation of a jail and other local confinement facilities.

(19) Joint Undertakings. - To cooperate with any other county, city, or political subdivision of the State in providing any of the functions, services, or activities listed in this subsection.

(20) Libraries. - To establish and maintain public libraries.

(21) Mosquito Control.

(22) Off-Street Parking. - To provide off-street lots and garages for the parking and storage of motor vehicles.

(23) Open Space. - To acquire open space land and easements in accordance with Article 19, Part 4, of this Chapter.

(24) Parks and Recreation. - To establish, support and maintain public parks and programs of supervised recreation.

(25) Planning. - To provide for a program of planning and regulation of development in accordance with Article 19 of this Chapter.

(26) Police. - To provide for law enforcement.

(26a) Ports and Harbors. - To participate in programs with the North Carolina Ports Authority and to provide for harbor masters.

(27) Public Transportation. - To provide public transportation by rail, motor vehicle, or another means of conveyance other than a ferry, including any facility or equipment needed to provide the public transportation.

(27a) Railroad Corridor Preservation. - To acquire property for railroad corridor preservation.

(27b) Senior Citizens Programs. - To undertake programs for the assistance and care of its senior citizens.

(28) Sewage. - To provide sewage collection and treatment services as defined in G.S. 160A-311(3).

(29) Solid Waste. - To provide solid waste collection and disposal services, and to acquire and operate landfills.

(30) Streets. - To provide for the public streets, sidewalks, and bridges of the city.

(31) Traffic Control and On-Street Parking. - To provide for the regulation of vehicular and pedestrian traffic within the city, and for the parking of motor vehicles on the public streets.

(31a) Urban Redevelopment. - To provide for urban redevelopment.

(32) Water. - To provide water supply and distribution services.

(33) Water Resources. - To participate in federal water resources development projects.

(34) Watershed Improvement. - To undertake watershed improvement projects.

(d) Property taxes may be levied for one or more of the purposes listed in subsection (c) up to a combined rate of one dollar and fifty cents ($1.50) on the one hundred dollars' ($100.00) appraised value of property subject to taxation.

(e) With an approving vote of the people, any city may levy property taxes for any purpose for which the city is authorized by its charter or general law to appropriate money. Any property tax levy approved by a vote of the people shall not be counted for purposes of the rate limitation imposed in subsection (d).

The city council may call a referendum on approval of a property tax levy. The referendum may be held at the same time as any other city referendum or city election, but may not be otherwise held (i) on the day of any federal, State, district, or county election already validly called or scheduled by law at the time the tax referendum is called, or (ii) within the period of time beginning 30 days before and ending 10 days after the day of any other city referendum or city election already validly called or scheduled by law at the time the tax referendum is called. The referendum shall be conducted by the same board of elections that conducts regular city elections. A notice of referendum shall be published in accordance with G.S. 163-287. The notice shall state the date of the referendum, the purpose for which it is being held, and a statement as to the last day for registration for the referendum under the election laws then in effect.

The proposition submitted to the voters shall be substantially in one of the following forms:

(1) Shall the Cityown of _____ be authorized to levy annually a property tax at a rate not in excess of ____ cents on the one hundred dollars ($100.00) value of property subject to taxation for the purpose of _____?

(2) Shall the Cityown of _____ be authorized to levy annually a property tax at a rate not in excess of that which will produce $ _____ for the purpose of _____?

(3) Shall the Cityown of _____ be authorized to levy annually a property tax without restriction as to rate or amount for the purpose of _____?

If a majority of those participating in the referendum approve the proposition, the city council may proceed to levy annually a property tax within the limitations (if any) described in the proposition.

The board of elections shall canvass the referendum and certify the results to the city council. The council shall then certify and declare the result of the referendum and shall publish a statement of the result once, with the following statement appended: "Any action or proceeding challenging the regularity or validity of this tax referendum must be begun within 30 days after (date of publication)." The statement of results shall be filed in the clerk's office and inserted in the minutes of the council.

Any action or proceeding in any court challenging the regularity or validity of a tax referendum must be begun within 30 days after the publication of the results of the referendum. After the expiration of this period of limitation, no right of action or defense based upon the invalidity of or any irregularity in the referendum shall be asserted, nor shall the validity of the referendum be open to question in any court upon any ground whatever, except in an action or proceeding begun within the period of limitation prescribed herein.

Except for tax referendums on functions not included in subsection (c) of this section, any referendum held before July 1, 1973, on the levy of property taxes is not valid for the purposes of this subsection. Cities in which such referendums have been held may support programs formerly supported by voted property taxes within the general rate limitations set out in subsection (d) at any appropriate level and are not subject to the former voted rate limitation.

(f) With an approving vote of the people, any city may increase the property tax rate limitation imposed in subsection (c) and may call a referendum for that purpose. The referendum may be held at the same time as any other city referendum or election, but may not be otherwise held (i) on the day of any federal, State, district, or county election, or (ii) within the period of time beginning 30 days before and ending 30 days after the day of any other city referendum or city election. The election shall be conducted by the same board of elections that conducts regular city elections.

The proposition submitted to the voters shall be substantially in the following form: "Shall the property tax rate limitation applicable to the Cityown of _____ be increased from _____ on the one hundred dollars ($100.00) value of property subject to taxation to ____ on the one hundred dollars ($100.00) value of property subject to taxation?"

If a majority of those participating in the referendum approve the proposition, the rate limitation imposed in subsection (c) shall be increased for the city.

(g)   With respect to any of the categories listed in subsections (b) and (c) of this section, the city may provide the necessary personnel, land, buildings, equipment, supplies, and financial support from property tax revenues for the program, function, or service.

(h)   This section does not authorize any city to undertake any program, function, joint undertaking, or service not otherwise authorized by law. It is intended only to authorize the levy of property taxes within the limitations set out herein to finance programs, functions, or services authorized by other portions of the General Statutes or by city charters. (1917, c. 138, s. 37; 1919, c. 178, s. 3(37); C.S., s. 2963; 1921, c. 8, s. 1; Ex. Sess. 1921, c. 106, s. 1; 1947, c. 506; 1959, c. 1250, s. 3; 1971, c. 698, s. 1; 1973, c. 426, s. 31; c. 803, s. 2; 1975, c. 664, s. 7; 1977, c. 187, s. 2; c. 834, s. 2; 1979, c. 619, s. 5; 1979, 2nd Sess., c. 1247, s. 21; 1981, c. 66, s. 1; 1983, c. 511, ss. 3, 4; c. 828; 1985, c. 665, ss. 4, 7; 1987, c. 464, s. 6; 1989, c. 600, s. 8; 1989 (Reg. Sess., 1990), c. 1005, ss. 6, 7; 1991 (Reg. Sess., 1992), c. 896, s. 2; 2002-159, s. 50(b); 2002-172, s. 2.4(b); 2003-416, s. 2; 2010-167, s. 4(d).)

§ 160A-210. Repealed by Session Laws 1979, 2nd Session, c. 1247, s. 22.

§ 160A-211. Privilege license taxes.

(a)   (See editor's note) Repealed by Session Laws 2013-414, s. 58(b), effective January 1, 2014.

(b) Barbershop and Salon Restriction. - A privilege license tax levied by a city on a barbershop or a beauty salon may not exceed two dollars and fifty cents ($2.50) for each barber, manicurist, cosmetologist, beautician, or other operator employed in the barbershop or beauty salon.

(c) (Effective until July 1, 2014) Prohibition. - A city may not impose a license, franchise, or privilege tax on a person engaged in any of the businesses listed in this subsection. These businesses are subject to a State tax for which the city receives a share of the tax revenue:

(1) Supplying piped natural gas taxed under Article 5E of Chapter 105 of the General Statutes.

(2) Providing telecommunications service taxed under G.S. 105-164.4(a)(4c).

(3) Providing video programming taxed under G.S. 105-164.4(a)(6).

(c) (Effective July 1, 2014) Prohibition. - A city may not impose a license, franchise, or privilege tax on a person engaged in any of the businesses listed in this subsection. These businesses are subject to sales tax at the combined general rate for which the city receives a share of the tax revenue or they are subject to the local sales tax:

(1) Supplying piped natural gas.

(2) Providing telecommunications service taxed under G.S. 105-164.4(a)(4c).

(3) Providing video programming taxed under G.S. 105-164.4(a)(6).

(4) Providing electricity. A city may continue to impose and collect the license, franchise, or privilege taxes on an electric power company that it imposed and collected on or before January 1, 1947, but it may not impose or collect any greater franchise, privilege, or license taxes, in the aggregate, on an electric power company that was imposed and collected on or before January 1, 1947.

(d) Repealed by Session Laws 2006-151, s. 12, effective January 1, 2007. (R.C., c. 111, s. 13; 1862, c. 51; Code, s. 3800; Rev., s. 2924; C.S., s. 2677; 1949, c. 933; 1971, c. 698, s. 1; 1996, 2nd Ex. Sess., c. 14, s. 23; 1998-22, s.

12; 2001-430, s. 17; 2006-151, s. 12; 2013-316, s. 4.4(a); 2013-414, s. 58(b), (d).)

§ 160A-211.1. Privilege license tax on low-level radioactive and hazardous waste facilities.

(a)   Cities in which hazardous waste facilities as defined in G.S. 130A-290 or low-level radioactive waste facilities as defined in G.S. 104E-5(9b) are located may levy an annual privilege license tax on persons or firms operating such facilities only in accordance with this section.

(b)   The rate or rates of a tax levied under authority of this section shall be in an amount calculated to compensate the city for the additional costs incurred by it from having a hazardous waste facility or a low-level radioactive waste facility located in its jurisdiction to the extent to which compensation for such costs is not otherwise provided, which costs may include the loss of ad valorem property tax revenues from the property on which a facility is located, the cost of providing any additional emergency services, the cost of monitoring air, surface water, groundwater, and other environmental media to the extent other monitoring data is not available, and other costs the municipality established as being associated with the facilities and for which it is not otherwise compensated.

(c)   Any person or firm taxed pursuant to this section may appeal the tax rate to the Board, but shall pay the tax when due, subject to a refund when the appeal is resolved by the Board or in the courts. (1981, c. 704, s. 15; 1985, c. 462, s. 10; 1987, c. 850, s. 22; 1989, c. 168, s. 35.)

§ 160A-212. Animal taxes.

A city shall have power to levy an annual license tax on the privilege of keeping any domestic animal, including dogs and cats, within the city. This section shall not limit the city's authority to enact ordinances under G.S. 160A-186. (R.C., c. 111, s. 13; 1862, c. 51; Code, s. 3800; Rev., s. 2924; C.S., s. 2677; 1949, c. 933; 1971, c. 698, s. 1.)

§ 160A-213. Motor vehicle taxes.

(a) A city may impose an annual license tax on motor vehicles as permitted by G.S. 20-97.

(b) By ordinance a city may provide that the annual license tax imposed under subsection (a) above may be waived for individuals serving as firemen or as members of emergency medical teams. A city may also provide such individuals with tags or decals with distinctive coloring, or other means, to identify the individual as a fireman or a member of an emergency medical team. (1971, c. 698, s. 1; 1979, c. 442.)

§ 160A-214: Repealed by Session Laws 2006-151, s. 13, effective January 1, 2007.

§ 160A-214.1. Uniform penalties for local meals taxes.

(a) Penalties. - Notwithstanding any other provision of law, the civil and criminal penalties that apply to State sales and use taxes under Chapter 105 of the General Statutes apply to local meals taxes. The governing board of a taxing city has the same authority to waive the penalties for a meals tax that the Secretary of Revenue has to waive the penalties for State sales and use taxes.

(b) Scope. - This section applies to every city authorized by the General Assembly to levy a meals tax.

(c) Definitions. - The following definitions apply in this section:

(1) City. - A municipality.

(2) Meals tax. - A tax on prepared food and drink. (2001-264, s. 2.)

§ 160A-215. Uniform provisions for room occupancy taxes.

(a) Scope. - This section applies only to municipalities the General Assembly has authorized to levy room occupancy taxes. For the purpose of this section, the term "city" means a municipality.

(b) Levy. - A room occupancy tax may be levied only by resolution, after not less than 10 days' public notice and after a public hearing held pursuant thereto.

A room occupancy tax shall become effective on the date specified in the resolution levying the tax. That date must be the first day of a calendar month, however, and may not be earlier than the first day of the second month after the date the resolution is adopted.

(c) Collection. - A retailer who is required to remit to the Department of Revenue the State sales tax imposed by G.S. 105-164.4(a)(3) on accommodations is required to remit a room occupancy tax to the taxing city on and after the effective date of the levy of the room occupancy tax. The room occupancy tax applies to the same gross receipts as the State sales tax on accommodations and is calculated in the same manner as that tax. A rental agent or a facilitator, as defined in G.S. 105-164.4(a)(3), has the same responsibility and liability under the room occupancy tax as the rental agent or facilitator has under the State sales tax on accommodations.

If a taxable accommodation is furnished as part of a package, the bundled transaction provisions in G.S. 105-164.4D apply in determining the sales price of the taxable accommodation. If those provisions do not address the type of package offered, the person offering the package may determine an allocated price for each item in the package based on a reasonable allocation of revenue that is supported by the person's business records kept in the ordinary course of business and calculate tax on the allocated price of the taxable accommodation.

A retailer must separately state the room occupancy tax. Room occupancy taxes paid to a retailer are held in trust for and on account of the taxing city.

The taxing city shall design and furnish to all appropriate businesses and persons in the city the necessary forms for filing returns and instructions to ensure the full collection of the tax. An operator of a business who collects a room occupancy tax may deduct from the amount remitted to the taxing city a discount equal to the discount the State allows the retailer for State sales and use tax.

(d) Administration. - The taxing city shall administer a room occupancy tax it levies. A room occupancy tax is due and payable to the city finance officer in monthly installments on or before the 20th day of the month following the month in which the tax accrues. Every person, firm, corporation, or association liable for the tax shall, on or before the 20th day of each month, prepare and render a return on a form prescribed by the taxing city. The return shall state the total gross receipts derived in the preceding month from rentals upon which the tax is levied. A room occupancy tax return filed with the city finance officer is not a public record and may not be disclosed except in accordance with G.S. 153A-148.1 or G.S. 160A-208.1.

(e) Penalties. - A person, firm, corporation, or association who fails or refuses to file a room occupancy tax return or pay a room occupancy tax as required by law is subject to the civil and criminal penalties set by G.S. 105-236 for failure to pay or file a return for State sales and use taxes. The governing board of the taxing city has the same authority to waive the penalties for a room occupancy tax that the Secretary of Revenue has to waive the penalties for State sales and use taxes.

(f) Repeal or Reduction. - A room occupancy tax levied by a city may be repealed or reduced by a resolution adopted by the governing body of the city. Repeal or reduction of a room occupancy tax shall become effective on the first day of a month and may not become effective until the end of the fiscal year in which the resolution was adopted. Repeal or reduction of a room occupancy tax does not affect a liability for a tax that was attached before the effective date of the repeal or reduction, nor does it affect a right to a refund of a tax that accrued before the effective date of the repeal or reduction.

(f1) Use. - The proceeds of a room occupancy tax shall not be used for development or construction of a hotel or another transient lodging facility.

(g) Applicability. - Subsection (c) of this section applies to all cities that levy an occupancy tax. To the extent subsection (c) conflicts with any provision of a local act, subsection (c) supersedes that provision. The remainder of this section applies only to Beech Mountain District W, to the Cities of Belmont, Conover, Eden, Elizabeth City, Gastonia, Goldsboro, Greensboro, Hickory, High Point, Jacksonville, Kings Mountain, Lenoir, Lexington, Lincolnton, Lowell, Lumberton, Monroe, Mount Airy, Mount Holly, Reidsville, Roanoke Rapids, Salisbury, Shelby, Statesville, Washington, and Wilmington, to the Towns of Ahoskie, Beech Mountain, Benson, Bermuda Run, Blowing Rock, Boiling Springs, Boone, Burgaw, Carolina Beach, Carrboro, Cooleemee, Cramerton, Dallas, Dobson, Elkin, Fontana Dam, Franklin, Grover, Hillsborough, Jonesville, Kenly, Kure Beach, Leland, McAdenville, Mocksville, Mooresville, Murfreesboro, North Topsail Beach, Pembroke, Pilot Mountain, Ranlo, Robbinsville, Selma, Smithfield, St. Pauls, Swansboro, Troutman, Tryon, West Jefferson, Wilkesboro, Wrightsville Beach, Yadkinville, and Yanceyville, and to the municipalities in Avery and Brunswick Counties. (1997-361, s. 4; 1997-364, s. 5; 1997-410, s. 3; 1997-447, s. 2; 1998-112, s. 4; 1999-258, s. 3; 1999-302, s. 2; 2000-103, s. 9; 2001-11, s. 2; 2001-365, s. 3; 2001-434, s. 9; 2001-439, s. 18.1; 2002-94, s. 4;

2002-95, s. 3; 2002-138, s. 2; 2002-139, s. 2; 2002-159, s. 62; 2003-281, s. 14; 2004-105, s. 3; 2004-170, ss. 36(b), 42(b); 2004-199, s. 60(b); 2005-16, s. 3; 2005-46, s. 2.3; 2005-49, s. 3; 2005-220, s. 5; 2005-233, s. 6.2; 2005-435, s. 45; 2006-118, s. 4; 2006-120, ss. 8.2, 10.2; 2006-148, s. 3; 2006-162, s. 20(b); 2006-164, s. 3; 2006-167, s. 3; 2006-264, ss. 19, 81(a); 2007-224, s. 6; 2007-317, s. 3; 2007-340, s. 10; 2007-484, s. 43; 2007-527, s. 42; 2008-64, s. 2; 2008-134, s. 12(c); 2009-169, s. 8; 2009-291, s. 2; 2009-428, s. 4; 2009-429, s. 8; 2010-31, s. 31.6(e), (f); 2010-78, s. 11; 2010-123, s. 10.2; 2011-69, s. 2; 2011-170, s. 6; 2012-107, s. 2; 2013-351, s. 1.3.)

§ 160A-215.1. Gross receipts tax on short-term leases or rentals.

(a) As a substitute for and in replacement of the ad valorem tax, which is excluded by G.S. 105-275(42), a city may levy a gross receipts tax on the gross receipts from the short-term lease or rental of vehicles at retail to the general public. The tax rate shall not exceed one and one-half percent (1.5%) of the gross receipts from such short-term leases or rentals. This tax on gross receipts is in addition to the privilege taxes authorized by G.S. 160A-211.

(b) If a city enacts the substitute and replacement gross receipts tax pursuant to this section, any entity required to collect the tax shall include a provision in each retail short-term lease or rental agreement noting that the percentage amount enacted by the city of the total lease or rental price, excluding highway use tax, is being charged as a tax on gross receipts. For purposes of this section, the transaction giving rise to the tax shall be deemed to have occurred at the location of the entity from which the customer takes delivery of the vehicle. The tax shall be collected at the time of lease or rental and placed in a segregated account until remitted to the city.

(c) The collection and use of taxes under this section are not subject to highway use tax and are not included in the gross receipts of the entity. The proceeds collected under this section belong to the city and are not subject to creditor liens against the entity.

(d) A tax levied under this section shall be collected by the city but otherwise administered in the same manner as the tax levied under G.S. 105-164.4(a)(2).

(e) The following definitions apply in this section:

(1) Short-term lease or rental. - Defined in G.S. 105-187.1.

(2) Vehicle. - Any of the following:

a. A motor vehicle of the passenger type, including a passenger van, minivan, or sport utility vehicle.

b. A motor vehicle of the cargo type, including cargo van, pickup truck, or truck with a gross vehicle weight rating of 26,000 pounds or less used predominantly in the transportation of property for other than commercial freight and that does not require the operator to posses a commercial drivers license.

c. A trailer or semitrailer with a gross vehicle weight of 6,000 pounds or less.

(f) The penalties and remedies that apply to local sales and use taxes levied under Subchapter VIII of Chapter 105 of the General Statutes apply to a tax levied under this section. The governing body of the city may exercise any power the Secretary of Revenue may exercise in collecting local sales and use taxes. (2000-2, s. 3; 2000-140, s. 75(c); 2001-414, s. 51.)

§ 160A-215.2. Heavy equipment gross receipts tax in lieu of property tax.

(a) Definitions. - The following definitions apply in this section:

(1) Heavy equipment. - Defined in G.S. 153A-156.1.

(2) Short-term lease or rental. - Defined in G.S. 105-187.1.

(b) Tax Authorized. - A city may, by ordinance, impose a tax at the rate of eight tenths percent (0.8%) on the gross receipts from the short-term lease or rental of heavy equipment by a person whose principal business is the short-term lease or rental of heavy equipment at retail. The heavy equipment subject to this tax is exempt from property tax under G.S. 105-275, and this tax provides an alternative to a property tax on the equipment. A person is not considered to be in the short-term lease or rental business if the majority of the person's lease and rental gross receipts are derived from leases and rentals to a person who is a related person under G.S. 105-163.010.

The tax authorized by this section applies to gross receipts that are subject to tax under G.S. 105-164.4(a)(2). Gross receipts from the short-term lease or rental of heavy equipment are subject to a tax imposed by a city under this section if the place of business from which the heavy equipment is delivered is located in the city.

(c) Payment. - A person whose principal business is the short-term lease or rental of heavy equipment is required to remit a tax imposed by this section to the city. The tax is payable quarterly and is due by the last day of the month following the end of the quarter. The tax is intended to be added to the amount charged for the short-term lease or rental of heavy equipment and paid to the heavy equipment business by the person to whom the heavy equipment is leased or rented.

(d) Enforcement. - The penalties and collection remedies that apply to the payment of sales and use taxes under Article 5 of Chapter 105 of the General Statutes apply to a tax imposed under this section. The city finance officer has the same authority as the Secretary of Revenue in imposing these penalties and remedies.

(e) Effective Date. - A tax imposed under this section becomes effective on the date set in the ordinance imposing the tax. The date must be the first day of a calendar quarter and may not be sooner than the first day of the calendar quarter that begins at least two months after the date the ordinance is adopted.

(f) Repeal. - A city may, by ordinance, repeal a tax imposed under this section. The repeal is effective on the date set in the ordinance. The date must be the first day of a calendar quarter and may not be sooner than the first day of the calendar quarter that begins at least two months after the date the ordinance is adopted. (2008-144, s. 3; 2009-445, s. 27(a).)

Article 10.

Special Assessments.

§ 160A-216. Authority to make special assessments.

Any city is authorized to make special assessments against benefited property within its corporate limits for:

(1) Constructing, reconstructing, paving, widening, installing curbs and gutters, and otherwise building and improving streets;

(2) Constructing, reconstructing, paving, widening, and otherwise building or improving sidewalks in any public street;

(3) Constructing, reconstructing, extending, and otherwise building or improving water systems;

(4) Constructing, reconstructing, extending, or otherwise building or improving sewage collection and disposal systems of all types, including septic tank systems or other on-site collection or disposal facilities or systems;

(5) Constructing, reconstructing, extending, and otherwise building or improving storm sewer and drainage systems. (1971, c. 698, s. 1; 1975, c. 664, s. 8; 1979, c. 619, s. 12.)

§ 160A-217. Petition for street or sidewalk improvements.

(a) A city shall have no power to levy special assessments for street or sidewalk improvements unless it receives a petition for the improvements signed by at least a majority in number of the owners of property to be assessed, who must represent at least a majority of all the lineal feet of frontage of the lands abutting on the street or portion thereof to be improved. Unless the petition specifies another percentage, not more than fifty percent (50%) of the cost of the improvement may be assessed (not including the cost of improvements made at street intersections).

(b) Property owned by the United States shall not be included in determining the lineal feet of frontage on the improvement, nor shall the United States be included in determining the number of owners of property abutting the improvement. Property owned by the State of North Carolina shall be included in determining frontage and the number of owners only if the State has consented to assessment in the manner provided in G.S. 160A-221. Property owned by railroad companies shall be included in determining frontage and the number of owners to the extent that the property is subject to assessment under G.S. 160A-222. Property owned by railroad companies that is not subject to assessment shall not be included in determining frontage and the number of owners. If it is necessary to exclude property owned by the United States, the State of North Carolina, or a railroad company in order to obtain a valid petition under subsection (a), not more than fifty percent (50%) of the cost (not including the cost of improvement at street intersections) may be assessed unless all of the owners subject to assessment agree to a higher percentage.

(c) No right of action or defense asserting the invalidity of street or sidewalk assessments on grounds that the city did not comply with this section in securing a valid petition shall be asserted except in an action or proceeding begun within 90 days after publication of the notice of adoption of the preliminary assessment resolution. (1915, c. 56, ss. 4, 5; C.S., ss. 2706, 2707; 1955, c. 675; 1963, c. 1000, s. 1; 1971, c. 698, s. 1; 1973, c. 426, s. 33.)

§ 160A-218. Basis for making assessments.

Assessments may be made on the basis of:

(1) The frontage abutting on the project, at an equal rate per foot of frontage, or

(2) The area of land served, or subject to being served, by the project, at an equal rate per unit of area, or

(3) The value added to the land served by the project, or subject to being served by it, being the difference between the appraised value of the land without improvements as shown on the tax records of the county, and the appraised value of the land with improvements according to the appraisal standards and rules adopted by the county at its last revaluation, at an equal rate per dollar of value added; or

(4) The number of lots served, or subject to being served, where the project involves extension of an existing system to a residential or commercial subdivision, at an equal rate per lot; or

(5) A combination of two or more of these bases.

Whenever the basis selected for assessment is either area or value added, the council may provide for the laying out of benefit zones according to the distance of benefited property from the project being undertaken, and may establish differing rates of assessment to apply uniformly throughout each benefit zone.

For each project, the council shall endeavor to establish an assessment method from among the bases set out in this section which will most accurately assess each lot or parcel of land according to the benefit conferred upon it by the project. The council's decision as to the method of assessment shall be final and conclusive and not subject to further review or challenge. (1971, c. 698, s. 1.)

§ 160A-219. Corner lot exemptions.

The council shall have authority to establish schedules of exemptions from assessments for corner lots when a project is undertaken along both sides of such lots. The schedules of exemptions shall be based on categories of land use (residential, commercial, industrial, or agricultural) and shall be uniform for each category. The schedule of exemptions may not provide exemption of more than seventy-five percent (75%) of the frontage of any side of a corner lot, or 150 feet, whichever is greater. (1971, c. 698, s. 1.)

§ 160A-220. Lands exempt from assessment.

No lands within a city, except as herein provided, shall be exempt from special assessments except lands belonging to the United States that are exempt under the provisions of federal statutes. (1971, c. 698, s. 1.)

§ 160A-221. Assessments against lands owned by the State.

When any city proposes to make local improvements that would benefit lands owned by the State of North Carolina or any board, agency, commission, or institution thereof, the council may request the Council of State to consent to special assessments against the property. The Council of State may authorize the Secretary of Administration to give consent for special assessments against State property, but the city may appeal to the Council of State if the Secretary of Administration refuses to give consent. When consent is given for special assessments against State lands, the Council of State may direct that the assessment be paid from the Contingency and Emergency Fund of the State of North Carolina or from any other available funds. If consent to the assessment is refused, the state-owned property shall be exempt from assessment. (1971, c. 698, s. 1; 1975, c. 879, s. 46.)

§ 160A-222. Assessments against railroads.

Assessments shall not be made against land owned, leased or controlled by a railroad company, except that if there is a building on the land, the portion of railroad property subject to assessment shall be a lot whose frontage equals the actual front footage occupied by the building plus 25 feet on each side thereof, but not more than the amount of land owned, leased, or controlled by the railroad. If a building is placed on land that would have been subject to assessment but for the limitations imposed by this section after an improvement is made, then the railroad company shall be subject to an assessment without interest on the same basis as if the building had been on the property when the improvement was made.

It is the intent of this section to make uniform the law concerning assessments against railroads. To this end, all provisions of law, whether general or local, in conflict with this section are repealed; and no local act taking effect on or after January 1, 1972, shall be construed to modify, amend, or repeal any portion of this section unless it shall specifically so provide by reference hereto. (1965, c. 839, s. 2; 1971, c. 698, s. 1.)

§ 160A-223. Preliminary resolution; contents.

Whenever the council decides to finance a proposed project by special assessments, it shall first adopt a preliminary resolution that shall contain the following:

(1)   A statement of intent to undertake the project;

(2)   A general description of the nature and location of the project;

(3)   A statement as to the proposed basis for making assessments, which shall include a general description of the boundaries of the area benefited if the basis of assessment is either area or value added;

(4)   A statement as to the percentage of the cost of the work that is to be assessed;

(5)   A statement as to which, if any, assessments shall be held in abeyance and for how long;

(6) A statement as to the proposed terms of payment of the assessment; and

(7) An order setting a time and place for a public hearing on all matters covered by the preliminary resolution which shall be not earlier than three weeks nor later than 10 weeks from the date of the adoption of the preliminary resolution. (1971, c. 698, s. 1.)

§ 160A-224. Notice of preliminary resolution.

At least 10 days before the date set for the public hearing, the council shall publish a notice that a preliminary assessment resolution has been adopted and that a public hearing will be held on it at a specified time and place. The notice shall generally describe the nature and location of the improvement. In addition, at least 10 days prior to the hearing, the council shall cause a copy of the preliminary resolution to be mailed to the owners, as shown on the county tax records, of all property subject to assessment if the project should be undertaken. The person designated to mail these resolutions shall file with the council a certificate showing that they were mailed by first-class mail and on what date. The certificate shall be conclusive as to compliance with the mailing provisions of this section in the absence of fraud. (1971, c. 698, s. 1.)

§ 160A-225. Hearing on preliminary resolution; assessment resolution.

At the public hearing, the council shall hear all interested persons who appear with respect to any matter covered by the preliminary resolution. After the public hearing, the council may adopt a resolution directing that the project or portions thereof be undertaken. The assessment resolution shall describe the project in general terms (which may be by reference to projects described in the preliminary resolution) and shall set forth the following:

(1) The basis on which the special assessments shall be levied, together with a general description of the boundaries of the area benefited if the basis of assessment is either area or value added;

(2) The percentage of the cost to be specially assessed;

(3) The terms of payment, including the conditions under which assessments are to be held in abeyance, if any.

The percentage of cost to be assessed may not be different from the percentage proposed, and the projects authorized may not be greater in scope than the projects described in the preliminary resolution. If the council decides that a different percentage of the cost should be assessed than that proposed in the preliminary resolution, or that any project should be enlarged, it shall adopt and advertise a new preliminary resolution as herein provided. (1915, c. 56, s. 6; C.S., s. 2708; 1971, c. 698, s. 1.)

§ 160A-226. Determination of costs.

When the project is complete, the council shall ascertain the total cost. In addition to construction costs, the cost of all necessary legal services, the amount of interest paid during construction, costs of rights-of-way, and the costs of publication of notices and resolutions may be included. The determination of the council as to the total cost of any project shall be conclusive. (1915, c. 56, s. 9; C.S., s. 2711; 1971, c. 698, s. 1.)

§ 160A-226.1. Discounts authorized.

The council is authorized to establish a schedule of discounts to be applied to assessments paid before the expiration of 30 days from the date that notice is published of confirmation of the assessment roll pursuant to G.S. 160A-229. Such a schedule of discounts may be established even though it was not included among the terms of payment as specified in the preliminary assessment resolution or assessment resolution. The amount of any discount may not exceed thirty percent (30%). (1983, c. 381, s. 4.)

§ 160A-227. Preliminary assessment roll; publication.

When the total cost of a project has been determined, the council shall have a preliminary assessment roll prepared. The preliminary roll shall contain a brief description of each lot, parcel, or tract of land assessed, the basis for the assessment, the amount assessed against each, the terms of payment, including the schedule of discounts, if such a schedule is to be established and the name of the owner of each parcel of land as far as this can be ascertained from the county tax records. A map of the project on which is shown each parcel assessed with the basis of its assessment, the amount assessed against it, and the name of the owner, as far as this can be ascertained from the county tax records, shall be a sufficient assessment roll.

After the preliminary assessment roll has been completed, it shall be filed in the city clerk's office where it shall be available for public inspection. A notice of the completion of the assessment roll, setting forth in general terms a description of the project, noting the availability of the assessment roll in the clerk's office for inspection, and stating the time and place for a hearing on the preliminary assessment roll, shall be published at least 10 days before the date set for the hearing on the preliminary assessment roll. The council shall also cause a notice of the hearing on the preliminary assessment roll to be mailed to the owners of property listed thereon at least 10 days before the hearing. The notice mailed to each property owner shall give notice of the time and place of the hearing, shall note the availability of the preliminary assessment roll for inspection in the city clerk's office and shall state the amount of the assessment against the property of the owner as shown on the preliminary assessment roll. The person designated to mail these notices shall file with the council a certificate showing they were mailed by first-class mail and on what date. Such a certificate shall be conclusive as to compliance with the mailing provisions of this section in the absence of fraud. (1915, c. 56, s. 9; C.S., s. 2712; 1971, c. 698, s. 1; 1983, c. 381, s. 5.)

§ 160A-228. Hearing on preliminary assessment roll; revision; confirmation; lien.

At the public hearing, which may be adjourned from time to time until all persons have had an opportunity to be heard, the council shall hear objections to the preliminary assessment roll from all interested persons who appear. Then or thereafter, the council shall annul, modify, or confirm the assessments, in whole or in part, either by confirming the preliminary assessments against any or all of the lots or parcels described in the preliminary assessment roll, or by canceling, increasing, or reducing them as may be proper in compliance with the basis of assessment. If any property is omitted from the preliminary assessment roll, the council may place it on the roll and levy the proper assessment. Whenever the council confirms assessments for any project, the city clerk shall enter in the minutes of the council the date, hour, and minute of confirmation. From and after the time of confirmation, the assessments shall be a lien on the property assessed of the same nature and to the same extent as the lien for county and city property taxes, according to the priorities set out in G.S. 160A-233(c). After the assessment roll is confirmed, a copy of it shall be delivered to the city tax collector for collection in the same manner as property taxes, except as herein provided. (1915, c. 56, s. 9; C.S., s. 2713; 1971, c. 698, s. 1; 1973, c. 426, s. 34.)

§ 160A-229. Publication of notice of confirmation of assessment roll.

After the expiration of 20 days from the confirmation of the assessment roll, the city tax collector shall publish once a notice that the assessment roll has been confirmed, and that assessments may be paid without interest at any time before the expiration of 30 days from the date that the notice is published, and that if they are not paid within this time, all installments thereof shall bear interest as provided in G.S. 160A-233. The notice shall also state the schedule of discounts, if one has been established, to be applied to assessments paid before the expiration date for payment of assessments without interest. (1971, c. 698, s. 1; 1983, c. 381, s. 6.)

§ 160A-230. Appeal to General Court of Justice.

If the owner of, or any person interested in, any lot or parcel of land against which an assessment is made is dissatisfied with the amount of the assessment, he may, within 10 days after the confirmation of the assessment roll, file a notice of appeal to the appropriate division of the General Court of Justice. He shall then have 20 days after the confirmation of the assessment roll to serve on the council or the city clerk a statement of facts upon which the appeal is based. The appeal shall be tried like other actions at law. (1915, c. 56, s. 9; C.S., s. 2714; 1971, c. 698, s. 1.)

§ 160A-231. Reassessment.

The council shall have the power, when in its judgment any irregularity, omission, error or lack of jurisdiction in any of the proceedings related thereto, has occurred, to set aside the whole of any special assessment made by it and thereupon to make a reassessment. In that case, all additional interest paid, or to be paid, as a result of the delay in confirming the assessment shall be included as a part of the project cost. The proceeding shall, as far as practicable, in all respects take place as it had with the original assessments, and the reassessment shall have the same force as if it had originally been properly made. (1915, c. 56, s. 9; C.S., s. 2715; 1971, c. 698, s. 1.)

§ 160A-232. Payment of assessments in cash or by installments.

The owners of assessed property shall have the option, within 30 days after the publication of the notice that the assessment roll has been confirmed, of paying the assessment either in cash or in not more than 10 annual installments, as may have been determined by the council in the resolution directing the project giving rise to the assessment to be undertaken. With respect to payment by installment, the council may provide

(1)   That the first installment with interest shall become due and payable on the date when property taxes are due and payable, and one subsequent installment and interest shall be due and payable on the same date in each successive year until the assessment is paid in full, or

(2)   That the first installment with interest shall become due and payable 60 days after the date that the assessment roll is confirmed, and one subsequent installment and interest shall be due and payable on the same day of the month in each successive year until the assessment is paid in full. (1915, c. 56, s. 10; C.S., s. 2716; 1971, c. 698, s. 1.)

§ 160A-233. Enforcement of assessments; interests; foreclosure; limitations.

(a)   Any portion of an assessment that is not paid within 30 days after publication of the notice that the assessment roll has been confirmed shall bear interest until paid at a rate to be fixed in the assessment resolution but not more than eight percent (8%) per annum.

(b)   If any installment of an assessment is not paid on or before the due date, all of the installments remaining unpaid shall immediately become due and payable, unless the council waives acceleration. The council may waive acceleration and permit the property owner to pay all installments in arrears together with interest due thereon and the cost to the city of attempting to obtain payment. If this is done, the remaining installments shall be reinstated so that they fall due as if there had been no default. Waiver of acceleration and reinstatement of future installments may be done at any time before foreclosure proceedings have been instituted.

(c)   Assessment liens may be foreclosed under any procedure prescribed by law for the foreclosure of property tax liens, except that lien sales and lien sale certificates shall not be required, and foreclosure may be begun at any time after 30 days after the due date. The city shall not be entitled to a deficiency judgment in an action to foreclose an assessment lien. The lien of special assessments shall be inferior to all prior and subsequent liens for State, local, and federal taxes, and superior to all other liens.

(d)   No city may maintain an action or proceeding to enforce any remedy for the foreclosure of special assessment liens unless the action or proceeding is begun within 10 years from the date that the assessment or the earliest installment thereof included in the action or proceeding became due. Acceleration of installments under subsection (b) shall not have the effect of shortening the time within which foreclosure may be begun, but in that event the statute of limitations shall continue to run as to each installment as if acceleration had not occurred. (1915, c. 56, s. 11; C.S., s. 2717; 1923, c. 87; 1929, c. 331, s. 1; 1971, c. 698, s. 1.)

§ 160A-234. Assessments on property held by tenancy for life or years.

(a)   Assessments upon real property in the possession or enjoyment of a tenant for life, or a tenant for a term of years, shall be paid by the holder of the remainder or reversion, as the case may be.

(b)   Repealed by Session Laws 1979, c. 107, s. 12. (1911, c. 7, ss. 1, 2, 3; C.S., ss. 2718, 2719, 2720; 1971, c. 698, s. 1; 1979, c. 107, s. 12; 2003-232, s. 6.)

§ 160A-235. Lien in favor of a cotenant or joint owner paying special assessments.

Any one of several tenants in common, or joint tenants, or copartners shall have the right to pay the whole or any part of any special assessment levied against property held jointly or in common, and all sums by him so paid in excess of his share of the assessment, interests, costs, and amounts required for redemption, shall constitute a lien upon the shares of his cotenants or associates, which he may enforce in proceedings for partition, actual or by sale, or in any other appropriate judicial proceeding. The lien herein provided for shall not be effective against an innocent purchaser for value unless and until notice thereof is filed in the office of the clerk of superior court in the county in which the land lies and indexed and docketed in the same manner as other liens required by law to be filed in the clerk's office. (1935, c. 174; 1971, c. 698, s. 1.)

§ 160A-236. Apportionment of assessments.

When special assessments are made against property which has been or is about to be subdivided, the council may, with the consent of the owner of the property, apportion the assessment among the lots or tracts within the subdivision, or release certain lots or tracts from the assessments if, in the opinion of the council, some of the lots or tracts in the subdivision are not benefited by the project. Upon an apportionment, each of the lots and tracts in the subdivision shall be released from the lien of the original assessment, and the portions of the original assessment assessed against each lot or tract shall have the same force and effect as the original assessment as to the particular lot or tract assessed. At the time of making an apportionment under this section, the council shall enter on its minutes a statement to the effect that the apportionment is made with the consent of the owners of the property affected, and this entry shall be conclusive in the absence of fraud. Reassessments made under this section may include past due installments of principal and interest as well as installments not then due, and any installments not then due shall fall due at the same dates as they would have under the original assessment. The council may delegate authority to make apportionment of assessments to the chief financial officer, but apportionments shall in all cases be reported to the council at its next regular meeting and entered in the minutes. (1929, c. 331, s. 1; 1935, c. 125; 1971, c. 698, s. 1.)

§ 160A-237. Authority to hold water and sewer assessments in abeyance.

The assessment resolution may provide that assessments levied under this Article for water or sewer improvements be held in abeyance without interest until improvements on the assessed property are actually connected to the water or sewer system for which the assessment was levied, or a date certain not more than 10 years from the date of confirmation of the assessment roll, whichever event first occurs. Upon termination of the period of abeyance, the assessment shall be paid in accordance with the terms set out in the assessment resolution. If assessments are to be held in abeyance, the assessment resolution shall classify the property assessed according to general land use, location with respect to the water or sewer system, or other relevant factors, and shall provide that the period of abeyance shall be the same for all assessed property in the same class.

All statutes of limitations are suspended during the time that any assessment is held in abeyance without interest. (1973, c. 426, s. 35.)

§ 160A-238. Authority to make assessments for beach erosion control and flood and hurricane protection works.

A city may make special assessments, according to the procedures of this Article, against benefited property within the city for all or part of the costs of acquiring, constructing, reconstructing, extending, or otherwise building or improving beach erosion control or flood and hurricane protection works. Assessments for these projects may be made on the basis of:

(1)   The frontage abutting on the project, at an equal rate per foot of frontage; or

(2)   The frontage abutting on a beach or shoreline protected or benefited by the project, at an equal rate per foot of frontage; or

(3)   The area of land benefited by the project, at an equal rate per unit of area; or

(4)   The valuation of land benefited by the project, being the value of the land without improvements as shown on the tax records of the county, at an equal rate per dollar of valuation; or

(5)   A combination of two or more of these bases.

Whenever the basis selected for assessment is either area or valuation, the council shall provide for the laying out of one or more benefit zones according to the distance from the shoreline, the distance from the project, the elevation of the land, or other relevant factors. If more than one benefit zone is established, the council shall establish differing rates of assessment to apply uniformly throughout each benefit zone. (1973, c. 822, s. 7.)

§ 160A-239. Reserved for future codification purposes.

Article 10A.

Special Assessments for Critical Infrastructure Needs.

§ 160A-239.1. (See note for expiration of Article) Purpose; sunset.

(a) Purpose. - This Article enables cities that face increased demands for infrastructure improvements as a result of rapid growth and development to issue revenue bonds payable from special assessments imposed under this Article on benefited property. This Article supplements the authority cities have in Article 10 of this Chapter. The provisions of Article 10 of this Chapter apply to this Article, to the extent they do not conflict with this Article.

(b) Sunset. - This Article expires July 1, 2015. The expiration does not affect the validity of assessments imposed or bonds issued or authorized under the provisions of this Article prior to the effective date of the expiration. (2008-165, s. 3; 2013-371, ss. 2(a), 3.)

§ 160A-239.2. (See note for expiration of Article) Assessments.

(a) Projects. - The council of a city may make special assessments as provided in this Article against benefited property within the city for the purpose of financing the capital costs of projects for which project development financing debt instruments may be issued under G.S. 159-103 or for the purpose of financing the installation of distributed generation renewable energy sources or energy efficiency improvements that are permanently fixed to residential, commercial, industrial, or other real property.

(b) Costs. - The city council must determine a project's total estimated cost. In addition to the costs allowed under G.S. 153A-193, the costs may include any expenses allowed under G.S. 159-84. A preliminary assessment roll may be prepared before the costs are incurred based on the estimated cost of the project.

(c) Method. - The city council must establish an assessment method that will most accurately assess each lot or parcel of land subject to the assessments according to the benefits conferred upon it by the project for which the assessment is made. In addition to other bases upon which assessments may be made under G.S. 160A-218, the council may select any other method designed to allocate the costs in accordance with benefits conferred. In doing so, the council may provide that the benefits conferred are measured on the basis of use being made on the lot or parcel of land and provide for adjustments of assessments upon a change in use, provided that the total amount of all assessments is sufficient to pay the costs of the project after the adjustments have been made. (2008-165, s. 3; 2008-187, s. 47.5(b); 2009-525, s. 2(a); 2013-371, ss. 2(b), 3.)

§ 160A-239.3. (See note for expiration of Article) Petition required.

(a) Petition. - The city council may not impose a special assessment under this Article unless it receives a petition for the project to be financed by the assessment signed by (i) at least a majority of the owners of real property to be assessed and (ii) owners who represent at least sixty-six percent (66%) of the assessed value of all real property to be assessed. For purposes of determining whether the petition has been signed by a majority of owners, an owner who holds title to a parcel of real property alone shall be treated as having one vote each, and an owner who shares title to a parcel of real property with one or more other owners shall have a vote equal to one vote multiplied by a fraction, the numerator of which is one, and the denominator of which is the total number of owners of the parcel. For purposes of determining whether the assessed value represented by those signing the petition constitutes at least sixty-six percent (66%) of the assessed value of all real property to be assessed, an owner who holds title to a parcel of real property alone shall have the full assessed value of the parcel included in the calculation, and an owner who shares title to a parcel of real property with one or more other owners shall have their proportionate share of the full assessed value of the parcel included in the calculation. The petition must include the following:

(1) A statement of the project proposed to be financed in whole or in part by the imposition of an assessment under this Article.

(2) An estimate of the cost of the project.

(3) An estimate of the portion of the cost of the project to be assessed.

(b) Petition Withdrawn. - The city council must wait at least 10 days after the public hearing on the preliminary assessment resolution before adopting a final assessment resolution. A petition submitted under subsection (a) of this section may be withdrawn if notice of petition withdrawal is given in writing to the council signed by at least a majority of the owners who signed the petition submitted under subsection (a) of this section representing at least fifty percent (50%) of the assessed value of all real property to be assessed. The council may not adopt a final assessment resolution if it receives a timely notice of petition withdrawal.

(c) Validity of Assessment. - No right of action or defense asserting the invalidity of an assessment on grounds that the city did not comply with this section may be asserted except in an action or proceeding begun within 90 days after publication of the notice of adoption of the preliminary assessment resolution. (2008-165, s. 3; 2013-371, ss. 2(c), 3.)

§ 160A-239.4. (See note for expiration of Article) Financing a project for which an assessment is imposed.

(a) Financing Sources. - A city council may provide for the payment of the cost of a project for which an assessment may be imposed under this Article from one or more financing sources listed in this subsection. The assessment resolution must include the estimated cost of the project and the amount of the cost to be derived from the respective financing source.

(1) Revenue bonds issued under G.S. 160A-239.6.

(2) Project development financing debt instruments issued under the North Carolina Project Development Financing Act, Article 6 of Chapter 159 of the General Statutes.

(3) General obligation bonds issued under the Local Government Bond Act, Article 4 of Chapter 159 of the General Statutes.

(4) General revenues.

(b) Assessments Pledged. - An assessment imposed under this Article may be pledged to secure revenue bonds under G.S. 160A-239.6 or as additional security for a project development financing debt instrument under G.S. 159-111. If an assessment imposed under this Article is pledged to secure financing, the city council must covenant to enforce the payment of the assessments. (2008-165, s. 3; 2009-525, s. 2(b); 2010-95, s. 40; 2013-371, s. 3.)

§ 160A-239.5. (See note for expiration of Article) Payment of assessments by installments.

An assessment imposed under this Article is payable in annual installments. The city council must set the number of annual installments, which may not be more than 30. The installments are due on the date that property taxes are due. (2008-165, s. 3; 2013-371, s. 3.)

§ 160A-239.6. (See note for expiration of Article) Revenue bonds.

(a) Authorization. - A city council that imposes an assessment under this Article may issue revenue bonds under Article 5 of Chapter 159 of the General Statutes to finance the project for which the assessment is imposed and use the proceeds of the assessment imposed as revenues pertaining to the project.

(b) Modifications. - This Article specifically modifies the authority of a city to issue revenue bonds under Article 5 of Chapter 159 of the General Statutes by extending the authority in that Article to include a project for which an assessment may be imposed under this Article. In applying the provisions of Article 5, the following definitions apply:

(1) Revenue bond project. - Defined in G.S. 159-81(3). The term includes projects for which an assessment is imposed under this Article.

(2) Revenues. - Defined in G.S. 159-81(4). The term includes assessments imposed under this Article to finance a project allowed under this Article. (2008-165, s. 3; 2013-371, s. 3.)

§ 160A-239.7. (See note for expiration of Article) Project implementation.

A city may act directly, through one or more contracts with other public agencies, through one or more contracts with private agencies, or by any combination thereof to implement the project financed in whole or in part by the imposition of an assessment imposed under this Article. If no more than twenty-five percent (25%) of the estimated cost of a project is to be funded from the proceeds of general obligation bonds or general revenue, a private agency that enters into a contract with a city for the implementation of all or part of the project is subject to the provisions of Article 8 of Chapter 143 of the General Statutes only to the extent specified in the contract. In the event any contract relating to construction a substantial portion of which is to be performed on publicly owned property is excluded from the provisions of Article 8 of Chapter 143, the city or any trustee or fiduciary responsible for disbursing funds shall obtain certification acceptable to the city in the amount due for work done or materials supplied for which payment will be paid from such disbursement. If the city or any trustee or fiduciary responsible for disbursing funds receives notice of a claim from any person who would be entitled to a mechanic's or materialman's lien but for the fact that the claim relates to work performed on or supplies provided to publicly owned property, then either no disbursement of funds may be made until the city, trustee, or fiduciary receives satisfactory proof of resolution of the claim or funds in the amount of the claim shall be set aside for payment thereof upon resolution of the claim. (2009-525, s. 2(c); 2013-371, s. 3.)

Article 11.

Eminent Domain.

§ 160A-240. Repealed by Session Laws 1981, c. 919, s. 28, effective January 1, 1982.

§ 160A-240.1. Power to acquire property.

A city may acquire, by gift, grant, devise, exchange, purchase, lease, or any other lawful method, the fee or any lesser interest in real or personal property for use by the city or any department, board, commission or agency of the city. In exercising the power of eminent domain a city shall use the procedures of Chapter 40A. (1981, c. 919, s. 29; 1983, c. 768, s. 23; 2011-284, s. 112.)

§§ 160A-241 through 160A-261. Repealed by Session Laws 1981, c. 919, s. 28, effective January 1, 1982.

§ 160A-262. Repealed by Session Laws 1973, c. 426, s. 42.

§ 160A-263. Repealed by Session Laws 1981, c. 919, s. 28, effective January 1, 1982.

§ 160A-264. Reserved for future codification purposes.

Article 12.

Sale and Disposition of Property.

§ 160A-265. Use and disposal of property.

In the discretion of the council, a city may: (i) hold, use, change the use thereof to other uses, or (ii) sell or dispose of real and personal property, without regard to the method or purpose of its acquisition or to its intended or actual governmental or other prior use. (1981 (Reg. Sess., 1982), c. 1236.)

§ 160A-266. Methods of sale; limitation.

(a) Subject to the limitations prescribed in subsection (b) of this section, and according to the procedures prescribed in this Article, a city may dispose of real or personal property belonging to the city by:

(1) Private negotiation and sale;

(2) Advertisement for sealed bids;

(3) Negotiated offer, advertisement, and upset bid;

(4) Public auction; or

(5) Exchange.

(b) Private negotiation and sale may be used only with respect to personal property valued at less than thirty thousand dollars ($30,000) for any one item or group of similar items. Real property, of any value, and personal property valued at thirty thousand dollars ($30,000) or more for any one item or group of similar items may be exchanged as permitted by G.S. 160A-271, or may be sold by any method permitted in this Article other than private negotiation and sale, except as permitted in G.S. 160A-277 and G.S. 160A-279.

Provided, however, a city may dispose of real property of any value and personal property valued at thirty thousand dollars ($30,000) or more for any one item or group of similar items by private negotiation and sale where (i) said real or personal property is significant for its architectural, archaeological, artistic, cultural or historical associations, or significant for its relationship to other property significant for architectural, archaeological, artistic, cultural or historical associations, or significant for its natural, scenic or open condition; and (ii) said real or personal property is to be sold to a nonprofit corporation or trust whose purposes include the preservation or conservation of real or personal properties of architectural, archaeological, artistic, cultural, historical, natural or scenic significance; and (iii) where a preservation agreement or conservation agreement as defined in G.S. 121-35 is placed in the deed conveying said property from the city to the nonprofit corporation or trust. Said nonprofit corporation or trust shall only dispose of or use said real or personal property subject to covenants or other legally binding restrictions which will promote the preservation or conservation of the property, and, where appropriate, secure rights of public access.

(c) A city council may adopt regulations prescribing procedures for disposing of personal property valued at less than thirty thousand dollars ($30,000) for any one item or group of items in substitution for the requirements of this Article. The regulations shall be designed to secure for the city fair market value for all property disposed of and to accomplish the disposal efficiently and economically. The regulations may, but need not, require published notice, and may provide for either public or private exchanges and sales. The council may authorize one or more city officials to declare surplus any personal property valued at less than thirty thousand dollars ($30,000) for any one item or group of items, to set its fair market value, and to convey title to the property for the city in accord with the regulations. A city official authorized under this section to dispose of property shall keep a record of all property sold under this section and that record shall generally describe the property sold or exchanged, to whom it was sold, or with whom exchanged, and the amount of money or other consideration received for each sale or exchange.

(d) A city may discard any personal property that: (i) is determined to have no value; (ii) remains unsold or unclaimed after the city has exhausted efforts to sell the property using any applicable procedure under this Article; or (iii) poses a potential threat to the public health or safety. (1971, c. 698, s. 1; 1973, c. 426, s. 42.1; 1983, c. 130, s. 1; c. 456; 1987, c. 692, s. 2; 1987 (Reg. Sess., 1988), c. 1108, s. 9; 1997-174, s. 6; 2001-328, s. 4; 2005-227, s. 3.)

§ 160A-267. Private sale.

When the council proposes to dispose of property by private sale, it shall at a regular council meeting adopt a resolution or order authorizing an appropriate city official to dispose of the property by private sale at a negotiated price. The resolution or order shall identify the property to be sold and may, but need not, specify a minimum price. A notice summarizing the contents of the resolution or order shall be published once after its adoption, and no sale shall be consummated thereunder until 10 days after its publication. (1971, c. 698, s. 1; 1979, 2nd Sess., c. 1247, s. 24.)

§ 160A-268. Advertisement for sealed bids.

The sale of property by advertisement for sealed bids shall be done in the manner prescribed by law for the purchase of property, except that in the case of real property the advertisement for bids shall be begun not less than 30 days before the date fixed for opening bids. (1971, c. 698, s. 1.)

§ 160A-269. Negotiated offer, advertisement, and upset bids.

A city may receive, solicit, or negotiate an offer to purchase property and advertise it for upset bids. When an offer is made and the council proposes to accept it, the council shall require the offeror to deposit five percent (5%) of his bid with the city clerk, and shall publish a notice of the offer. The notice shall contain a general description of the property, the amount and terms of the offer, and a notice that within 10 days any person may raise the bid by not less than ten percent (10%) of the first one thousand dollars ($1,000) and five percent (5%) of the remainder. When a bid is raised, the bidder shall deposit with the city clerk five percent (5%) of the increased bid, and the clerk shall readvertise the offer at the increased bid. This procedure shall be repeated until no further qualifying upset bids are received, at which time the council may accept the offer and sell the property to the highest bidder. The council may at any time reject any and all offers. (1971, c. 698, s. 1; 1979, 2nd Sess., c. 1247, s. 25.)

§ 160A-270. Public auction.

(a)   Real Property. - When it is proposed to sell real property at public auction, the council shall first adopt a resolution authorizing the sale, describing the property to be sold, specifying the date, time, place, and terms of sale, and stating that any offer or bid must be accepted and confirmed by the council before the sale will be effective. The resolution may, but need not, require the highest bidder at the sale to make a bid deposit in a specified amount. The council shall then publish a notice of the sale at least once and not less than 30 days before the sale. The notice shall contain a general description of the land sufficient to identify it, the terms of the sale, and a reference to the authorizing resolution. After bids have been received, the highest bid shall be reported to the council, and the council shall accept or reject it within 30 days thereafter. If the bid is rejected, the council may readvertise the property for sale.

(b) Personal Property. - When it is proposed to sell personal property at public auction, the council shall at a regular council meeting adopt a resolution or order authorizing an appropriate city official to dispose of the property at public auction. The resolution or order shall identify the property to be sold and set out the date, time, place, and terms of the sale. The resolution or order (or a notice summarizing its contents) shall be published at least once and not less than 10 days before the date of the auction.

(c) The council may conduct auctions of real or personal property electronically by authorizing the establishment of an electronic auction procedure or by authorizing the use of existing private or public electronic auction services. Notice of an electronic auction of property shall identify, in addition to the information required in subsections (a) and (b) of this section, the electronic address where information about the property to be sold can be found and the electronic address where electronic bids may be posted. Notice may be published in a newspaper having general circulation in the political subdivision or by electronic means, or both. A decision to publish notice solely by electronic means for a particular auction or for all auctions under this subsection shall be approved by the governing board of the political subdivision. Except as provided in this subsection, all requirements of subsections (a) and (b) of this section apply to electronic auctions. (1971, c. 698, s. 1; 1973, c. 426, s. 43; 2001-328, s. 5; 2005-227, s. 4; 2006-264, s. 74.)

§ 160A-271. Exchange of property.

A city may exchange any real or personal property belonging to the city for other real or personal property by private negotiation if the city receives a full and fair consideration in exchange for its property. A city may also exchange facilities of a city-owned enterprise for like facilities located within or outside the corporate limits. Property shall be exchanged only pursuant to a resolution authorizing the exchange adopted at a regular meeting of the council upon 10 days' public notice. Notice shall be given by publication describing the properties to be exchanged, stating the value of the properties and other consideration changing hands, and announcing the council's intent to authorize the exchange at its next regular meeting. (1971, c. 698, s. 1; 1973, c. 426, s. 42.1.)

§ 160A-272. Lease or rental of property.

(a) Any property owned by a city may be leased or rented for such terms and upon such conditions as the council may determine, but not for longer than

10 years (except as otherwise provided herein) and only if the council determines that the property will not be needed by the city for the term of the lease. In determining the term of a proposed lease, periods that may be added to the original term by options to renew or extend shall be included. Property may be rented or leased only pursuant to a resolution of the council authorizing the execution of the lease or rental agreement adopted at a regular council meeting upon 10 days' public notice. Notice shall be given by publication describing the property to be leased or rented, stating the annual rental or lease payments, and announcing the council's intent to authorize the lease or rental at its next regular meeting.

(b) No public notice need be given for resolutions authorizing leases or rentals for terms of one year or less, and the council may delegate to the city manager or some other city administrative officer authority to lease or rent city property for terms of one year or less. Leases for terms of more than 10 years shall be treated as a sale of property and may be executed by following any of the procedures authorized for sale of real property.

(c) (Effective until June 30, 2015) The council may approve a lease for the siting and operation of a renewable energy facility, as that term is defined in G.S. 62-133.8(a)(7), for a term up to 20 years without treating the lease as a sale of property and without giving notice by publication of the intended lease. This subsection applies to Catawba, Mecklenburg, and Wake Counties, the Cities of Asheville, Raleigh, and Winston-Salem, and the Towns of Apex, Carrboro, Cary, Chapel Hill, Fuquay-Varina, Garner, Holly Springs, Knightdale, Morrisville, Rolesville, Wake Forest, Wendell, and Zebulon only.

(c) (Effective June 30, 2015) The council may approve a lease for the siting and operation of a renewable energy facility, as that term is defined in G.S. 62-133.8(a)(7), for a term up to 20 years without treating the lease as a sale of property and without giving notice by publication of the intended lease. This subsection applies to Catawba, Mecklenburg, and Wake Counties, the Cities of Raleigh and Winston-Salem, and the Towns of Apex, Cary, Fuquay-Varina, Garner, Holly Springs, Knightdale, Morrisville, Rolesville, Wake Forest, Wendell, and Zebulon only. (1971, c. 698, s. 1; 1979, 2nd Sess., c. 1247, s. 26; 2009-149, ss. 2, 3; 2010-57, s. 2; 2010-63, s. 2(b); 2011-150, s. 1.)

§ 160A-272.1. Lease of utility or enterprise property.

Subject to G.S. 160A-321, a city-owned utility or public service enterprise, or part thereof, may be leased. (1979, 2nd Sess., c. 1247, s. 27.)

§ 160A-273. Grant of easements.

A city shall have authority to grant easements over, through, under, or across any city property or the right-of-way of any public street or alley that is not a part of the State highway system. Easements in a street or alley right-of-way shall not be granted if the easement would substantially impair or hinder the use of the street or alley as a way of passage. A grant of air rights over a street right-of-way or other property owned by the city for the purpose of erecting a building or other permanent structure (other than utility wires or pipes) shall be treated as a sale of real property, except that a grant of air rights over a street right-of-way for the purpose of constructing a bridge or passageway between existing buildings on opposite sides of the street shall be treated as a grant of an easement. (1971, c. 698, s. 1.)

§ 160A-274. Sale, lease, exchange and joint use of governmental property.

(a) For the purposes of this section, "governmental unit" means a city, county, school administrative unit, sanitary district, fire district, the State, or any other public district, authority, department, agency, board, commission, or institution.

(b) Any governmental unit may, upon such terms and conditions as it deems wise, with or without consideration, exchange with, lease to, lease from, sell to, or purchase from any other governmental unit any interest in real or personal property.

(c) Action under this section shall be taken by the governing body of the governmental unit. Action hereunder by any State agency, except the Department of Transportation, shall be taken only after approval by the Department of Administration. Action with regard to State property under the control of the Department of Transportation shall be taken by the Department of Transportation or its duly authorized delegate. Provided, any county board of education or board of education for any city administrative unit may, upon such terms and conditions as it deems wise, lease to another governmental unit for one dollar ($1.00) per year any real property owned or held by the board which has been determined by the board to be unnecessary or undesirable for public school purposes. (1969, c. 806; 1971, c. 698, s. 1; 1973, c. 507, s. 5; 1975, c. 455; c. 664, s. 9; c. 879, s. 46; 1977, c. 464, s. 34; 2001-328, s. 6.)

§ 160A-275. Warranty deeds.

Any city, county, or other municipal corporation is authorized to execute and deliver deeds to any real property with full covenants of warranty, without regard to how the property was acquired, when, in the opinion of the governing body, it is in the best interest of the city, county, or other municipal corporation to convey by warranty deed. Members of the governing boards of counties, cities, and other municipal corporations are hereby relieved of any personal or individual liability by reason of the execution of warranty deeds to governmentally owned property unless they act in fraud, malice, or bad faith. (1945, c. 962; 1955, c. 935; 1969, cc. 48, 223, 332; c. 1003, s. 5; 1971, c. 698, s. 1.)

§ 160A-276. Sale of stocks, bonds, and other securities.

A city may sell through a broker without complying with the preceding sections of this Article shares of common and preferred stock, bonds, options, and warrants or other rights with respect to stocks and bonds, and other securities, when the stock, bond, or other right or security has an established market and is traded in the usual course of business on a national stock exchange or over-the-counter by reputable brokers and securities dealers. The city may pay the usual fees and taxes incident to such transactions. Nothing in this section authorizes a city to deal in its own bonds in any manner inconsistent with Chapter 159 of the General Statutes, nor to invest in any securities not authorized by G.S. 159-30. (1973, c. 426, s. 44.)

§ 160A-277. Sale of land to volunteer fire departments and rescue squads; procedure.

(a) A city, upon such terms and conditions as it deems wise, with or without monetary consideration may lease, sell or convey to a volunteer fire department or to a volunteer rescue squad any land or interest in land, for the purpose of constructing or expanding fire department or rescue squad facilities, if the volunteer fire department or volunteer rescue squad provides fire protection or rescue services to the city.

(b) Any lease, sale or conveyance under this section must be approved by the city council by resolution adopted at a regular meeting of the council upon 10 days' public notice. Notice shall be given by publication describing the property to be leased or sold, stating the value of the properties, the proposed monetary consideration or lack thereof, and the council's intent to authorize the lease, sale or conveyance. (1979, c. 583.)

§ 160A-278. Lease of land for housing.

A city may lease land upon such terms and conditions as it deems wise to any person, firm or corporation who will use the land to construct housing for the benefit of persons of low income, or moderate income, or low and moderate income. Such a housing project may also provide housing to persons of other than low or moderate income, as long as at least twenty percent (20%) of the units in the project are set aside for the exclusive use of persons of low income. Despite the provisions of G.S. 160A-272, a lease authorized pursuant to this section may be made by private negotiation and may extend for longer than 10 years. Property may be leased under this section only pursuant to a resolution of the council authorizing the execution of the lease adopted at a regular council meeting upon 10 days' public notice. Notice shall be given by publication describing the property to be leased, stating the value of the property, stating the proposed consideration for the lease, and stating the council's intention to authorize the lease. (1987, c. 464, s. 9.)

§ 160A-279. Sale of property to entities carrying out a public purpose; procedure.

(a) Whenever a city or county is authorized to appropriate funds to any public or private entity which carries out a public purpose, the city or county may, in lieu of or in addition to the appropriation of funds, convey by private sale to such an entity any real or personal property which it owns; provided no property acquired by the exercise of eminent domain may be conveyed under this section; provided that no such conveyance may be made to a for-profit corporation. The city or county shall attach to any such conveyance covenants or conditions which assure that the property will be put to a public use by the recipient entity. The procedural provisions of G.S. 160A-267 shall apply. Provided, however, that a city or county may convey to any public or private entity, which is authorized to receive appropriations from a city or county, surplus automobiles without compensation or without the requirement that the automobiles be used for a public purpose. Provided, however, this conveyance is conditioned upon conveyance by the public or private entity to Work First participants selected by the county department of social services under the rules adopted by the local department of social services. In the discretion of the public or private entity to which the city or county conveys the surplus automobile, when that entity conveys the vehicle to a Work First participant it may arrange for an appropriate security interest in the vehicle, including a lien or lease, until such time as the Work First participant satisfactorily completes the requirements of the Work First program. This subsequent conveyance by the public or private entity to the Work First participant may be without compensation. The participant may be required to pay for license, tag, and/or title.

(b)   Notwithstanding any other provision of law, this section applies only to cities and counties and not to any other entity which this Article otherwise applies to.

(c)   Repealed by Session Laws 1993, c. 491, s. 1.

(d)   This section does not limit the right of any entity to convey property by private sale when that right is conferred by another law, public, or local. (1987, c. 692, s. 1; 1993, c. 491, s. 1; 1998-195, s. 1.)

§ 160A-280. Donations of personal property to other governmental units.

(a)   A city may donate to another governmental unit within the United States, a sister city, or a nonprofit organization incorporated by (i) the United States, (ii) the District of Columbia, or (iii) one of the United States, any personal property, including supplies, materials, and equipment, that the governing board deems to be surplus, obsolete, or unused. The governing board of the city shall post a public notice at least five days prior to the adoption of a resolution approving the donation. The resolution shall be adopted prior to making any donation of surplus, obsolete, or unused personal property. For purposes of this section a sister city is a city in a nation other than the United States that has entered into a formal, written agreement or memorandum of understanding with the donor city for the purposes of establishing a long term partnership to promote communication, understanding, and goodwill between peoples and to develop mutually beneficial activities, programs, and ideas. The agreement or memorandum of understanding establishing the sister city relationship shall be signed by the mayors or chief elective officer of both the donor and recipient cities.

(b)   For the purposes of this section, the term "governmental unit" shall have the same meaning as defined by G.S. 160A-274(a) and shall include North Carolina charter schools.

(c)   The authority granted to a city under this section is in addition to any authority granted under any other provision of law. (2007-430, s. 1; 2009-141, ss. 1, 2, 3.)

Article 13.

Law Enforcement.

§ 160A-281. Policemen appointed.

A city is authorized to appoint a chief of police and to employ other police officers who may reside outside the corporate limits of the city unless the council provides otherwise. (R.C., c. 111, s. 16; Code, c. 3803; Rev., s. 2926; C.S., s. 2641; 1969, c. 23, s. 1; 1971, c. 698, s. 1; 1973, c. 426, s. 45.)

§ 160A-282. Auxiliary law-enforcement personnel; workers' compensation benefits.

(a)   A city may by ordinance provide for the organization of an auxiliary police department made up of volunteer members.

(b)   A city, by enactment of an ordinance, may provide that, while undergoing official training and while performing duties on behalf of the city pursuant to orders or instructions of the chief of police of the city, auxiliary law-enforcement personnel shall be entitled to benefits under the North Carolina Workers' Compensation Act and to any fringe benefits for which such volunteer personnel qualify.

(c)   The board of commissioners of any county may provide that persons who are deputized by the sheriff of the county as special deputy sheriffs or persons who are serving as volunteer law-enforcement officers at the request of the sheriff and under his authority, while undergoing official training and while performing duties on behalf of the county pursuant to orders or instructions of the sheriff, shall be entitled to benefits under the North Carolina Workers' Compensation Act and to any fringe benefits for which such persons qualify.

This subsection shall not apply to volunteer school safety resource officers as described in G.S. 162-26. (1969, c. 206, s. 1; 1971, c. 698, s. 1; 1973, c. 1263, s. 1; 1979, c. 714, s. 2; 1979, 2nd Sess., c. 1247, s. 28; 2013-360, s. 8.45(d).)

§ 160A-283. Joint county and city auxiliary police.

The governing body of any city, town, or county is hereby authorized to create and establish a joint law-enforcement officers' auxiliary force with one or more cities, towns, or counties. Each participating city, town, or county shall, by resolution or ordinance, establish the joint auxiliary police force. The resolution or ordinance shall specify whether the members of the joint auxiliary police force shall be volunteers or shall be paid. Members shall be appointed by the respective governmental units and shall take the oath required for regular police officers. The joint auxiliary force may be called into active service at any time by the mayor or chief of police of the participating town or city or the chairman of the board of commissioners or sheriff of a participating county. Members of the joint auxiliary force, while undergoing official training and while on active duty shall be members of the unit which called the auxiliary force into active duty and shall be entitled to all powers, privileges and immunities afforded by law to regularly employed law-enforcement officers of that unit including benefits under the Workers' Compensation Act. Members of the joint auxiliary force shall not be considered as public officers within the meaning of the North Carolina Constitution. Such members shall be dressed in the uniform prescribed by such auxiliary force at any time such members or member exercises any of the duties or authority herein provided for. (1971, c. 607; c. 896, s. 4; 1979, c. 714, s. 2.)

§ 160A-284. Oath of office; holding other offices.

Each person appointed or employed as chief of police, policeman, or auxiliary policeman shall take and subscribe before some person authorized by law to administer oaths the oath of office required by Article VI, Sec. 7, of the Constitution. The oath shall be filed with the city clerk. The offices of policeman, chief of police, and auxiliary policeman are hereby declared to be offices that may be held concurrently with any other appointive office pursuant to Article VI, Sec. 9, of the Constitution. The office of auxiliary policeman is hereby declared to be an office that may be held concurrently with any elective office pursuant to Article VI, Sec. 9, of the Constitution. (1971, c. 698, s. 1; c. 896, s. 4; 1975, c. 664, s. 10.)

§ 160A-285. Powers and duties of policemen.

As a peace officer, a policeman shall have within the corporate limits of the city all of the powers invested in law-enforcement officers by statute or common law. He shall also have power to serve all civil and criminal process that may be directed to him by any officer of the General Court of Justice and may enforce the ordinances and regulations of the city as the council may direct. (Code, s. 3811; Rev., s. 2927; C.S., s. 2642; 1971, c. 698, s. 1; c. 896, s. 4.)

§ 160A-286. Extraterritorial jurisdiction of policemen.

In addition to their authority within the corporate limits, city policemen shall have all the powers invested in law-enforcement officers by statute or common law within one mile of the corporate limits of the city, and on all property owned by or leased to the city wherever located.

Any officer pursuing an offender outside the corporate limits or extraterritorial jurisdiction of the city shall be entitled to all of the privileges, immunities, and benefits to which he would be entitled if acting within the city, including coverage under the workers' compensation laws. (1971, c. 698, s. 1; c. 896, s. 4; 1973, c. 426, s. 46; c. 1286, s. 24; 1991, c. 636, s. 3.)

§ 160A-287. City lockups.

A city shall have authority to establish, erect, repair, maintain and operate a lockup for the temporary detention of prisoners pending their transferal to the county or district jail or the State Department of Corrections. (Code, ss. 704, 3117; 1901, c. 283; 1905, c. 526; Rev., s. 2916; 1907, c. 978; P.L. 1917, c. 223; C.S., s. 2623; Ex. Sess. 1921, c. 58; 1927, c. 14; 1933, c. 69; 1949, c. 938; 1955, c. 77; 1959, c. 391; 1961, c. 308; 1967, c. 100, s. 2; c. 1122, s. 1; 1969, c. 944; 1971, c. 698, s. 1; c. 896, s. 4.)

§ 160A-288. Cooperation between law-enforcement agencies.

(a)   In accordance with rules, policies, or guidelines officially adopted by the governing body of the city or county by which he is employed, and subject to any conditions or restrictions included therein, the head of any law-enforcement agency may temporarily provide assistance to another agency in enforcing the laws of North Carolina if so requested in writing by the head of the requesting agency. The assistance may comprise allowing officers of the agency to work temporarily with officers of the requesting agency (including in an undercover capacity) and lending equipment and supplies. While working with the requesting agency under the authority of this section, an officer shall have the same jurisdiction, powers, rights, privileges and immunities (including those relating to the defense of civil actions and payment of judgments) as the officers of the requesting agency in addition to those he normally possesses. While on duty with the requesting agency, he shall be subject to the lawful operational commands of his superior officers in the requesting agency, but he shall for personnel and administrative purposes, remain under the control of his own agency, including for purposes of pay. He shall furthermore be entitled to workers' compensation and the same benefits when acting pursuant to this section to the same extent as though he were functioning within the normal scope of his duties.

(b)   As used in this section:

(1)   "Head" means any director or chief officer of a law-enforcement agency including the chief of police of a local department, chief of police of county police department, and the sheriff of a county, or an officer of one of the above named agencies to whom the head of that agency has delegated authority to make or grant requests under this section, but only one officer in the agency shall have this delegated authority at any time.

(2)   "Law-enforcement agency" means only a municipal police department, a county police department, or a sheriff's department. All other State and local agencies are exempted from the provisions of this section.

(c)   This section in no way reduces the jurisdiction or authority of State law-enforcement officers.

(d)   For purposes of this section, the following shall be considered the equivalent of a municipal police department:

(1) Campus law-enforcement agencies established pursuant to G.S. 115D-21.1(a) or G.S. 116-40.5(a).

(2) Colleges or universities which are licensed, or exempted from licensure, by G.S. 116-15 and which employ company police officers commissioned by the Attorney General pursuant to Chapter 74E or Chapter 74G of the General Statutes.

(3) Law enforcement agencies operated or eligible to be operated by a municipality pursuant to G.S. 63-53(2).

(4) Repealed by Session Laws 2013-360, s. 16B.4(d), effective July 1, 2013.

(5) A Company Police agency of the Department of Agriculture and Consumer Services commissioned by the Attorney General pursuant to Chapter 74E of the General Statutes. (1967, c. 846; 1971, c. 698, s.1; c. 896, s.4; 1977, c. 534; 1981, c. 93, s. 2; 1987, c. 671, s. 4; 1989, c. 518, s. 2; 1991, c. 636, s. 3; 1991 (Reg. Sess., 1992), c. 1043, s. 6; 1997-143, s. 1; 1999-68, s. 4; 2005-231, s. 8; 2006-159, s. 4; 2009-94, s. 1; 2011-260, s. 4; 2013-360, s. 16B.4(d).)

§ 160A-288.1. Assistance by State law-enforcement officers; rules; cost.

(a) The governing body of any city or county may request the Governor to assign temporarily State law-enforcement officers with statewide authority to provide law-enforcement protection when local law-enforcement officers: (i) are engaged in a strike; (ii) are engaged in a slowdown; (iii) otherwise refuse to fulfill their law-enforcement responsibilities; or (iv) submit mass resignations. The request from the governing body of the city or county shall be in writing. The request from a county governing board shall be upon the advice of the sheriff of the county.

(b) The Governor shall formulate such rules, policies or guidelines as may be necessary to establish a plan under which temporary State law-enforcement assistance will be provided to cities and counties. The Governor may delegate the responsibility for developing appropriate rules, policies or guidelines to the head of any State department. The Governor may also delegate to a department head the authority to determine the number of officers to be assigned in a particular case, if any, and the length of time they are to be assigned.

(c) While providing assistance to a city or county, a State law-enforcement officer shall be considered an employee of the State for all purposes, including compensation and fringe benefits.

(d) While providing assistance to the city or county, a State officer shall be subject to the lawful operational commands of his State superior officers. The ranking representative of each State law-enforcement agency providing assistance shall consult with the appropriate city or county officials prior to deployment of the State officers under his command. (1979, c. 639, s. 1.)

§ 160A-288.2. Assistance to State law-enforcement agencies.

(a) In accordance with rules, policies, or guidelines officially adopted by the governing body of the city or county by which he is employed, and subject to any conditions or restrictions included therein, the head of any local law-enforcement agency may temporarily provide assistance to a State law-enforcement agency in enforcing the laws of North Carolina if so requested in writing by the head of the State agency. The assistance may comprise allowing officers of the local agency to work temporarily with officers of the State agency (including in an undercover capacity) and lending equipment and supplies. While working with the State agency under the authority of this section, an officer shall have the same jurisdiction, powers, rights, privileges and immunities (including those relating to the defense of civil actions and the payment of judgments) as the officers of the State agency in addition to those he normally possesses. While on duty with the State agency, he shall be subject to the lawful operational commands of his superior officers in the State agency, but he shall for personnel and administrative purposes, remain under the control of the local agency, including for purposes of pay. He shall furthermore be entitled to workers' compensation and the same benefits when acting pursuant to this section to the same extent as though he were functioning within the normal scope of his duties.

(b) As used in this section:

(1) "Head" means any director or chief officer of any State or local law-enforcement agency including the chief of police of a local department, chief of police of a county police department, and the sheriff of a county, or an officer of the agency to whom the head of that agency has delegated authority to make or grant requests under this section, but only one officer in the agency shall have this delegated authority at any time.

(2) "Local law-enforcement agency" means any municipal police department, a county police department, or a sheriff's department.

(3) "State law-enforcement agency" means any State agency, force, department, or unit responsible for enforcing criminal laws.

(c) This section in no way reduces the jurisdiction or authority of State law-enforcement officers.

(d) For the purposes of this section, the following shall be considered the equivalent of a municipal police department:

(1) Campus law-enforcement agencies established pursuant to G.S. 116-40.5(a).

(2) Colleges or universities which are licensed, or exempted from licensure, by G.S. 116-15 and which employ company police officers commissioned by the Attorney General pursuant to Chapter 74E or Chapter 74G of the General Statutes.

(3) Repealed by Session Laws 2013-360, s. 16B.4(e), effective July 1, 2013. (1981, c. 878; 1989, c. 518, s. 3; 1991, c. 636, s. 3; 1991 (Reg. Sess., 1992), c. 1043, s. 7; 2005-231, s. 9; 2006-159, s. 5; 2011-260, s. 5; 2011-326, s. 10; 2013-360, s. 16B.4(e).)

§ 160A-288.3. Expired.

§ 160A-288.4. Police chief may establish volunteer school safety resource officer program.

(a) The chief of police of a local police department or of a county police department may establish a volunteer school safety resource officer program to provide nonsalaried special law enforcement officers to serve as school safety resource officers in public schools. To be a volunteer in the program, a person must have prior experience as either (i) a sworn law enforcement officer or (ii) a military police officer with a minimum of two years' service. If a person with experience as a military police officer is no longer in the armed services, the person must also have an honorable discharge. A program volunteer must receive training on research into the social and cognitive development of elementary, middle, and high school children and must also meet the selection standards and any additional criteria established by the chief of police.

(b) Each volunteer shall report to the chief of police and shall work under the direction and supervision of the chief of police or the chief's designee when carrying out the volunteer's duties as a school safety resource officer. No volunteer may be assigned to a school as a school safety resource officer until the volunteer has updated or renewed the volunteer's law enforcement training and has been certified by the North Carolina Criminal Justice Education and Training Standards Commission as meeting the educational and firearms proficiency standards required of persons serving as criminal justice officers. A volunteer is not required to meet the physical standards required by the North Carolina Criminal Justice Education and Training Standards Commission but must have a standard medical exam to ensure the volunteer is in good health. A person selected by the chief of police to serve as a volunteer under this section shall have the power of arrest while performing official duties as a volunteer school safety resource officer.

(c) The chief of police may enter into an agreement with the local board of education to provide volunteer school safety resource officers who meet both the criteria established by this section and the selection and training requirements set by the chief of police of the municipality or county in which the schools are located. The chief of police shall be responsible for the assignment of any volunteer school safety resource officer assigned to a public school and for the supervision of the officer.

(d) There shall be no liability on the part of and no cause of action shall arise against a volunteer school safety resource officer, the chief of police or employees of the local law enforcement agency supervising a volunteer school safety officer, or the public school system or its employees for any good-faith action taken by them in the performance of their duties with regard to the volunteer school safety resource officer program established pursuant to this section. (2013-360, s. 8.45(f).)

§ 160A-289. Training and development programs for law enforcement.

A city shall have authority to plan and execute training and development programs for law-enforcement agencies, and for that purpose may

(1) Contract with other cities, counties, and the State and federal governments and their agencies;

(2) Accept, receive, and disburse funds, grants and services;

(3) Create joint agencies to act for and on behalf of participating counties and cities;

(4) Make applications for, receive, administer, and expend federal grant funds; and

(5) Appropriate and expend available tax or nontax funds. (1969, c. 1145, s. 3; 1971, c. 698, s. 1; c. 896, s. 4.)

§ 160A-289.1. Resources to protect the public.

Subject to the requirements of G.S. 7A-41, 7A-44.1, 7A-64, 7A-102, 7A-133, and 7A-498.7, a city may appropriate funds under contract with the State for the provision of services for the speedy disposition of cases involving drug offenses, domestic violence, or other offenses involving threats to public safety. Nothing in this section shall be construed to obligate the General Assembly to make any appropriation to implement the provisions of this section. Further, nothing in this section shall be construed to obligate the Administrative Office of the Courts or the Office of Indigent Defense Services to maintain positions or services initially provided for under this section. (1999-237, s. 17.17(c); 2000-67, s. 15.4(f); 2001-424, s. 22.11(f).)

§ 160A-289.2. Neighborhood crime watch programs.

A city may establish neighborhood crime watch programs within the city to encourage residents and business owners to promote citizen involvement in securing homes, businesses, and personal property against criminal activity and to report suspicious activities to law enforcement officials. (2006-181, s. 2.)

§ 160A-290. Reserved for future codification purposes.

Article 14.

Fire Protection.

§ 160A-291. Firemen appointed.

A city is authorized to appoint a fire chief; to employ other firemen; to establish, organize, equip, and maintain a fire department; and to prescribe the duties of the fire department. (1917, c. 136, subch. 8, s. 1; C.S., s. 2801; 1969, c. 1065, s. 3; 1971, c. 698, s. 1.)

§ 160A-292. Duties of fire chief.

Where not otherwise prescribed, the duties of the fire chief shall be to preserve and care for fire apparatus, have charge of fighting and extinguishing fires and training the fire department, seek out and have corrected all places and conditions dangerous to the safety of the city and its citizens from fire, and make annual reports to the council concerning these duties. If these duties include State Building Code enforcement, they shall follow the provisions as defined in G.S. 143-151.13. (1969, c. 1065, s. 3; 1971, c. 698, s. 1; 1989, c. 681, s. 13.)

§ 160A-293. Fire protection outside city limits; immunity; injury to firemen.

(a)   A city may install and maintain water mains, pipes, hydrants, buildings and equipment outside its corporate limits and may send its firemen and equipment outside its corporate limits to provide fire protection to rural or unincorporated areas pursuant to agreements between the city and the county, or between the city and the owner of the property to be protected. Counties are hereby authorized to enter into these agreements and to make from tax funds any payments agreed upon for rural fire protection.

(b)   No city or any officer or employee thereof shall be held to answer in any civil action or proceeding for failure or delay in answering calls for fire protection outside the corporate limits, nor shall any city be held to answer in any civil action or proceeding for the acts or omissions of its officers or employees in rendering fire protection services outside its corporate limits.

(c)   Any employee of a city fire department, while engaged in any duty or activity outside the corporate limits of the city pursuant to orders of the fire chief or council, shall have all of the jurisdiction, authority, rights, privileges, and immunities, including coverage under the workers' compensation laws, which they have within the corporate limits of the city. (1919, c. 244; C.S., s. 2804; 1941, c. 188; 1947, c. 669; 1949, c. 89; 1971, c. 698, s. 1; 1991, c. 636, s. 3.)

§ 160A-294. Loss of rural fire employment.

(a) Whenever a city annexes any territory under Parts 2 or 3 of Article 4A of this Chapter, and because of the annexation the rural fire department must terminate the employment of any full-time employee, then the annexing city must take one of the three actions listed below with respect to any person who has been in such full-time employment for two years or more at the time of adoption of the resolution of intent:

(1) The annexing city may offer employment without loss of salary or seniority and place the person in a position as near as possible in type to the position that was held in the rural fire department; or

(2) The annexing city may offer employment in some other department of the city at a comparable salary and seniority; or

(3) The city may choose to pay to the person a sum equal to the person's salary for one year as the equivalent of severance pay. For the purpose of this subsection, the person's salary was his total salary with the rural fire department for the 12-month period ending on the last pay period before the resolution of consideration was adopted, plus any increased salary due to reasonable cost-of-living increases and bona fide promotions; provided that if no resolution of consideration was required to be adopted because of either G.S. 160A-37(j) or G.S. 160A-49(j), or because the resolution of intent was adopted prior to July 1, 1984, the person's salary was his total salary with the rural fire department for the 12-month period ending on the last pay period before the resolution of intent was adopted, plus any increased salary due to reasonable cost-of-living increases and bona fide promotions.

(b) This section is effective with respect to all annexations where an annexation ordinance is adopted on or after January 1, 1983, except that it is also effective with respect to all annexations where an annexation ordinance was adopted before January 1, 1983, but on January 1, 1983, the annexation ordinance:

(1) Was under review under G.S. 160A-38 or G.S. 160A-50, and a stay is in effect under G.S. 160A-38(e) or G.S. 160A-50(e); or

(2) Was subject to the Voting Rights Act of 1965 but had not yet been approved under that act. (1983, c. 636, s. 25.)

§ 160A-294.1. Honoring deceased or retiring firefighters.

A fire department established by a municipality pursuant to this Article may, in the discretion of the governing body of the municipality, award to a retiring firefighter or a surviving relative of a deceased firefighter, upon request, the fire helmet of the deceased or retiring firefighter, at a price determined in a manner authorized by the governing body. The price may be less than the fair market value of the helmet. (2003-145, s. 2.)

Article 14A.

Municipal Firefighters.

§ 160A-295. (Contingent effective date - see Editor's note) Definitions.

As used in this Article, the following terms mean:

(1) Compensatory time. - Time off with regular compensation in lieu of immediate overtime premium pay when a fire department, under certain conditions, compensates the firefighter for overtime hours worked.

(2) Firefighter. - A full-time, paid employee of an employer, maintaining a fire department certified by the North Carolina Department of Insurance, who is actively serving in a position with assigned primary duties and responsibilities for the prevention, detection, and suppression of fire.

(3) Supervisory personnel. - An individual employed by a public safety employer who (i) has the authority in the interest of the employer to hire, direct, assign, promote, reward, transfer, furlough, lay off, recall, suspend, discipline, or remove public safety officers, or to adjust their grievances or effectively recommend an adjustment, provided that the exercise of the authority is not merely routine or clerical in nature, but requires consistent exercise of

independent judgment; and (ii) devotes a majority of time at work exercising that authority.

(4) Trade time. - The time one individual substitutes for another during scheduled work hours in performance of work in the same capacity when two individuals are employed in any occupation by the same fire department, as agreed to solely at the individual's option and with the approval of the management of the fire department. The hours worked are excluded by the employer in the calculation of the hours for which the substituting employee would otherwise be entitled to overtime compensation under this Article. Where one employee substitutes for another, the employee being substituted for is credited as if he or she had worked his or her normal work schedule for that shift. (2008-151, s. 1.)

§ 160A-295.1. (Contingent effective date - see Editor's note) Municipal firefighters; hours of labor; overtime pay.

(a) A firefighter or a member of a fire department who provides emergency medical services, other than supervisory personnel, and who is required or permitted to work, on average, more than 53 hours in a seven-day work period or up to the number of hours that bears the same ratio to 212 hours as the number of days in the work period bears to 28 days is considered to have worked overtime. A person included under this subsection is entitled to be compensated for the overtime as provided by subsection (d) of this section.

(b) A member of a fire department, other than supervisory personnel, who does not fight fires or provide emergency medical services, including a mechanic, clerk, investigator, inspector, fire marshal, fire alarm dispatcher, or maintenance worker, and who is required or permitted to average more hours in a week than the number of hours in a normal workweek of the majority of the employees of the municipality other than firefighters, emergency medical service personnel, and police officers, is considered to have worked overtime. A person included under this subsection is entitled to be compensated for the overtime as provided by subsection (d) of this section.

(c) In computing the hours worked in a workweek or the average number of hours worked in a workweek during a work cycle of a firefighter or other member of a fire department covered by this section, all hours are counted during which the firefighter or other member of a fire department is required to remain on call on the employer's premises or so close to the employer's premises that the person cannot use those hours effectively for that person's own purposes. Hours in which the firefighter or other member of a fire department is required only to leave a telephone number at which that person may be reached or to remain accessible by radio or pager are not to be used in computing the hours worked. In computing the hours in a workweek or the average number of hours in a workweek during a work cycle of a firefighter or a member of a fire department who provides emergency medical services, vacation, sick time, holidays, time in lieu of holidays, compensatory time, or trade time may be excluded as hours worked.

(d) A firefighter or other member of a fire department may be required or permitted to work overtime. A firefighter, other than supervisory personnel, who is required or permitted to work overtime as provided by subsection (a) of this section is entitled to be paid overtime for the excess hours worked without regard to the number of hours worked in any one week of the work cycle. Overtime hours as computed under this Article are to be paid at a rate equal to one and one-half times the compensation paid to the firefighter or member of the fire department for regular hours. To the extent that the municipality complies with the requirements of section 7(o) of the Fair Labor Standards Act (29 U.S.C. § 207(o)), it may compensate firefighters for their overtime hours with compensatory time in lieu of pay. A member of a fire department included under subsection (b) of this section shall be paid overtime in the same manner as other employees of the municipality entitled to overtime pay, excluding firefighters. (2008-151, s. 1.)

§ 160A-295.2. (Contingent effective date - see Editor's note) Authority of Department of Labor.

The Department of Labor shall have the authority to enforce the provisions of this Article to the extent that these provisions are not subject to enforcement under the Fair Labor Standards Act (29 U.S.C. § 207). (2008-151, s. 1.)

§ 160A-295.3. (Contingent effective date - see Editor's note) Applicability.

This Article applies only to full-time paid firefighters and other full-time paid members of a fire department of a municipality that employs five or more employees in fire protection during the workweek. (2008-151, s. 1.)

Article 15.

Streets, Traffic and Parking.

§ 160A-296. Establishment and control of streets; center and edge lines.

(a)   A city shall have general authority and control over all public streets, sidewalks, alleys, bridges, and other ways of public passage within its corporate limits except to the extent that authority and control over certain streets and bridges is vested in the Board of Transportation. General authority and control includes but is not limited to all of the following:

(1)   The duty to keep the public streets, sidewalks, alleys, and bridges in proper repair.

(2)   The duty to keep the public streets, sidewalks, alleys, and bridges open for travel and free from unnecessary obstructions.

(3)   The power to open new streets and alleys, and to widen, extend, pave, clean, and otherwise improve existing streets, sidewalks, alleys, and bridges, and to acquire the necessary land therefor by dedication and acceptance, purchase, or eminent domain.

(4)   The power to close any street or alley either permanently or temporarily.

(5)   The power to regulate the use of the public streets, sidewalks, alleys, and bridges.

(6)   The power to regulate, license, and prohibit digging in the streets, sidewalks, or alleys, or placing therein or thereon any pipes, poles, wires, fixtures, or appliances of any kind either on, above, or below the surface. To the extent a municipality is authorized under applicable law to impose a fee or charge with respect to activities conducted in its rights-of-way, the fee or charge must apply uniformly and on a competitively neutral and nondiscriminatory basis to all comparable activities by similarly situated users of the rights-of-way.

(7)   The power to provide for lighting the streets, alleys, and bridges of the city.

(8)   The power to grant easements in street rights-of-way as permitted by G.S. 160A-273.

(a1)   A city with a population of 250,000 or over according to the most recent decennial federal census may also exercise the power granted by subdivision (a)(3) of this section within its extraterritorial planning jurisdiction. Before a city makes improvements under this subsection, it shall enter into a memorandum of understanding with the Department of Transportation to provide for maintenance.

(b)   Repealed by Session Laws 1991, c. 530, s. 6, effective January 1, 1992. (1917, c. 136, subch. 5, s. 1; subch. 10, s. 1; 1919, cc. 136, 237; C.S., ss. 2787, 2793; 1925, c. 200; 1963, c. 986; 1971, c. 698, s. 1; 1973, c. 507, s. 5; 1979, c. 598; 1991, c. 530, s. 6; 2001-261, s. 1; 2006-151, s. 14.)

§ 160A-297. Streets under authority of Board of Transportation.

(a)   A city shall not be responsible for maintaining streets or bridges under the authority and control of the Board of Transportation, and shall not be liable for injuries to persons or property resulting from any failure to do so.

(b)   Nothing in this Article shall authorize any city to interfere with the rights and privileges of the Board of Transportation with respect to streets and bridges under the authority and control of the Board of Transportation. (1925, c. 71, s. 3; 1957, c. 65, s. 11; 1971, c. 698, s. 1; 1973, c. 507, s. 5; 1987, c. 747, s. 3.1.)

§ 160A-298. Railroad crossings.

(a)   A city shall have authority to direct, control, and prohibit the laying of railroad tracks and switches in public streets and alleys and to require that all railroad tracks, crossings, and bridges be constructed so as not to interfere with drainage patterns or with the ordinary travel and use of the public streets and alleys.

(b)   The costs of constructing, reconstructing, and improving public streets and alleys, including the widening thereof, within areas covered by railroad cross ties, including cross timbers, shall be borne equally by the city and the railroad company. The costs of maintaining and repairing such areas after construction shall be borne by the railroad company.

(c)   A city shall have authority to require the installation, construction, erection, reconstruction, and improvement of warning signs, gates, lights, and other safety devices at grade crossings, and the city shall bear ninety percent (90%) of the costs thereof and the railroad company shall bear ten percent (10%) of the costs. The costs of maintaining warning signs, gates, lights, and other safety devices installed after January 1, 1972, shall be borne equally by the city and the railroad company. The maintenance shall be performed by the railroad company and the city shall pay annually to the railroad company fifty percent (50%) of these costs. In maintaining maintenance cost records and determining such costs, the city and the railroad company shall use the same methods and procedures as are now or may hereafter be used by the Board of Transportation.

(d) A city shall have authority to require that a grade crossing be eliminated and replaced by a railroad bridge or by a railroad underpass, if the council finds as a fact that the grade crossing constitutes an unreasonable hazard to vehicular or pedestrian traffic. In such event, the city shall bear ninety percent (90%) of the costs and the railroad company shall bear ten percent (10%) of the costs. If the city constructs a new street which requires a grade separation and which does not replace an existing street, the city shall bear all of the costs. If a railroad company constructs a new track across at grade, or under, or over an existing street, the railroad company shall pay the entire cost thereof. The city shall pay the costs of maintaining street bridges which cross over railroads. Railroad companies shall pay the cost of maintaining railroad bridges over streets, except that cities shall pay the costs of maintaining street pavement, sidewalks, street drainage, and street lighting where streets cross under railroads.

(e) Whenever the widening, improving, or other changes in a street require that a railroad bridge be relocated, enlarged, heightened, or otherwise reconstructed, the city shall bear ninety percent (90%) of the costs and the railroad company shall bear ten percent (10%) of the costs.

(f) It is the intent of this section to make uniform the law concerning the construction and maintenance of railroad crossings, bridges, underpasses, and warning devices within cities. To this end, all general laws and local acts in conflict with this section are repealed, and no local act taking effect on or after January 1, 1972, shall be construed to modify, amend, or repeal any portion of this section unless it specifically so provides by express reference to this section. (1917, c. 136, subch. 5, s. 1; 1919, cc. 136, 237; C.S., s. 2787; 1971, c. 698, s. 1; 1973, c. 507, s. 5.)

§ 160A-299. Procedure for permanently closing streets and alleys.

(a)   When a city proposes to permanently close any street or public alley, the council shall first adopt a resolution declaring its intent to close the street or alley and calling a public hearing on the question. The resolution shall be published once a week for four successive weeks prior to the hearing, a copy thereof shall be sent by registered or certified mail to all owners of property adjoining the street or alley as shown on the county tax records, and a notice of the closing and public hearing shall be prominently posted in at least two places along the street or alley. If the street or alley is under the authority and control of the Department of Transportation, a copy of the resolution shall be mailed to the Department of Transportation. At the hearing, any person may be heard on the question of whether or not the closing would be detrimental to the public interest, or the property rights of any individual. If it appears to the satisfaction of the council after the hearing that closing the street or alley is not contrary to the public interest, and that no individual owning property in the vicinity of the street or alley or in the subdivision in which it is located would thereby be deprived of reasonable means of ingress and egress to his property, the council may adopt an order closing the street or alley. A certified copy of the order (or judgment of the court) shall be filed in the office of the register of deeds of the county in which the street, or any portion thereof, is located.

(b)   Any person aggrieved by the closing of any street or alley including the Department of Transportation if the street or alley is under its authority and control, may appeal the council's order to the General Court of Justice within 30 days after its adoption. In appeals of streets closed under this section, all facts and issues shall be heard and decided by a judge sitting without a jury. In addition to determining whether procedural requirements were complied with, the court shall determine whether, on the record as presented to the city council, the council's decision to close the street was in accordance with the statutory standards of subsection (a) of this section and any other applicable requirements of local law or ordinance.

No cause of action or defense founded upon the invalidity of any proceedings taken in closing any street or alley may be asserted, nor shall the validity of the order be open to question in any court upon any ground whatever, except in an action or proceeding begun within 30 days after the order is adopted. The failure to send notice by registered or certified mail shall not invalidate any ordinance adopted prior to January 1, 1989.

(c) Upon the closing of a street or alley in accordance with this section, subject to the provisions of subsection (f) of this section, all right, title, and interest in the right-of-way shall be conclusively presumed to be vested in those persons owning lots or parcels of land adjacent to the street or alley, and the title of such adjoining landowners, for the width of the abutting land owned by them, shall extend to the centerline of the street or alley.

The provisions of this subsection regarding division of right-of-way in street or alley closings may be altered as to a particular street or alley closing by the assent of all property owners taking title to a closed street or alley by the filing of a plat which shows the street or alley closing and the portion of the closed street or alley to be taken by each such owner. The plat shall be signed by each property owner who, under this section, has an ownership right in the closed street or alley.

(d) This section shall apply to any street or public alley within a city or its extraterritorial jurisdiction that has been irrevocably dedicated to the public, without regard to whether it has actually been opened. This section also applies to unopened streets or public alleys that are shown on plats but that have not been accepted or maintained by the city, provided that this section shall not abrogate the rights of a dedicator, or those claiming under a dedicator, pursuant to G.S. 136-96.

(e) No street or alley under the control of the Department of Transportation may be closed unless the Department of Transportation consents thereto.

(f) A city may reserve its right, title, and interest in any utility improvement or easement within a street closed pursuant to this section. Such reservation shall be stated in the order of closing. Such reservation also extends to utility improvements or easements owned by private utilities which at the time of the street closing have a utility agreement or franchise with the city.

(g) The city may retain utility easements, both public and private, in cases of streets withdrawn under G.S. 136-96. To retain such easements, the city council shall, after public hearing, approve a "declaration of retention of utility easements" specifically describing such easements. Notice by certified or registered mail shall be provided to the party withdrawing the street from dedication under G.S. 136-96 at least five days prior to the hearing. The declaration must be passed prior to filing of any plat or map or declaration of withdrawal with the register of deeds. Any property owner filing such plats, maps, or declarations shall include the city declaration with the declaration of withdrawal and shall show the utilities retained on any map or plat showing the withdrawal. (1971, c. 698, s. 1; 1973, c. 426, s. 47; c. 507, s. 5; 1977, c. 464, s. 34; 1981, c. 401; c. 402, ss. 1, 2; 1989, c. 254; 1993, c. 149, s. 1.)

§ 160A-299.1. Applications for intermittent closing of roads within watershed improvement project by municipality; notice; costs; markers.

(a) Upon proper application by the board of commissioners of a drainage district established under the provisions of Chapter 156 of the General Statutes by the board of trustees of a watershed improvement district established under the provisions of Article 2 of Chapter 139 of the General Statutes, by the board of county commissioners of any county operating a county watershed improvement program under the provisions of Article 3 of Chapter 139 of the General Statutes, by the board of commissioners of any watershed improvement commission appointed by a board of county commissioners, or by the board of supervisors of any soil and water conservation district designated by a board of county commissioners to exercise authority in carrying out a county watershed improvement program, any municipality for roads or streets coming under its jurisdictional control is hereby authorized to permit the intermittent closing of any highway or public road within the boundaries of any watershed improvement project operated by the applicants, whenever in the judgment of the municipality it is necessary to do so, and when the highway or public road will be intermittently subject to inundation by floodwaters retained by an approved watershed improvement project.

(b) Before any permit may be issued for the temporary inundation and closing of such a road, an application for such permit shall be made to the appropriate municipality by the public body having jurisdiction over the watershed improvement project. The application shall specify the highway, road, or street involved, and shall request that a permit be granted to the applicant public body to allow the intermittent closing of the road.

(c) Upon receipt of such an application the municipality shall give public notice of the proposed action by publication in a newspaper of general circulation in the county or counties, within which the proposed intermittent closing of road or roads would occur; and such notices shall contain a description of the places of beginning and the places of ending of such intermittent closing. In addition, the municipality shall give notice to all public utilities or common carriers having facilities located within the rights-of-way of any roads being closed by mailing copies of such notices to the appropriate offices of the public utility or common carrier having jurisdiction over the affected facilities of the public utility or common carrier. Not sooner than 14 days after publication and mailing of notices, the municipality may issue its permit with respect to such road.

(d)   All cost in connection with the publication and mailing of notices shall be paid by the applicant. In the event any municipality issues a permit allowing the intermittent closing of a road, the permit shall contain a provision that the applicant public body having jurisdiction over the watershed improvement project causing the potential flooding shall cause suitable markers to be installed on the road to advise the general public of the intermittent closing of the road. (1975, c. 639, s. 2.)

§ 160A-300. Traffic control.

A city may by ordinance prohibit, regulate, divert, control, and limit pedestrian or vehicular traffic upon the public streets, sidewalks, alleys, and bridges of the city. (1917, c. 136, subch. 5, s. 1; 1919, cc. 136, 237; C.S., s. 2787; 1941, c. 153, ss. 1, 2; c. 272; 1947, c. 7; 1953, c. 171; 1965, c. 945; 1971, c. 698, s. 1.)

§ 160A-300.1. Use of traffic control photographic systems.

(a)   A traffic control photographic system is an electronic system consisting of a photographic, video, or electronic camera and a vehicle sensor installed to work in conjunction with an official traffic control device to automatically produce photographs, video, or digital images of each vehicle violating a standard traffic control statute or ordinance.

(b)   Any traffic control photographic system or any device which is a part of that system, as described in subdivision (a) of this section, installed on a street or highway which is a part of the State highway system shall meet requirements established by the North Carolina Department of Transportation. Any traffic control system installed on a municipal street shall meet standards established by the municipality and shall be consistent with any standards set by the Department of Transportation.

(b1)   Any traffic control photographic system installed on a street or highway must be identified by appropriate advance warning signs conspicuously posted not more than 300 feet from the location of the traffic control photographic system. All advance warning signs shall be consistent with a statewide standard adopted by the Department of Transportation in conjunction with local governments authorized to install traffic control photographic systems.

(c) Municipalities may adopt ordinances for the civil enforcement of G.S. 20-158 by means of a traffic control photographic system, as described in subsection (a) of this section. Notwithstanding the provisions of G.S. 20-176, in the event that a municipality adopts an ordinance pursuant to this section, a violation of G.S. 20-158 at a location at which a traffic control photographic system is in operation shall not be an infraction. An ordinance authorized by this subsection shall provide that:

(1) The owner of a vehicle shall be responsible for a violation unless the owner can furnish evidence that the vehicle was, at the time of the violation, in the care, custody, or control of another person. The owner of the vehicle shall not be responsible for the violation if the owner of the vehicle, within 30 days after notification of the violation, furnishes the officials or agents of the municipality which issued the citation either of the following:

a. An affidavit stating the name and address of the person or company who had the care, custody, and control of the vehicle.

b. An affidavit stating that the vehicle involved was, at the time, stolen. The affidavit must be supported with evidence that supports the affidavit, including insurance or police report information.

(1a) Subdivision (1) of this subsection shall not apply, and the registered owner of the vehicle shall not be responsible for the violation, if notice of the violation is given to the registered owner of the vehicle more than 90 days after the date of the violation.

(2) A violation detected by a traffic control photographic system shall be deemed a noncriminal violation for which a civil penalty of fifty dollars ($50.00) shall be assessed, and for which no points authorized by G.S. 20-16(c) shall be assigned to the owner or driver of the vehicle nor insurance points as authorized by G.S. 58-36-65.

(3) The owner of the vehicle shall be issued a citation which shall clearly state the manner in which the violation may be challenged, and the owner shall comply with the directions on the citation. The citation shall be processed by officials or agents of the municipality and shall be forwarded by personal service

or first-class mail to the address given on the motor vehicle registration. If the owner fails to pay the civil penalty or to respond to the citation within the time period specified on the citation, the owner shall have waived the right to contest responsibility for the violation, and shall be subject to a civil penalty not to exceed one hundred dollars ($100.00). The municipality may establish procedures for the collection of these penalties and may enforce the penalties by civil action in the nature of debt.

(4)   The municipality shall institute a nonjudicial administrative hearing to review objections to citations or penalties issued or assessed under this section.

(c1)   The duration of the yellow light change interval at intersections where traffic control photographic systems are in use shall be no less than the yellow light change interval duration specified on the traffic signal plan of record signed and sealed by a professional engineer, licensed in accordance with the provisions of Chapter 89C of the General Statutes, and shall comply with the provisions of the Manual on Uniform Traffic Control Devices.

(d)   This section applies only to the Cities of Albemarle, Charlotte, Durham, Fayetteville, Greensboro, Greenville, High Point, Locust, Lumberton, Newton, Rocky Mount, and Wilmington, to the Towns of Chapel Hill, Cornelius, Huntersville, Matthews, Nags Head, Pineville, and Spring Lake, and to the municipalities in Union County. (1997-216, ss. 1, 2; 1999-17, s. 1; 1999-181, ss. 1, 2; 1999-182, s. 2; 1999-456, s. 48(c); 2000-37, s. 1; 2000-97, s. 2; 2001-286, ss. 1, 2; 2001-487, s. 37; 2003-86, s. 1; 2003-380, s. 2; 2007-341, s. 2; 2010-132, s. 17.)

§ 160A-300.5: Repealed by Session Laws 2009-459, s. 2, effective October 1, 2009.

§ 160A-300.6. Regulation of golf carts on streets, roads, and highways.

(a)   Notwithstanding the provisions of G.S. 20-50 and G.S. 20-54, a city may, by ordinance, regulate the operation of golf carts, as defined in G.S. 20-4.01(12a), on any public street, road, or highway where the speed limit is 35 miles per hour or less within its municipal limits or on any property owned or leased by the city.

(b) By ordinance, a city may require the registration of golf carts, charge a fee for the registration, specify who is authorized to operate golf carts, and specify the required equipment, load limits, and the hours and methods of operation of golf carts. No person less than 16 years of age may operate a golf cart on a public street, road, or highway. (2009-459, s. 3.)

§ 160A-301. Parking.

(a) On-Street Parking. - A city may by ordinance regulate, restrict, and prohibit the parking of vehicles on the public streets, alleys, and bridges within the city. When parking is permitted for a specified period of time at a particular location, a city may install a parking meter at that location and require any person parking a vehicle therein to place the meter in operation for the entire time that the vehicle remains in that location, up to the maximum time allowed for parking there. Parking meters may be activated by coins or tokens. Proceeds from the use of parking meters on public streets must be used to defray the cost of enforcing and administering traffic and parking ordinances and regulations.

(b) Off-Street Parking. - A city may by ordinance regulate the use of lots, garages, or other facilities owned or leased by the city and designated for use by the public as parking facilities. The city may impose fees and charges for the use of these facilities, and may provide for the collection of these fees and charges through parking meters, attendants, automatic gates, or any other feasible means. The city may make it unlawful to park any vehicle in an off-street parking facility without paying the established fee or charge and may ordain other regulations pertaining to the use of such facilities.

Revenues realized from off-street parking facilities may be pledged to amortize bonds issued to finance such facilities, or used for any other public purpose.

(c) Nothing contained in Public Laws 1921, Chapter 2, Section 29, or Public Laws 1937, Chapter 407, Section 61, shall be construed to affect the validity of a parking meter ordinance or the revenues realized therefrom.

(d) The governing body of any city may, by ordinance, regulate the stopping, standing, or parking of vehicles in specified areas of any parking areas or driveways of a hospital, shopping center, apartment house, condominium complex, or commercial office complex, or any other privately owned public vehicular area, or prohibit such stopping, standing, or parking during any specified hours, provided the owner or person in general charge of the operation and control of that area requests in writing that such an ordinance be adopted. The owner of a vehicle parked in violation of an ordinance adopted pursuant to this subsection shall be deemed to have appointed any appropriate law-enforcement officer as his agent for the purpose of arranging for the transportation and safe storage of such vehicle.

(e) The registered owner of a vehicle that has been leased or rented to another person or company shall not be liable for a violation of an ordinance adopted pursuant to this section if, after receiving notification of the civil violation within 90 days of the date of occurrence, the owner, within 30 days thereafter, files with the officials or agents of the municipality an affidavit including the name and address of the person or company that leased or rented the vehicle. If notification is given to the owner of the vehicle after 90 days have elapsed from the date of the violation, the owner is not required to provide the name and address of the lessee or renter, and the owner shall not be held responsible for the violation. (1917, c. 136, subch. 5, s. 1; 1919, cc. 136, 237; C.S., s. 2787; 1941, c. 153, ss. 1, 2; c. 272; 1947, c. 7; 1953, c. 171; 1965, c. 945; 1971, c. 698, s. 1; 1973, c. 426, s. 48; 1979, c. 745, s. 2; 2003-380, s. 1.)

§ 160A-302. Off-street parking facilities.

A city shall have authority to own, acquire, establish, regulate, operate, and control off-street parking lots, parking garages, and other facilities for parking motor vehicles, and to make a charge for the use of such facilities. (1917, c. 136, subch. 5, s. 1; 1919, cc. 136, 237; C.S., s. 2787; 1941, c. 153, ss. 1, 2; c. 272; 1947, c. 7; 1953, c. 171; 1965, c. 945; 1971, c. 698, s. 1.)

§ 160A-302.1. Fishing from bridges regulated.

The governing body of any city is hereby authorized to enact an ordinance prohibiting or regulating fishing from any bridge for the purpose of protecting persons fishing on the bridge from passing vehicular or rail traffic. Such ordinance may also prohibit or regulate fishing from any bridge one mile beyond the corporate limits of the city where the board or boards of county commissioners by resolution agree to such prohibition or regulation; provided, however, that the board or boards of county commissioners may upon 30 days' written notice withdraw their respective approval of the municipal ordinance, and that ordinance shall have no further effect within that county's jurisdiction. The ordinance shall provide that signs shall be posted on any bridge where fishing is prohibited or regulated reflecting such prohibition or regulation. In any event, no one may fish from the drawspan of any regularly attended drawbridge.

The police department of the city is hereby vested with the jurisdiction and authority to enforce any ordinance passed pursuant to this section.

The authority granted under the provisions of this section shall be subject to the authority of the Board of Transportation to prohibit fishing on any bridge on the State highway system. (1971, c. 690, ss. 2, 3, 6; c. 896, s. 15; 1973, c. 426, s. 49; c. 507, s. 5.)

§ 160A-303. Removal and disposal of junked and abandoned motor vehicles.

(a)   A city may by ordinance prohibit the abandonment of motor vehicles on the public streets or on public or private property within the city, and may enforce any such ordinance by removing and disposing of junked or abandoned motor vehicles according to the procedures prescribed in this section.

(b)   A motor vehicle is defined to include all machines designed or intended to travel over land or water by self-propulsion or while attached to any self-propelled vehicle.

(b1)   An abandoned motor vehicle is one that:

(1)   Has been left upon a street or highway in violation of a law or ordinance prohibiting parking; or

(2)   Is left on property owned or operated by the city for longer than 24 hours; or

(3)   Is left on private property without the consent of the owner, occupant, or lessee thereof for longer than two hours; or

(4)   Is left on any public street or highway for longer than seven days or is determined by law enforcement to be a hazard to the motoring public.

(b2)   A junked motor vehicle is an abandoned motor vehicle that also:

(1)   Is partially dismantled or wrecked; or

(2)   Cannot be self-propelled or moved in the manner in which it was originally intended to move; or

(3)   Is more than five years old and worth less than one hundred dollars ($100.00) or is more than five years old and worth less than five hundred dollars ($500.00) as provided by the municipality in an ordinance adopted under this section; or

(3a)   Repealed by Session Laws 2009-97, s. 1, effective October 1, 2009.

(4)   Does not display a current license plate.

(c)   Any junked or abandoned motor vehicle found to be in violation of an ordinance adopted under this section may be removed to a storage garage or area, but no such vehicle shall be removed from private property without the written request of the owner, lessee, or occupant of the premises unless the council or a duly authorized city official or employee has declared it to be a health or safety hazard. The city may require any person requesting the removal of a junked or abandoned motor vehicle from private property to indemnify the city against any loss, expense, or liability incurred because of the removal, storage, or sale thereof. When an abandoned or junked motor vehicle is removed, the city shall give notice to the owner as required by G.S. 20-219.11(a) and (b).

(d)   Hearing Procedure. - Regardless of whether a city does its own removal and disposal of motor vehicles or contracts with another person to do so, the city, shall provide a hearing procedure for the owner. For purposes of this subsection, the definitions in G.S. 20-219.9 apply.

(1)   If the city operates in such a way that the person who tows the vehicle is responsible for collecting towing fees, all provisions of Article 7A, Chapter 20, apply.

(2)   If the city operates in such a way that it is responsible for collecting towing fees, it shall:

a.   Provide by contract or ordinance for a schedule of reasonable towing fees,

b.   Provide a procedure for a prompt fair hearing to contest the towing,

c. Provide for an appeal to district court from that hearing,

d. Authorize release of the vehicle at any time after towing by the posting of a bond or paying of the fees due, and

e. Provide a sale procedure similar to that provided in G.S. 44A-4, 44A-5, and 44A-6, except that no hearing in addition to the probable cause hearing is required. If no one purchases the vehicle at the sale and if the value of the vehicle is less than the amount of the lien, the city may destroy it.

(e) Repealed by Session Laws 1983, c. 420, s. 13.

(f) No person shall be held to answer in any civil or criminal action to any owner or other person legally entitled to the possession of any abandoned, lost, or stolen motor vehicle for disposing of the vehicle as provided in this section.

(g) Nothing in this section shall apply to any vehicle in an enclosed building or any vehicle on the premises of a business enterprise being operated in a lawful place and manner if the vehicle is necessary to the operation of the enterprise, or to any vehicle in an appropriate storage place or depository maintained in a lawful place and manner by the city.

(h) Repealed by Session Laws 1983, c. 420, s. 13, effective July 1, 1983. (1965, c. 1156; 1967, cc. 1215, 1250; 1971, c. 698, s. 1; 1973, c. 426, s. 50; 1975, c. 716, s. 5; 1983, c. 420, ss. 11-13; 1997-456. s. 27; 2005-10, ss. 1, 3; 2006-15, s. 1; 2006-166, s. 2; 2006-171, s. 1; 2007-208, s. 1; 2009-97, s. 1; 2010-132, s. 20.)

§ 160A-303.1. Regulation of the placing of trash, refuse and garbage within municipal limits.

The governing body of any municipality is hereby authorized to enact an ordinance prohibiting the placing, discarding, disposing or leaving of any trash, refuse or garbage upon a street or highway located within that municipality or upon property owned or operated by the municipality unless such garbage, refuse or trash is placed in a designated location or container for removal by a specific garbage or trash service collector. Any ordinance adopted pursuant hereto may prohibit the placing, discarding, disposing or leaving of any trash, refuse or garbage upon private property located within the municipality without the consent of the owner, occupant, or lessee thereof and may provide that the placing, discarding, disposing or leaving of the articles forbidden by this section shall, for each day or portion thereof the articles or matter are left, constitute a separate offense.

The governing body of a municipality, in any ordinance adopted pursuant hereto, may provide that a person who violates the ordinance may be punished by a fine not exceeding fifty dollars ($50.00) or imprisoned not exceeding 30 days, or both, for each offense. (1973, c. 953.)

§ 160A-303.2. Regulation of abandonment of junked motor vehicles.

(a)   A municipality may by ordinance regulate, restrain or prohibit the abandonment of junked motor vehicles on public grounds and on private property within the municipality's ordinance-making jurisdiction upon a finding that such regulation, restraint or prohibition is necessary and desirable to promote or enhance community, neighborhood or area appearance, and may enforce any such ordinance by removing or disposing of junked motor vehicles subject to the ordinance according to the procedures prescribed in this section. The authority granted by this section shall be supplemental to any other authority conferred upon municipalities. Nothing in this section shall be construed to authorize a municipality to require the removal or disposal of a motor vehicle kept or stored at a bona fide "automobile graveyard" or "junkyard" as defined in G.S. 136-143.

For purposes of this section, the term "junked motor vehicle" means a vehicle that does not display a current license plate and that:

(1)   Is partially dismantled or wrecked; or

(2)   Cannot be self-propelled or moved in the manner in which it originally was intended to move; or

(3)   Is more than five years old and appears to be worth less than one hundred dollars ($100.00) or is more than five years old and appears to be worth less than five hundred dollars ($500.00) as provided by the municipality in an ordinance adopted under this section.

(4)   Repealed by Session Laws 2009-97, s. 2, effective October 1, 2009.

(a1) Any junked motor vehicle found to be in violation of an ordinance adopted pursuant to this section may be removed to a storage garage or area, but no such vehicle shall be removed from private property without the written request of the owner, lessee, or occupant of the premises unless the council or a duly authorized city official or employee finds in writing that the aesthetic benefits of removing the vehicle outweigh the burdens imposed on the private property owner. Such finding shall be based on a balancing of the monetary loss of the apparent owner against the corresponding gain to the public by promoting or enhancing community, neighborhood or area appearance. The following, among other relevant factors, may be considered:

(1) Protection of property values;

(2) Promotion of tourism and other economic development opportunities;

(3) Indirect protection of public health and safety;

(4) Preservation of the character and integrity of the community; and

(5) Promotion of the comfort, happiness, and emotional stability of area residents.

(a2) The city may require any person requesting the removal of a junked or abandoned motor vehicle from private property to indemnify the city against any loss, expense, or liability incurred because of the removal, storage, or sale thereof. When an abandoned or junked motor vehicle is removed, the city shall give notice to the owner as required by G.S. 20-219.11(a) and (b).

(a3) Hearing Procedure. - Regardless of whether a city does its own removal and disposal of motor vehicles or contracts with another person to do so, the city shall provide a prior hearing procedure for the owner. For purposes of this subsection, the definitions in G.S. 20-219.9 apply.

(1) If the city operates in such a way that the person who tows the vehicle is responsible for collecting towing fees, all provisions of Article 7A, Chapter 20, apply.

(2) If the city operates in such a way that it is responsible for collecting towing fees, it shall:

a. Provide by contract or ordinance for a schedule of reasonable towing fees,

b. Provide a procedure for a prompt fair hearing to contest the towing,

c. Provide for an appeal to district court from that hearing,

d. Authorize release of the vehicle at any time after towing by the posting of a bond or paying of the fees due, and

e. Provide a sale procedure similar to that provided in G.S. 44A-4, 44A-5, and 44A-6, except that no hearing in addition to the probable cause hearing is required. If no one purchases the vehicle at the sale and if the value of the vehicle is less than the amount of the lien, the city may destroy it.

(a4) Any person who removes a vehicle pursuant to this section shall not be held liable for damages for the removal of the vehicle to the owner, lienholder or other person legally entitled to the possession of the vehicle removed; however, any person who intentionally or negligently damages a vehicle in the removal of such vehicle, or intentionally or negligently inflicts injury upon any person in the removal of such vehicle, may be held liable for damages.

(b) Any ordinance adopted pursuant to this section shall include a prohibition against removing or disposing of any motor vehicle that is used on a regular basis for business or personal use. (1983, c. 841, s. 2; 1985, c. 737, s. 2; 1987, c. 42, s. 2; c. 451, s. 2; 1989, c. 3; c. 743, s. 2; 2005-10, ss. 2, 3; 2006-15, s. 3; 2006-166, s. 2; 2006-171, s. 1; 2007-208, s. 2; 2007-505, s. 3; 2009-97, s. 2.)

§ 160A-304. Regulation of taxis.

(a) A city may by ordinance license and regulate all vehicles operated for hire in the city. The ordinance may require that the drivers and operators of taxicabs engaged in the business of transporting passengers for hire over the public streets shall obtain a license or permit from the city; provided, however, that the license or permit fee for taxicab drivers shall not exceed fifteen dollars ($15.00). As a condition of licensure, the city may require an applicant for licensure to pass a controlled substance examination. The ordinances may also specify the types of taxicab services that are legal in the municipality; provided, that in all cases shared-ride services as well as exclusive-ride services shall be legal. Shared-ride service is defined as a taxi service in which two or more persons with either different origins or with different destinations, or both, occupy a taxicab at one time. Exclusive-ride service is defined as a taxi service in which the first passenger or party requests exclusive use of the taxicab. In the event the applicant is to be subjected to a national criminal history background check, the ordinance shall specifically authorize the use of FBI records. The ordinance shall require any applicant who is subjected to a national criminal history background check to be fingerprinted.

The Department of Justice may provide a criminal record check to the city for a person who has applied for a license or permit through the city. The city shall provide to the Department of Justice, along with the request, the fingerprints of the applicant, any additional information required by the Department of Justice, and a form signed by the applicant consenting to the check of the criminal record and to the use of the fingerprints and other identifying information required by the State or national repositories. The applicant's fingerprints shall be forwarded to the State Bureau of Investigation for a search of the State's criminal history record file, and the State Bureau of Investigation shall forward a set of the fingerprints to the Federal Bureau of Investigation for a national criminal history check. The city shall keep all information pursuant to this subsection privileged, in accordance with applicable State law and federal guidelines, and the information shall be confidential and shall not be a public record under Chapter 132 of the General Statutes.

The Department of Justice may charge each applicant a fee for conducting the checks of criminal history records authorized by this subsection.

The following factors shall be deemed sufficient grounds for refusing to issue a permit or for revoking a permit already issued:

(1) Conviction of a felony against this State, or conviction of any offense against another state which would have been a felony if committed in this State;

(2) Violation of any federal or State law relating to the use, possession, or sale of alcoholic beverages or narcotic or barbiturate drugs;

(3) Addiction to or habitual use of alcoholic beverages or narcotic or barbiturate drugs;

(4) Violation of any federal or State law relating to prostitution;

(5) Noncitizenship in the United States;

(6) Habitual violation of traffic laws or ordinances.

The ordinance may also require operators and drivers of taxicabs to display prominently in each taxicab, so as to be visible to the passengers, the city taxi permit, the schedule of fares, a photograph of the driver, and any other identifying matter that the council may deem proper and advisable. The ordinance may also establish rates that may be charged by taxicab operators, may limit the number of taxis that may operate in the city, and may grant franchises to taxicab operators on any terms that the council may deem advisable.

(b) When a city ordinance grants a taxi franchise for operation of a stated number of taxis within the city, the holder of the franchise shall report at least quarterly to the council the average number of taxis actually in operation during the preceding quarter. The council may amend a taxi franchise to reduce the number of authorized vehicles by the average number not in actual operation during the preceding quarter, and may transfer the unused allotment to another franchised operator. Such amendments of taxi franchises shall not be subject to G.S. 160A-76. Allotments of taxis among franchised operators may be transferred only by the city council, and it shall be unlawful for any franchised operator to sell, assign, or otherwise transfer allotments under a taxi franchise.

(c) Nothing in this Chapter authorizes a city to adopt an ordinance doing any of the following:

(1) Requiring licensing or regulation of digital dispatching services for prearranged transportation services for hire connected with vehicles operated for hire in the city if the business providing the digital dispatching services does not own or operate the vehicles for hire in the city.

(2) Setting a minimum rate or minimum increment of time used to calculate a rate for prearranged transportation services for hire.

(3) Requiring an operator to use a particular formula or method to calculate rates charged.

(4) Setting a minimum waiting period between requesting prearranged transportation services and the provision of those transportation services when the prearranged transportation services are digitally dispatched.

(5) Requiring a final destination to be set at the time of requesting prearranged transportation services through digital dispatching services.

(6) Requiring or prohibiting taxi franchises or taxi operators from contracting with a person in the business of digital dispatching services for prearranged transportation services for hire. (1943, c. 639, s. 1; 1945, c. 564, s. 2; 1971, c. 698, s. 1; 1981, c. 412, s. 4; c. 606, s. 5; c. 747, s. 66; 1987, c. 777, s. 7; 2002-147, s. 14; 2003-65, s. 1; 2013-413, s. 12.1(b).)

§ 160A-305. Agreements under National Highway Safety Act.

Any city is hereby authorized to enter into agreements with the State of North Carolina and its agencies, and with the federal government and its agencies, to secure the full benefits available to the city under the National Highway Safety Act of 1966, and to cooperate with State and federal agencies, other public and private agencies, interested organizations, and individuals, to effectuate the purposes of the act and subsequent amendments thereof. (1967, c. 1255; 1971, c. 698, s. 1.)

§ 160A-306. Building setback lines.

(a) A city shall have authority to (i) classify all or a portion of the streets in the city according to their size, present and anticipated traffic loads, and other characteristics relevant to the achievement of the purposes of this section, and (ii) establish by ordinance minimum distances that buildings and other permanent structures or improvements constructed along each class or type of street shall be set back from the right-of-way line or the center line of an existing or proposed street. Portions of any street may be classified in a manner different from other portions of the same street where the characteristics of the portions differ.

(b) Any setback line shall be designed

(1) To promote the public safety by providing adequate sight distances for persons using the street and its sidewalks, lessening congestion in the street and sidewalks, facilitating the safe movement of vehicular and pedestrian traffic on the street and sidewalks and providing adequate fire lanes between buildings, and

(2) To protect the public health by keeping dwellings and other structures an adequate distance from the dust, noise, and fumes created by traffic on the street and by insuring an adequate supply of light and air.

(c) A setback-line ordinance shall permit affected property owners to appeal to the council for variance or modification of setback requirements as they apply to a particular piece of property. The council may vary or modify the requirements upon a showing that

(1) The peculiar nature of the property results in practical difficulties or unnecessary hardships that impede carrying out the strict letter of the requirement,

(2) The property will not yield a reasonable return or cannot be put to reasonable use unless relief is granted, and

(3) Balancing the public interest in enforcing the setback requirements and the interest of the owner, the grant of relief is required by considerations of justice and equity.

In granting relief, the council may impose reasonable and appropriate conditions and safeguards to protect the interest of neighboring properties. The council may delegate authority to hear appeals under setback-line ordinances to any authorized body to hear appeals under zoning ordinances. If this is done, appeal to the council from the board shall be governed by the same laws and rules as appeals from decisions granting or denying variances or modifications under the zoning ordinance. (1971, c. 698, s. 1; 1987, c. 747. ss. 13, 14.)

§ 160A-307. Curb cut regulations.

A city may by ordinance regulate the size, location, direction of traffic flow, and manner of construction of driveway connections into any street or alley. The ordinance may require the construction or reimbursement of the cost of construction and public dedication of medians, acceleration and deceleration lanes, and traffic storage lanes for driveway connections into any street or alley if:

(1) The need for such improvements is reasonably attributable to the traffic using the driveway; and

(2) The improvements serve the traffic of the driveway.

No street or alley under the control of the Department of Transportation may be improved without the consent of the Department of Transportation. However, if there is a conflict between the written driveway regulations of the Department of Transportation and the related driveway improvements required by the city, the more stringent requirement shall apply. (1971, c. 698, s. 1; 1987, c. 747, s. 16.)

§ 160A-308. Regulation of dune buggies.

A municipality may by ordinance regulate, restrict and prohibit the use of dune or beach buggies, jeeps, motorcycles, cars, trucks, or any other form of power-driven vehicle specified by the governing body of the municipality on the foreshore, beach strand and the barrier dune system. Violation of any ordinance adopted by the governing body of a municipality pursuant to this section is a Class 3 misdemeanor.

Provided, a municipality shall not prohibit the use of such specified vehicles from the foreshore, beach strand and barrier dune system by commercial fishermen for commercial activities. Commercial fishermen, however, shall abide by all other regulations or restrictions duly enacted by municipalities under this section. (1973, cc. 856, 1401; 1993, c. 539, s. 1086; 1994, Ex. Sess., c. 14, s. 68, c. 24, s. 14(c).)

§ 160A-309. Intersection and roadway improvements.

A city may contract with a developer or property owner, or with a private party who is under contract with the developer or property owner, for public intersection or roadway improvements that are adjacent or ancillary to a private land development project. Such a contract is not subject to Article 8 of Chapter 143 of the General Statutes if the public cost will not exceed two hundred fifty thousand dollars ($250,000) and the city or its designated agency determines that: (i) the public cost will not exceed the estimated cost of providing for those public intersection or roadway improvements through either eligible force account qualified labor or through a public contract let pursuant to Article 8 of Chapter 143 of the General Statutes; or (ii) the coordination of separately constructed public intersection or roadway improvements, and the adjacent or ancillary private land development improvements would be impracticable. A city may enact ordinances and policies setting forth the procedures, requirements, and terms for agreements authorized by this section. (2005-426, s. 8(c).)

§ 160A-310. Reserved for future codification purposes.

Article 16.

Public Enterprise.

Part 1. General Provisions.

§ 160A-311. Public enterprise defined.

As used in this Article, the term "public enterprise" includes:

(1)   Electric power generation, transmission, and distribution systems.

(2)   Water supply and distribution systems.

(3)   Wastewater collection, treatment, and disposal systems of all types, including septic tank systems or other on-site collection or disposal facilities or systems.

(4)   Gas production, storage, transmission, and distribution systems, where systems shall also include the purchase or lease of natural gas fields and natural gas reserves, the purchase of natural gas supplies, and the surveying, drilling and any other activities related to the exploration for natural gas, whether within the State or without.

(5)   Public transportation systems.

(6)   Solid waste collection and disposal systems and facilities.

(7)   Cable television systems.

(8)   Off-street parking facilities and systems.

(9)   Airports.

(10)   Stormwater management programs designed to protect water quality by controlling the level of pollutants in, and the quantity and flow of, stormwater and structural and natural stormwater and drainage systems of all types. (1971, c.

698, s. 1; 1975, c. 549, s. 2; c. 821, s. 3; 1977, c. 514, s. 2; 1979, c. 619, s. 2; 1989, c. 643, s. 5; 1991 (Reg. Sess., 1992), c. 944, s. 14; 2000-70, s. 3.)

§ 160A-312. Authority to operate public enterprises.

(a) A city shall have authority to acquire, construct, establish, enlarge, improve, maintain, own, operate, and contract for the operation of any or all of the public enterprises as defined in this Article to furnish services to the city and its citizens. Subject to Part 2 of this Article, a city may acquire, construct, establish, enlarge, improve, maintain, own, and operate any public enterprise outside its corporate limits, within reasonable limitations, but in no case shall a city be held liable for damages to those outside the corporate limits for failure to furnish any public enterprise service.

(b) A city shall have full authority to protect and regulate any public enterprise system belonging to or operated by it by adequate and reasonable rules. The rules shall be adopted by ordinance, shall apply to the public enterprise system both within and outside the corporate limits of the city, and may be enforced with the remedies available under any provision of law.

(c) A city may operate that part of a gas system involving the purchase and/or lease of natural gas fields, natural gas reserves and natural gas supplies and the surveying, drilling or any other activities related to the exploration for natural gas, in a partnership or joint venture arrangement with natural gas utilities and private enterprise. (1971, c. 698, s. 1; 1973, c. 426, s. 51; 1975, c. 821, s. 5; 1979, 2nd Sess., c. 1247, s. 29; 1991 (Reg. Sess., 1992), c. 836, s. 1.)

§ 160A-313. Financing public enterprise.

Subject to the restrictions, limitations, procedures, and regulations otherwise provided by law, a city shall have full authority to finance the cost of any public enterprise by levying taxes, borrowing money, and appropriating any other revenues therefor, and by accepting and administering gifts and grants from any source on behalf thereof. (1971, c. 698, s. 1.)

§ 160A-314. Authority to fix and enforce rates.

(a) A city may establish and revise from time to time schedules of rents, rates, fees, charges, and penalties for the use of or the services furnished by any public enterprise. Schedules of rents, rates, fees, charges, and penalties may vary according to classes of service, and different schedules may be adopted for services provided outside the corporate limits of the city.

(a1) (1) Before it establishes or revises a schedule of rates, fees, charges, or penalties for stormwater management programs and structural and natural stormwater and drainage systems under this section, the city council shall hold a public hearing on the matter. A notice of the hearing shall be given at least once in a newspaper having general circulation in the area, not less than seven days before the public hearing. The hearing may be held concurrently with the public hearing on the proposed budget ordinance.

(2) The fees established under this subsection must be made applicable throughout the area of the city. Schedules of rates, fees, charges, and penalties for providing stormwater management programs and structural and natural stormwater and drainage system service may vary according to whether the property served is residential, commercial, or industrial property, the property's use, the size of the property, the area of impervious surfaces on the property, the quantity and quality of the runoff from the property, the characteristics of the watershed into which stormwater from the property drains, and other factors that affect the stormwater drainage system. Rates, fees, and charges imposed under this subsection may not exceed the city's cost of providing a stormwater management program and a structural and natural stormwater and drainage system. The city's cost of providing a stormwater management program and a structural and natural stormwater and drainage system includes any costs necessary to assure that all aspects of stormwater quality and quantity are managed in accordance with federal and State laws, regulations, and rules.

(3) No stormwater utility fee may be levied under this subsection whenever two or more units of local government operate separate stormwater management programs or separate structural and natural stormwater and drainage system services in the same area within a county. However, two or more units of local government may allocate among themselves the functions, duties, powers, and responsibilities for jointly operating a stormwater management program and structural and natural stormwater and drainage system service in the same area within a county, provided that only one unit may levy a fee for the service within the joint service area. For purposes of this subsection, a unit of local government shall include a regional authority

providing stormwater management programs and structural and natural stormwater and drainage system services.

(4) A city may adopt an ordinance providing that any fee imposed under this subsection may be billed with property taxes, may be payable in the same manner as property taxes, and, in the case of nonpayment, may be collected in any manner by which delinquent personal or real property taxes can be collected. If an ordinance states that delinquent fees can be collected in the same manner as delinquent real property taxes, the fees are a lien on the real property described on the bill that includes the fee.

This subdivision applies only to the Cities of Creedmoor, Durham and Winston-Salem, the Towns of Butner, Garner, Kernersville, Knightdale, Morrisville, Stem, Wendell, and Zebulon, and the Village of Clemmons.

(a2) A fee for the use of a disposal facility provided by the city may vary based on the amount, characteristics, and form of recyclable materials present in solid waste brought to the facility for disposal. This section does not prohibit a city from providing aid to low-income persons to pay all or part of the cost of solid waste management services for those persons. A city may, upon a finding that a fund balance in a utility or public service enterprise fund used for operation of a landfill exceeds the requirements for funding the operation of that fund, including closure and post-closure expenditures, transfer excess funds accruing due to imposition of a surcharge imposed on another local government located within the State for use of the disposal facility, as authorized by G.S. 160A-314.1, to be used to support the other services supported by the city's general fund.

(a3) Revisions in the rates, fees, or charges for electric service for cities that are members of the North Carolina Eastern Municipal Power Agency must comply with the public hearing provisions applicable to those cities under G.S. 159B-17.

(b) A city shall have power to collect delinquent accounts by any remedy provided by law for collecting and enforcing private debts, and may specify by ordinance the order in which partial payments are to be applied among the various enterprise services covered by a bill for the services. A city may also discontinue service to any customer whose account remains delinquent for more than 10 days. When service is discontinued for delinquency, it shall be unlawful for any person other than a duly authorized agent or employee of the city to do any act that results in a resumption of services. If a delinquent customer is not the owner of the premises to which the services are delivered, the payment of the delinquent account may not be required before providing services at the request of a new and different tenant or occupant of the premises, but this restriction shall not apply when the premises are occupied by two or more tenants whose services are measured by the same meter.

(b1)   A city shall not do any of the following in its debt collection practices:

(1)   Suspend or disconnect service to a customer because of a past-due and unpaid balance for service incurred by another person who resides with the customer after service has been provided to the customer's household, unless one or more of the following apply:

a.   The customer and the person were members of the same household at a different location when the unpaid balance for service was incurred.

b.   The person was a member of the customer's current household when the service was established, and the person had an unpaid balance for service at that time.

c.   The person is or becomes responsible for the bill for the service to the customer.

(2)   Require that in order to continue service, a customer must agree to be liable for the delinquent account of any other person who will reside in the customer's household after the customer receives the service, unless one or more of the following apply:

a.   The customer and the person were members of the same household at a different location when the unpaid balance for service was incurred.

b.   The person was a member of the customer's current household when the service was established, and the person had an unpaid balance for service at that time.

(b2)   Notwithstanding the provisions of subsection (b1) of this section, if a customer misrepresents his or her identity in a written or verbal agreement for service or receives service using another person's identity, the city shall have the power to collect a delinquent account using any remedy provided by subsection (b) of this section from that customer.

(b3), (b4) Reserved.

(b5) (Applicable to certain localities) Except as provided in subsections (a1) and (d) of this section and G.S. 160A-314.1, rents, rates, fees, charges, and penalties for enterprisory services shall be legal obligations of the person contracting for them, and shall in no case be a lien upon the property or premises served, provided that no contract shall be necessary in the case of structural and natural stormwater and drainage systems.

This subsection applies only to the Cities of Creedmoor, Durham and Winston-Salem, the Towns of Butner, Garner, Kernersville, Knightdale, Morrisville, Stem, Wendell, and Zebulon, and the Village of Clemmons.

(c) (Applicable to other localities) Except as provided in subsection (d) of this section and G.S. 160A-314.1, rents, rates, fees, charges, and penalties for enterprisory services shall be legal obligations of the person contracting for them, and shall in no case be a lien upon the property or premises served, provided that no contract shall be necessary in the case of structural and natural stormwater and drainage systems.

(d) Notwithstanding subsection (b1) of this section, rents, rates, fees, charges, and penalties for enterprisory services shall be legal obligations of the owner of the premises served when:

(1) The property or premises is leased or rented to more than one tenant and services rendered to more than one tenant are measured by the same meter.

(2) Charges made for use of a sewage system are billed separately from charges made for the use of a water distribution system.

(e) Nothing in this section shall repeal any portion of any city charter inconsistent herewith. (1971, c. 698, s. 1; 1991, c. 591, s. 1; c. 652, s. 4; 1991 (Reg. Sess., 1992), c. 1007, s. 46; 1995 (Reg. Sess., 1996), c. 594, s. 28; 2000-70, s. 4; 2005-441, ss. 3(a), (b), 4; 2009-302, s. 3(a), (b); 2011-109, s. 1; 2012-55, s. 2; 2012-167, s. 2; 2013-413, s. 59.4(d).)

§ 160A-314.1. Availability fees for solid waste disposal facilities; collection of any solid waste fees.

(a) A city may impose a fee for the collection of solid waste. The fee may not exceed the costs of collection.

A city may impose a fee for the use of a disposal facility provided by the city. Except as provided in this subsection, the fee for use may not exceed the cost of operating the facility. The fee may exceed those costs if the city enters into a contract with another local government located within the State to accept the other local government's solid waste and the city by ordinance levies a surcharge on the fee. The fee authorized by this paragraph may only be used to cover the costs of operating the facility. The surcharge authorized by this paragraph may be used for any purpose for which the city may appropriate funds. A fee under this paragraph may be imposed only on those who use the facility. The fee for use may vary based on the amount, characteristics, and form of recyclable materials present in solid waste brought to the facility for disposal.

(a1) In addition to a fee that a city may impose for collecting solid waste or for using a disposal facility, a city may impose a fee for the availability of a disposal facility provided by the city. A fee for availability may not exceed the cost of providing the facility and may be imposed on all improved property in the city that benefits from the availability of the facility. A city may not impose an availability fee on property whose solid waste is collected by a county, a city, or a private contractor for a fee if the fee imposed by a county, a city, or a private contractor for the collection of solid waste includes a charge for the availability and use of a disposal facility provided by the city. Property served by a private contractor who disposes of solid waste collected from the property in a disposal facility provided by a private contractor that provides the same services as those provided by the city disposal facility is not considered to benefit from a disposal facility provided by the city and is not subject to a fee imposed by the city for the availability of a disposal facility provided by the city. To the extent that the services provided by the city disposal facility differ from the services provided by the disposal facility provided by a private contractor in the same city, the city may charge an availability fee to cover the costs of the additional services provided by the city disposal facility.

In determining the costs of providing and operating a disposal facility, a city may consider solid waste management costs incidental to a city's handling and disposal of solid waste at its disposal facility. A fee for the availability or use of a disposal facility may be based on the combined costs of the different disposal facilities provided by the city.

(b) A city may adopt an ordinance providing that any fee imposed under subsection (a) or under G.S. 160A-314 for collecting or disposing of solid waste may be billed with property taxes, may be payable in the same manner as property taxes, and, in the case of nonpayment, may be collected in any manner by which delinquent personal or real property taxes can be collected. If an ordinance states that delinquent fees can be collected in the same manner as delinquent real property taxes, the fees are a lien on the real property described on the bill that includes the fee. (1991, c. 652, s. 5; 2007-550, s. 10(b); 2013-413, s. 59.4(c).)

§ 160A-315. Billing and collecting agents for certain sewer systems.

Any city that maintains and operates a sewage collection and disposal system but does not maintain and operate a water distribution system is authorized to contract with the owner or operator of the water distribution system operating within the area served by the city sewer system to act as the billing and collection agent of the city for any charges, rents, or penalties imposed by the city for sewer services. (1933, c. 322, s. 1; 1941, c. 106; 1961, c. 1074; 1971, c. 698, s. 1.)

§ 160A-316. Independent water companies to supply information.

The owner or operator of any independent or private water distribution system operating within a city that maintains and operates a sewage collection and disposal system shall furnish to the city upon request copies of water meter readings and any other water consumption records and data that the city may require to bill and collect its sewer rents and charges. The city shall pay the reasonable cost of supplying this information. (1933, c. 322, s. 1; 1941, c. 106; 1961, c. 1074; 1971, c. 698, s. 1.)

§ 160A-317. Power to require connections to water or sewer service and the use of solid waste collection services.

(a) Connections. - A city may require an owner of developed property on which there are situated one or more residential dwelling units or commercial establishments located within the city limits and within a reasonable distance of any water line or sewer collection line owned, leased as lessee, or operated by the city or on behalf of the city to connect the owner's premises with the water or sewer line or both, and may fix charges for the connections. In lieu of requiring connection under this subsection and in order to avoid hardship, the city may require payment of a periodic availability charge, not to exceed the minimum periodic service charge for properties that are connected.

(b)   Solid Waste. - A city may require an owner of improved property to do any of the following:

(1)   Place solid waste in specified places or receptacles for the convenience of city collection and disposal.

(2)   Separate materials before the solid waste is collected.

(3)   Participate in a recycling program by requiring separation of designated materials by the owner or occupant of the property prior to disposal. An owner of recovered materials as defined by G.S. 130A-290(a)(24) retains ownership of the recovered materials until the owner conveys, sells, donates, or otherwise transfers the recovered materials to a person, firm, company, corporation, or unit of local government. A city may not require an owner to convey, sell, donate, or otherwise transfer recovered materials to the city or its designee. If an owner places recovered materials in receptacles or delivers recovered materials to specific locations, receptacles, and facilities that are owned or operated by the city or its designee, then ownership of these materials is transferred to the city or its designee.

(4)   Participate in any solid waste collection service provided by the city or by a person who has a contract with the city if the owner or occupant of the property has not otherwise contracted for the collection of solid waste from the property.

(c)   A city may impose a fee for the solid waste collection service provided under subdivision (4) of subsection (b) of this section. The fee may not exceed the costs of collection. (1917, c. 136, subch. 7, s. 2; C.S., s. 2806; 1971, c. 698, s. 1; 1979, c. 619, s. 14: 1981, c. 823; 1989, c. 741, s. 2; 1991, c. 698, s. 2; 1993, c. 165, s. 2; 1995, c. 511, s. 4.)

§ 160A-318. Mutual aid contracts.

(a)   Any two or more cities, counties, water and sewer authorities, metropolitan sewage districts, sanitary districts, or private utility companies or combination thereof may enter into contracts with each other to provide mutual aid and assistance in restoring electric, water, sewer, or gas services in the event of natural disasters or other emergencies under such terms and conditions as may be agreed upon. Mutual aid contracts may include provisions for furnishing personnel, equipment, apparatus, supplies and materials; for reimbursement or indemnification of the aiding party for loss or damage incurred by giving aid; for delegating authority to a designated official or employee to send aid upon request; and any other provisions not inconsistent with law.

(b) Officials and employees furnished by one party in aid of another party pursuant to a mutual aid contract entered into under authority of this section shall be conclusively deemed for all purposes to remain officials and employees of the aiding party. While providing aid to another and while traveling to and from another city or county pursuant to giving aid, they shall retain all rights, privileges, and immunities, including coverage under the North Carolina Workers' Compensation Act, as they enjoy while performing their normal duties.

(c) Notwithstanding any other provisions of law to the contrary, any party to a mutual aid contract entered into under authority of this section, may sell or otherwise convey or deliver to another party to the contract personal property to be used in restoring utility services pursuant to the contract, without following procedures for the sale or disposition of property prescribed by any general law, local act, or city charter.

(d) Nothing in this section shall be construed to deprive any party to a mutual aid contract of its discretion to send or decline to send its personnel, equipment, and apparatus in aid of another party to the contract under any circumstances, whether or not obligated by the contract to do so. In no case shall a party to a mutual aid contract or any of its officials or employees be held to answer in any civil or criminal action for declining to send personnel, equipment, or apparatus to another party to the contract, whether or not obligated by contract to do so. (1967, c. 450; 1971, c. 698, s. 1; 1991, c. 636, s. 3.)

§ 160A-319. Utility franchises.

(a) A city shall have authority to grant upon reasonable terms franchises for a telephone system and any of the enterprises listed in G.S. 160A-311, except a cable television system. A franchise granted by a city authorizes the operation of the franchised activity within the city. No franchise shall be granted for a period of more than 60 years, except that a franchise for solid waste collection or disposal systems and facilities shall not be granted for a period of more than 30 years. Except as otherwise provided by law, when a city operates an enterprise, or upon granting a franchise, a city may by ordinance make it unlawful to operate an enterprise without a franchise.

(b)   For the purposes of this section, "cable television system" means any system or facility that, by means of a master antenna and wires or cables, or by wires or cables alone, receives, amplifies, modifies, transmits, or distributes any television, radio, or electronic signal, audio or video or both, to subscribing members of the public for compensation. "Cable television system" does not include providing master antenna services only to property owned or leased by the same person, firm, or corporation, nor communication services rendered to a cable television system by a public utility that is regulated by the North Carolina Utilities Commission or the Federal Communications Commission in providing those services. (Code, ss. 704, 3117; 1901, c. 283; 1905, c. 526; Rev., s. 2916; 1907, c. 978; P.L. 1917, c. 223; C. S., s. 2623; Ex. Sess. 1921, c. 58; 1927, c. 14; 1933, c. 69; 1949, c. 938; 1955, c. 77; 1959, c. 391; 1961, c. 308; 1967, c. 100, s. 2; c. 1122, s. 1; 1969, c. 944; 1971, c. 698, s. 1; 1975, c. 664, s. 11; 1991 (Reg. Sess., 1992), c. 1013, s. 2; 2006-151, s. 15.)

§ 160A-320. Public enterprise improvements.

(a)   Authorization. - A city may contract with a developer or property owner, or with a private party who is under contract with the developer or property owner, for public enterprise improvements that are adjacent or ancillary to a private land development project. Such a contract shall allow the city to reimburse the private party for costs associated with the design and construction of improvements that are in addition to those required by the city's land development regulations. Such a contract is not subject to Article 8 of Chapter 143 of the General Statutes if the public cost will not exceed two hundred fifty thousand dollars ($250,000) and the city determines that: (i) the public cost will not exceed the estimated cost of providing for those improvements through either eligible force account qualified labor or through a public contract let pursuant to Article 8 of Chapter 143 of the General Statutes; or (ii) the coordination of separately constructed improvements would be impracticable. A city may enact ordinances and policies setting forth the procedures, requirements, and terms for agreements authorized by this section.

(b) Property Acquisition. - The improvements may be constructed on property owned or acquired by the private party or on property owned or acquired by the city. The private party may assist the city in obtaining easements in favor of the city from private property owners on those properties that will be involved in or affected by the project. The contract between the city and the private party may be entered into before the acquisition of any real property necessary to the project. (2005-426, s. 8(d).)

§ 160A-321. Sale, lease, or discontinuance of city-owned enterprise.

(a) A city is authorized to sell or lease as lessor any enterprise that it may own upon any terms and conditions that the council may deem best. However, except as to transfers to another governmental entity pursuant to G.S. 160A-274 or as provided in subsection (b) of this section, a city-owned enterprise shall not be sold, leased to another, or discontinued unless the proposal to sell, lease, or discontinue is first submitted to a vote of the people and approved by a majority of those who vote thereon. Voter approval shall not be required for the sale, lease, or discontinuance of airports, off-street parking systems and facilities, or solid waste collection and disposal systems.

(b) For the sale, lease, or discontinuance of water treatment systems, water distribution systems, or wastewater collection and treatment systems, a city may, but is not required to, submit to its voters the question of whether such sale, lease, or discontinuance shall be undertaken. The referendum is to be conducted pursuant to the general and local laws applicable to special elections in such city. (Code, ss. 704, 3117; 1901, c. 283; 1905, c. 526; Rev., s. 2916; 1907, c. 978; P.L. 1917, c. 223; C.S., s. 2623; Ex. Sess. 1921, c. 58; 1927, c. 14; 1933, c. 69; 1949, c. 938; 1955, c. 77; 1959, c. 391; 1961, c. 308; 1967, c. 100, s. 2; c. 1122, s. 1; 1969, c. 944; 1971, c. 698, s. 1; 1973, c. 489, s. 2; 2011-212, s. 1.)

§ 160A-322. Contracts for electric power and water.

A city is authorized to enter into contracts for a period not exceeding 40 years for the supply of water, and for a period not exceeding 30 years for the supply of electric power or other public commodity or services. (Code, ss. 704, 3117; 1901, c. 283; 1905, c. 526; Rev., s. 2916; 1907, c. 978; P.L. 1917, c. 223; C. S., s. 2623; Ex. Sess. 1921, c. 58; 1927, c. 14; 1933, c. 69; 1949, c. 938; 1955, c.

77; 1959, c. 391; 1961, c. 308; 1967, c. 100, s. 2; c. 1122, s. 1; 1969, c. 944; 1971, c. 698, s. 1.)

§ 160A-323. Load management and peak load pricing of electric power.

In addition and supplemental to the powers conferred upon municipalities by the laws of the State and for the purposes of conserving electricity and increasing the economy of operation of municipal electric systems, any municipality owning or operating an electric distribution system, any municipality engaging in a joint project pursuant to Chapter 159B of the General Statutes and any joint agency created pursuant to Chapter 159B of the General Statutes, shall have and may exercise the power and authority:

(1) To investigate, study, develop and place into effect procedures and to investigate, study, develop, purchase, lease, own, operate, maintain, and put into service devices, which will temporarily curtail or cut off certain types of appliances or equipment for short periods of time whenever an unusual peak demand threatens to overload the electric system or economies would result; and

(2) To fix rates and bill customers by a system of nondiscriminatory peak pricing, with incentive rates for off-peak use of electricity charging more for peak periods than for off-peak periods to reflect the higher cost of providing electric service during periods of peak demand on the electric system. (1977, c. 232.)

§ 160A-324. Contract with private solid waste collection firm(s).

(a) If the area to be annexed described in an act of the General Assembly includes an area where a firm (i) meets the requirements of subsection (a1) of this section, (ii) on the ninetieth day preceding the date of introduction in the House of Representatives or the Senate of the bill which became the act making the annexation, was providing solid waste collection services in the area to be annexed, (iii) is still providing such services on the date the act becomes law, and (iv) by reason of the annexation the firm's franchise with a county or arrangements with third parties for solid waste collection will be terminated, the city shall do one of the following:

(1) Contract with the firm for a period of two years after the effective date of the annexation ordinance to allow the firm to provide collection services to the

city in the area to be annexed for sums determined under subsection (d) of this section.

(2) Pay the firm for the firm's economic loss, with one-third of the economic loss to be paid within 30 days of the termination and the balance paid in 12 equal monthly installments during the next succeeding 12 months. Any remaining economic loss payment is forfeited if the firm terminates service to customers in the annexation area prior to the effective date of the annexation.

(3) Make other arrangements satisfactory to the parties.

(a1) To qualify for the options set forth in subsection (a) of this section, a firm must have, subsequent to receiving notice of the annexation in accordance with subsection (b) of this section, filed with the city clerk at least 10 days prior to the effective date of the annexation a written request to contract with the city to provide solid waste collection services containing a certification, signed by an officer or owner of the firm, that the firm serves at least 50 customers within the county at that time.

(a2) Firms shall file notice of provision of solid waste collection service with the city clerk of all cities located in the firm's collection area or within five miles thereof.

(b) The city shall make a good faith effort to provide at least 30 days before the effective date of the annexation a copy of the act to each private firm providing solid waste collection services in the area to be annexed. The notice shall be sent to all firms that filed notice in accordance with subsection (a2) of this section by certified mail, return receipt requested, to the address provided by the firm under subsection (a2) of this section.

(c) The city may require that the contract contain:

(1) A requirement that the firm post a performance bond and maintain public liability insurance coverage;

(2) A requirement that the firm agree to service customers in the annexed area that were not served by that firm on the effective date of annexation;

(3) A provision that divides the annexed area into service areas if there were more than one firm being contracted within the area, such that the entire

area is served by the firms, or by the city as to customers not served by the firms;

(4) A provision that the city may serve customers not served by the firm on the effective date of annexation;

(5) A provision that the contract can be cancelled in writing, delivered by certified mail to the firm in question with 30 days to cure, substantial violations of the contract, but no contract may be cancelled on these grounds unless the Local Government Commission finds that substantial violations have occurred, except that the city may suspend the contract for up to 30 days if it finds substantial violation of health laws;

(6) Performance standards, not exceeding city standards existing at the time of notice provided pursuant to subsection (b) of this section, with provision that the contract may be cancelled for substantial violations of those standards, but no contract may be cancelled on those grounds unless the Local Government Commission finds that substantial violations have occurred;

(7) A provision for monetary damages if there are violations of the contract or of performance standards.

(d) If the services to be provided to the city by reason of the annexation are substantially the same as rendered under the franchise with the county or arrangements with the parties, the amount paid by the city shall be at least ninety percent (90%) of the amount paid or required under the existing franchise or arrangements. If such services are required to be adjusted to conform to city standards or as a result of changes in the number of customers and as a result there are changes in disposal costs (including mileage and landfill charges), requirements for storage capacity (dumpsters and/or residential carts), and/or frequency of collection, the amount paid by the city for the service shall be increased or decreased to reflect the value of such adjusted services as if computed under the existing franchise or arrangements. In the event agreement cannot be reached between the city and the firm under this subsection, the matters shall be determined by the Local Government Commission.

(e), (f) Repealed by Session Laws 2006-193, s. 1, applicable to annexations for which the bill making the annexation is enacted on or after January 1, 2007.

(g) If the city fails to offer a contract to the firm within 30 days following the effective date of the annexation act, the firm may appeal within 60 days following the effective date of the annexation act to the Local Government Commission for an order directing the city to offer a contract. If the Local Government Commission finds that the city has not made an offer which complies with this section, it shall order the city to pay to the firm a civil penalty of the amount of payments it finds that the city would have had to make under the contract, during the noncompliance period until the contract offer is made. Either the firm or the city may obtain judicial review in accordance with Chapter 150B of the General Statutes.

(h) A firm which has given notice under subsection (a) of this section that it desires to contract, and any firm that the city believes is eligible to give such notice, shall make available to the city not later than 30 days following a written request of the city all information in its possession or control, including but not limited to operational, financial and budgetary information, necessary for the city to determine if the firm qualifies for the benefits of this section and to determine the nature and scope of the potential contract and/or economic loss. The firm forfeits its rights under this section if it fails to make a good faith response within 30 days following receipt of the written request for information from the city, provided that the city's written request so states by specific reference to this section.

(i) As used in this section, the following terms mean:

(1) Economic loss. - A sum equal to 15 times the average gross monthly revenue for the three months prior to the introduction of the bill under subsection (a) of this section, collected or due the firm for residential, commercial, and industrial collection service in the area annexed or to be annexed; provided that revenues shall be included in calculations under this subdivision only if policies of the city will provide solid waste collection to those customers such that arrangements between the firm and the customers will be terminated.

(2) Firm. - A private solid waste collection firm. (1989, c. 598, s. 1; 2006-193, s. 3.)

§ 160A-325. Selection or approval of sites for certain sanitary landfills; solid waste defined.

(a) The governing board of a city shall consider alternative sites and socioeconomic and demographic data and shall hold a public hearing prior to selecting or approving a site for a new sanitary landfill that receives residential solid waste that is located within one mile of an existing sanitary landfill within the State. The distance between an existing and a proposed site shall be determined by measurement between the closest points on the outer boundary of each site. The definitions set out in G.S. 130A-290 apply to this subsection. As used in this subsection:

(1) "Approving a site" refers to prior approval of a site under G.S. 130A-294(a)(4).

(2) "Existing sanitary landfill" means a sanitary landfill that is in operation or that has been in operation within the five-year period immediately prior to the date on which an application for a permit is submitted.

(3) "New sanitary landfill" means a sanitary landfill that includes areas not within the legal description of an existing sanitary landfill as set out in the permit for the existing sanitary landfill.

(4) "Socioeconomic and demographic data" means the most recent socioeconomic and demographic data compiled by the United States Bureau of the Census and any additional socioeconomic and demographic data submitted at the public hearing.

(b) As used in this Part, "solid waste" means nonhazardous solid waste, that is, solid waste as defined in G.S. 130A-290 but not including hazardous waste. (1991 (Reg. Sess., 1992), c. 1013, s. 3.)

§ 160A-326. Limitations on rail transportation liability.

(a) As used in this section:

(1) "Claim" means a claim, action, suit, or request for damages, whether compensatory, punitive, or otherwise, made by any person or entity against:

a. The City, a railroad, or an operating rights railroad; or

b. An officer, director, trustee, employee, parent, subsidiary, or affiliated corporation as defined in G.S. 105-130.2, or agent of: the City, a railroad, or an operating rights railroad.

(2) "Operating rights railroad" means a railroad corporation or railroad company that, prior to January 1, 2001, was granted operating rights by a State-Owned Railroad Company or operated over the property of a State-Owned Railroad Company under a claim of right over or adjacent to facilities used by or on behalf of the City.

(3) "Passenger rail services" means the transportation of rail passengers by or on behalf of the City and all services performed by a railroad pursuant to a contract with the City in connection with the transportation of rail passengers, including, but not limited to, the operation of trains; the use of right-of-way, trackage, public or private roadway and rail crossings, equipment, or station areas or appurtenant facilities; the design, construction, reconstruction, operation, or maintenance of rail-related equipment, tracks, and any appurtenant facilities; or the provision of access rights over or adjacent to lines owned by the City or a railroad, or otherwise occupied by the City or a railroad, pursuant to charter grant, fee-simple deed, lease, easement, license, trackage rights, or other form of ownership or authorized use.

(4) "Railroad" means a railroad corporation or railroad company, including a State-Owned Railroad Company as defined in G.S. 124-11, that has entered into any contracts or operating agreements of any kind with the City concerning passenger rail services.

(b) Contracts Allocating Financial Responsibility Authorized. - The City may contract with any railroad to allocate financial responsibility for passenger rail services claims, including, but not limited to, the execution of indemnity agreements, notwithstanding any other statutory, common law, public policy, or other prohibition against same, and regardless of the nature of the claim or the conduct giving rise to such claim.

(c) Insurance Required. -

(1) If the City enters into any contract authorized by subsection (b) of this section, the contract shall require the City to secure and maintain, upon and after the commencement of the operation of trains by or on behalf of the City, a liability insurance policy covering the liability of the parties to the contract, a State-Owned Railroad Company as defined in G.S. 124-11 that owns or claims an interest in any real property subject to the contract, and any operating rights railroad for all claims for property damage, personal injury, bodily injury, and death arising out of or related to passenger rail services. The policy shall name the parties to the contract, a State-Owned Railroad Company as defined in G.S.

124-11 that owns or claims an interest in any real property subject to the contract, and any operating rights railroad as named insureds and shall have policy limits of not less than two hundred million dollars ($200,000,000) per single accident or incident, and may include a self-insured retention in an amount of not more than five million dollars ($5,000,000).

(2) If the City does not enter into any contract authorized by subsection (b) of this section, upon and after the commencement of the operation of trains by or on behalf of the City, the City shall secure and maintain a liability insurance policy, with policy limits and a self-insured retention consistent with subdivision (1) of this subsection, for all claims for property damage, personal injury, bodily injury, and death arising out of or related to passenger rail services.

(d) Liability Limit. - The aggregate liability of the City, the parties to the contract or contracts authorized by subsection (b) of this section, a State-Owned Railroad Company as defined in G.S. 124-11, and any operating rights railroad for all claims arising from a single accident or incident related to passenger rail services for property damage, personal injury, bodily injury, and death is limited to two hundred million dollars ($200,000,000) per single accident or incident or to any proceeds available under any insurance policy secured pursuant to subsection (c) of this section, whichever is greater.

(e) Effect on Other Laws. - This section shall not affect the damages that may be recovered under the Federal Employers' Liability Act, 45 U.S.C. § 51, et seq., (1908); or under Article 1 of Chapter 97 of the General Statutes.

(f) Applicability. - This section shall apply only to municipalities with a population of more than 500,000 persons, according to the latest decennial census, or to municipalities that have entered into a transit governance interlocal agreement with, among other local governments, a city with a population of more than 500,000 persons. (2002-78, s. 3; 2012-79, s. 1.14(f).)

§ 160A-327. Displacement of private solid waste collection services.

(a) A unit of local government shall not displace a private company that is providing collection services for municipal solid waste or recovered materials, or both, except as provided for in this section.

(b) Before a local government may displace a private company that is providing collection services for municipal solid waste or recovered materials, or both, the unit of local government shall publish notice of the first meeting where the proposed change in solid waste collection service will be discussed. Notice shall be published once a week for at least four consecutive weeks in at least one newspaper of general circulation in the area in which the unit of local government and the proposed displacement area are located. The first public notice shall be given no less than 30 days but no more than 60 days prior to the displacement issue being placed on the agenda for discussion or action at an official meeting of the governing body of the unit of local government. The notice shall specify the date and place of the meeting, the geographic location in which solid waste collection services are proposed to be changed, and the types of solid waste collection services that may be affected. In addition, the unit of local government shall send written notice by certified mail, return receipt requested, to all companies that have filed notice with the unit of local government clerk pursuant to the provisions of subsection (f) of this section. The unit of local government shall deposit notice in the U.S. mail at least 30 days prior to the displacement issues being placed on the agenda for discussion or action at an official meeting of the governing body of the unit of local government.

(c) Following the public notice required by subsection (b) of this section, but in no event later than six months after the date of the first meeting pursuant to subsection (b) of this section, the unit of local government may proceed to take formal action to displace a private company. The unit of local government or other public or private entity selected by the unit of local government may not commence the actual provision of these services for a period of 15 months from the date of the first publication of notice, unless the unit of local government provides compensation to the displaced private company as follows:

(1) Subject to subdivision (3) of this subsection, if the private company has provided collection services in the displacement area prior to announcement of the displacement action, the unit of local government shall provide compensation to the displaced private company in an amount equal to the total gross revenues for collection services provided in the displacement area for the six months prior to the first publication of notice required under subsection (b) of this section.

(2) Subject to subdivision (3) of this subsection, if the displaced private company has provided collection services in the displacement area for less than six months prior to the first publication of notice required under subsection (b) of this section, the unit of local government shall provide compensation to the displaced private company in an amount equal to the total gross revenues for

the period of time that the private company provided such services in the displacement area.

(3)   If the displaced private company purchased an existing operation of another private company providing such services, compensation shall be for six months based on the monthly average total gross revenues for three months the immediate preceding the first publication of notice required under subsection (b) of this section.

(d)   If the local government elects to provide compensation pursuant to subsection (c) of this section, the amount due from the unit of local government to the displaced company shall be paid as follows: one-third of the compensation to be paid within 30 days of the displacement and the balance paid in six equal monthly installments during the next succeeding six months.

(e)   If the unit of local government fails to change the provision of solid waste services as described in the notices required under subsection (b) of this section within six months of the date of the first meeting pursuant to subsection (b) of this section, the unit of local government shall not take action to displace without complying again with the provisions of subsection (b) of this section.

(f)   Notice of the provision of solid waste collection service shall be filed with the unit of local government clerk of all cities and counties located in the private company's collection area or within five miles thereof.

(g)   This section shall not apply when a private company is displaced as the result of an annexation under Article 4A of Chapter 160A of the General Statutes or an annexation by an act of the General Assembly. The provisions of G.S. 160A-37.3, 160-49.3, or 160A-324 shall apply.

(h)   If a unit of local government intends to provide compensation under subsection (c) of this section to a private company that has given notice under subsection (f) of this section, the private company shall make available to the unit of local government not later than 30 days following a written request of the unit of local government, sent by certified mail, return receipt requested, all information in its possession or control, including operational, financial, and budgetary information necessary for the unit of local government to determine if the private company qualifies for compensation. The private company forfeits its rights under this section if it fails to make a good faith response within 30 days following receipt of the written request for information from the unit of local government provided that the unit of local government's written request so states by specific reference to this section.

(i) Nothing in this section shall affect the authority of a city or county to establish recycling service where recycling service is not currently being offered.

(j) As used in this section, the following terms mean:

(1) Collection. - The gathering of municipal solid waste, recovered materials, or recyclables from residential, commercial, industrial, governmental, or institutional customers and transporting it to a sanitary landfill or other disposal facility. Collection does not include transport from a transfer station or processing point to a disposal facility.

(2) Displacement. - Any formal action by a unit of local government that prohibits a private company from providing all or a portion of the collection services for municipal solid waste, recovered materials, or recyclables that the company is providing in the affected area at least 90 days prior to the date of the first publication of notice required by subsection (b) of this section. Displacement also means an action by a unit of local government to use an availability fee, nonoptional fee, or taxes to fund competing collection services for municipal solid waste, recovered materials, or recyclables that the private company is providing in the affected areas at least 90 days prior to the date of the first publication of notice required under subsection (b) of this section is given. Displacement does not include any of the following actions:

a. Failure to renew a franchise agreement or contract with a private company.

b. Taking action that results in a change in solid waste collection services because the private company's operations present an imminent and substantial threat to human health or safety or are causing a substantial public nuisance.

c. Taking action that results in a change in solid waste collection services because the private company has materially breached its franchise agreement or the terms of a contract with the local government, or the company has notified the local government that it no longer intends to honor the terms of the franchise agreement or contract. Notice of breach must be delivered in writing, delivered by certified mail to the firm in question with 30 days to cure the violation of the contract.

d. Terminating an existing contract or franchise in accordance with the provisions of the contract or franchise agreement.

e. Providing temporary collection services under a declared state of emergency.

f. Taking action that results in a change in solid waste collection services due to the existing providers' felony conviction of a violation in the State of federal or State law governing the solid waste collection or disposal.

g. Contracting with a private company to continue its existing services or provide a different level of service at a negotiated price on terms agreeable to the parties.

(3) Municipal solid waste. - As defined in G.S. 130A-290(18a).

(4) Unit of local government. - A county, municipality, authority, or political subdivision that is authorized by law to provide for collection of solid waste or recovered materials, or both. (2006-193, s. 4.)

§ 160A-328. Local government landfill liaison.

(a) A city that has planning jurisdiction over any portion of the site of a sanitary landfill may employ a local government landfill liaison. No person who is responsible for any aspect of the management or operation of the landfill may serve as a local government landfill liaison. A local government landfill liaison shall have a right to enter public or private lands on which the landfill facility is located at reasonable times to inspect the landfill operation in order to:

(1) Ensure that the facility meets all local requirements.

(2) Identify and notify the Department of suspected violations of applicable federal or State laws, regulations, or rules.

(3) Identify and notify the Department of potentially hazardous conditions at the facility.

(b) Entry pursuant to this section shall not constitute a trespass or taking of property. (2007-550, s. 11(b).)

§ 160A-329. Provision of municipal services to certain properties.

(a) A municipality shall provide municipal services as defined under subsection (b) of this section to any property if that property owner submitted a petition for voluntary annexation under Article 4A of this Chapter, and the municipal governing board voted on an annexation ordinance for that property but the annexation ordinance failed of adoption. This section applies if the property owner (i) submits to the governing board a notice exercising the provisions of this section within 60 days of this section becoming law and (ii) agrees in writing to all the requirements contained in any utility extension agreement that was presented to the governing board at the same meeting as the annexation that failed of adoption. The municipal governing board may not impose more burdensome requirements or commitments on the property owner that are inconsistent with the requirements and commitments that are contained in the utility extension agreement.

(b) For purposes of this section, prior to the effective date of the annexation of the property, the term "municipal services" only means water or sewer services, but only if the municipality has water or sewer capacity. For purposes of this section, prior to the effective date of annexation, the term "municipal services" specifically does not include any of the following services of the municipality: police protection, fire protection, solid waste services, or street maintenance services.

(c) Requirements and commitments contained in the utility extension agreement that was presented to the governing board at the same meeting as the annexation ordinance that failed of adoption shall continue as obligations of the agreement unless the city council relieves the property owner of the requirement or commitment. Those requirements and commitments include, but are not limited to, the committed elements of a development plan in a zoning map case approved by the county where the property is located. (2013-386, s. 1.)

§ 160A-330. Reserved for future codification purposes.

Part 2. Electric Service in Urban Areas.

§ 160A-331. Definitions.

Unless the context otherwise requires, the following words and phrases shall have the meanings indicated when used in this Part:

(1) "Assigned area" means any portion of an area annexed to or incorporated into a city which, on or before the effective date of annexation or incorporation, had been assigned by the North Carolina Utilities Commission to a specific electric supplier pursuant to G.S. 62-110.2.

(1a) "Assigned supplier" means a person, firm, or corporation to which the North Carolina Utilities Commission had assigned a specific area for service as an electric supplier pursuant to G.S. 62-110.2, which area, in whole or in part, is subsequently annexed to or incorporated into a city.

(1b) The "determination date" is

a. April 20, 1965, with respect to areas within the corporate limits of any city as of April 20, 1965;

b. The effective date of annexation with respect to areas annexed to any city after April 20, 1965;

c. The date a primary supplier comes into being with respect to any city first incorporated after April 20, 1965.

(2) "Line" means any conductor located inside the city, or any conductor within 300 feet of areas annexed by the city that is a primary supplier, for distributing or transmitting electricity, except as follows:

a. For overhead construction, a conductor from the pole nearest the premises of a consumer to such premises, or a conductor from a line tap to such premises.

b. For underground construction, a conductor from the transformer (or the junction point, if there be one) nearest the premises of a consumer to such premises.

(3) "Premises" means the building, structure, or facility to which electricity is being or is to be furnished. Two or more buildings, structures, or facilities that are located on one tract or contiguous tracts of land and are used by one electric consumer for commercial, industrial, institutional, or governmental purposes, shall together constitute one "premises," except that any such

building, structure, or facility shall not, together with any other building, structure, or facility, constitute one "premises" if the electric service to it is separately metered and the charges for such service are calculated independently of charges for service to any other building, structure, or facility.

(4)   "Primary supplier" means a city that owns and maintains its own electric system, or a person, firm, or corporation that furnishes electric service within a city pursuant to a franchise granted by, or contract with, a city, or that, having furnished service pursuant to a franchise or contract, is continuing to furnish service within a city after the expiration of the franchise or contract.

(5)   "Secondary supplier" means a person, firm, or corporation that is not a primary supplier, but that furnishes electricity at retail to one or more consumers other than itself within the limits of a city, or that has a conductor located within 300 feet of an area annexed by a city that is a primary supplier. A primary supplier that furnishes electric service within a city pursuant to a franchise or contract that limits or restricts the classes of consumers or types of electric service permitted to such supplier shall, in and with respect to any area annexed by the city after April 20, 1965, be a primary supplier for such classes of consumers or types of service, and if it furnishes other electric service in the annexed area on the effective date of annexation, shall be a secondary supplier, in and with respect to such annexed area, for all other electric service. A primary supplier that continues to furnish electric service after the expiration of a franchise or contract that limited or restricted such primary supplier with respect to classes of consumers or types of electric service shall, in and with respect to any area annexed by the city after April 20, 1965, be a secondary supplier for all electric service if it is furnishing electric service in the annexed area on the effective date of annexation. (1965, c. 287, s. 1; 1971, c. 698, s. 1; 1973, c. 426, s. 52; 1997-346, s. 1; 1999-111, s. 1; 2003-24, s. 1; 2005-150, s. 2.)

§ 160A-331.1: Repealed by Session Laws 2007-419, s. 3, effective August 21, 2007.

§ 160A-331.2. Agreements of electric suppliers.

(a)   The General Assembly finds and determines that, in order to avoid the unnecessary duplication of electric facilities and to facilitate the settlement of disputes between cities that are primary suppliers and other electric suppliers, it is desirable for the State to authorize electric suppliers to enter into agreements pursuant to which the parties to the agreements allocate to each other the right to provide electric service to premises each would not have the right to serve under this Article but for the agreement, provided that no agreement between a city that is a primary supplier and another electric supplier shall be enforceable by or against an electric supplier that is subject to the territorial assignment jurisdiction of the North Carolina Utilities Commission until the agreement has been approved by the Commission. The Commission shall approve an agreement entered into pursuant to this section unless it finds that such agreement is not in the public interest. Such agreements may allocate the right to serve premises by reference to specific premises, geographical boundaries, or amounts of unspecified load to be served, but no agreement shall affect in any way the rights of other electric suppliers who are not parties to the relevant agreement. The provisions of this section apply to agreements relating to electric service inside and outside the corporate limits of a city.

(b)   Repealed by Session Laws 2007-419, s. 1, effective August 21, 2007.

(c)   To the extent negotiations undertaken pursuant to subsection (b) of this section, as enacted by S.L. 2005-150, have not resulted in an agreement between a negotiating electric membership corporation and a negotiating city by May 31, 2007, jurisdiction shall immediately lie in the North Carolina Utilities Commission to resolve all issues related to those negotiations. Either party to the negotiations may petition the Commission to exercise the jurisdiction conferred in this subsection upon the filing of a petition and the payment of a filing fee of five hundred dollars ($500.00). In reaching its decision, the Commission shall include consideration of the public convenience and necessity. The Commission shall not consider rate differentials between the involved city and the involved electric membership corporation.

(d)   Notwithstanding an order of the Commission issued pursuant to subsection (c) of this section:

(1)   Any electric membership corporation or city may furnish electric service to any consumer who desires service from that electric membership corporation or city at any premises being served by another electric membership corporation or city, or at premises which another electric membership corporation or city has the right to serve pursuant to subsection (c) of this section, upon agreement of the affected electric membership corporation or city, subject to approval by the Commission.

(2) The Commission shall have the authority and jurisdiction, after notice to all affected electric membership corporations and cities and after a hearing, if a hearing is requested by any affected electric membership corporation or city, or any other interested party, to order any electric membership corporation or city which may reasonably do so to furnish electric service to any consumer who desires service from that electric membership corporation or city at any premises being served by another electric membership corporation or city pursuant to subsection (c) of this section or subdivision (1) of this subsection, or which another electric membership corporation or city has the right to serve pursuant to subsection (c) of this section or subdivision (1) of this subsection, and to order the other electric membership corporation or city to cease and desist from furnishing electric service to such premises, upon finding that service to the consumer by the electric membership corporation or city which is then furnishing service, or which has the right to furnish service to those premises, is or will be inadequate or undependable, or that the rates, conditions of service, or service regulations, applied to such consumer, are unreasonably discriminatory.

(e) Assignments or reassignments made or approved by the Commission pursuant to subsection (c) or (d) of this section shall be deemed to be service area agreements approved pursuant to subsection (a) of this section. (2005-150, s. 3; 2007-419, s. 1.)

§ 160A-332. Electric service within city limits.

(a) The suppliers of electric service inside the corporate limits of any city in which a secondary supplier was furnishing electric service on the determination date (as defined in G.S. 160A-331(1)) shall have rights and be subject to restrictions as follows:

(1) The secondary supplier shall have the right to serve all premises being served by it, or to which any of its facilities are attached, on the determination date.

(2) The secondary supplier shall have the right, subject to subdivision (3) of this section, to serve all premises initially requiring electric service after the determination date which are located wholly within 300 feet of its lines and located wholly more than 300 feet from the lines of the primary supplier, as such suppliers' lines existed on the determination date.

(3) Any premises initially requiring electric service after the determination date which are located wholly within 300 feet of a secondary supplier's lines and wholly within 300 feet of another secondary supplier's lines, but wholly more than 300 feet from the primary supplier's lines, as the lines of all suppliers existed on the determination date, may be served by the secondary supplier which the consumer chooses, and no other supplier shall thereafter furnish electric service to such premises, except with the written consent of the supplier then serving the premises.

(4) A primary supplier shall not furnish electric service to any premises which a secondary supplier has the right to serve as set forth in subdivisions (1), (2), and (3) of this section, except with the written consent of the secondary supplier.

(5) Any premises initially requiring electric service after the determination date which are located wholly or partially within 300 feet of the primary supplier's lines and are located wholly or partially within 300 feet of the secondary supplier's lines, as such suppliers' lines existed on the determination date, may be served by either the secondary supplier or the primary supplier, whichever the consumer chooses, and no other supplier shall thereafter furnish service to such premises, except with the written consent of the supplier then serving the premises.

(6) Any premises initially requiring electric service after the determination date, which are located only partially within 300 feet of the secondary supplier's lines and are located wholly more than 300 feet from the primary supplier's lines, as such supplier's lines existed on the determination date, may be served either by the secondary supplier or the primary supplier, whichever the consumer chooses, and no other supplier shall thereafter furnish service to such premises, except with the written consent of the supplier then serving the premises.

(6a) Notwithstanding any other provision of law, a secondary supplier, upon obtaining the prior written consent of the city, shall be the exclusive provider of electric service within (i) any assigned area for which that secondary supplier had been assigned supplier prior to the determination date; or (ii) any area previously unassigned by the North Carolina Utilities Commission pursuant to G.S. 62-110.2. However, any rights of other electric suppliers existing under G.S. 62-110.2 prior to the determination date to provide service shall continue to exist without impairment in the areas described in (i) and (ii) above.

(6b) A primary supplier or secondary supplier that, after the determination date, offers to serve any premises initially requiring electric service for which a consumer has a right to choose suppliers under subsections (5) or (6) of this section, without providing the consumer written notice that the consumer may be entitled to choose another electric supplier for the premises, shall not have the right to serve those premises.

(7) Except as provided in subdivisions (1), (2), (3), (5), (6), and (6a) of this section, a secondary supplier shall not furnish electric service within the corporate limits of any city unless it first obtains the written consent of the city and the primary supplier.

(b) In any city that is first incorporated after April 20, 1965, in which, on the effective date of the incorporation, there is more than one supplier of electric service, all suppliers of electric service therein shall continue to have the rights and be subject to the restrictions in effect before the city was incorporated until there is a primary supplier within the city.

(c) It shall be unlawful for a primary supplier or secondary supplier to serve premises within a city that the supplier does not have the right to serve under the provisions of this Article. Upon receiving written notice from another supplier of electric service that has authority to lawfully provide service to the premises in dispute that the provision of service by the current supplier is unlawful, the primary supplier or secondary supplier that is providing electric service shall be obligated to discontinue service and remove all of its facilities used in the provision of the unlawful service within 30 days after substitute electric service can be provided by an electric supplier with authority to lawfully provide service to the premises, unless the supplier currently providing service has a good faith basis for believing it has authority to continue rendering such service. If the primary or secondary supplier is determined to be providing electric services unlawfully, and is found to have unreasonably failed to fulfill its obligation to discontinue service as required above, the supplier of electric service that has authority to lawfully provide service to the premises may bring an action to compel performance of those obligations, and may recover in that action its costs of enforcing this subsection, including its reasonable attorneys' fees.
(1965, c. 287, s. 1; 1971, c. 698, s. 1; 1997-346, s. 2; 1999-111, s. 1; 2003-24, s. 1; 2005-150, ss. 4, 5.)

§ 160A-333. Temporary electric service.

No electric supplier shall furnish temporary electric service for the construction of premises which it would not have the right to serve under this Part if such premises were already constructed. The construction of lines for, and the furnishing of, temporary electric service for the construction of premises which any other electric supplier, if chosen by the consumer, would have the right to serve if such premises were already constructed, shall not impair the right of such other electric supplier to furnish service to such premises after the construction thereof, if then chosen by the consumer; nor, unless the consumer chooses to have such premises served by the supplier that furnished the temporary service, shall the furnishing of such temporary service or the construction of a line therefor impair the right of any other electric supplier to furnish service to any other premises which, without regard to the construction of such temporary service line, it has the right to serve. (1965, c. 287, s. 1; 1971, c. 698, s. 1; 1973, c. 426, s. 53.)

§ 160A-334. Authority and jurisdiction of Utilities Commission.

Notwithstanding G.S. 160A-332 and 160A-333, if the North Carolina Utilities Commission finds that service being furnished to or to be furnished to the consumer by a secondary supplier is or will be inadequate or undependable, or that rates, conditions of service or service regulations, applied to such consumer, are unreasonably discriminatory, the Commission shall have the authority and jurisdiction, after notice to each affected electric supplier, and after hearing, if a hearing is requested by an interested party, to:

(1)   Order a primary supplier that is subject to the jurisdiction of the Commission to furnish electric service to any consumer who desires service from the primary supplier at any premises served by a secondary supplier, or at premises which a secondary supplier has the right to serve pursuant to other sections of this Part, and to order such secondary supplier to cease and desist from furnishing electric service to such premises, or

(2)   Order any secondary supplier to cease and desist from furnishing electric service to any premises being served by it or to any premises which it has the right to serve pursuant to other sections of this Part, if the consumer desires service from a primary supplier that is not subject to the jurisdiction of the Commission and which is willing to furnish service to such premises. (1965, c. 287, s. 1; 1971, c. 698, s. 1; 1973, c. 426, s. 54.)

§ 160A-335. Discontinuance of service and transfer of facilities by secondary supplier.

A secondary supplier may voluntarily discontinue its service to any premises and remove any of its electric facilities located inside the corporate limits of a city or sell and transfer such facilities to a primary supplier in such city, subject to approval by the North Carolina Utilities Commission, if the Commission determines that the public interest will not thereby be adversely affected. (1965, c. 287, s. 1; 1971, c. 698, s. 1.)

§ 160A-336. Electric service for city facilities.

No provisions of this Part shall prevent a city that is a primary supplier from furnishing its own electric service for city facilities, or prevent any other primary supplier from furnishing electric street lighting service to a city inside its corporate limits. (1965, c. 287, s. 1; 1971, c. 698, s. 1.)

§ 160A-337. Effect of Part on rights and duties of primary supplier.

Except for the rights granted to and restrictions upon primary suppliers contained in the provisions of this Part, nothing in this Part shall diminish, enlarge, alter, or affect in any way the rights and duties of a primary supplier to furnish electric service to premises within the corporate limits of a city. (1965, c. 287, s. 1; 1971, c. 698, s. 1.)

§ 160A-338. Electric suppliers subject to police power.

No provisions of this Part shall restrict the exercise of the police power of a city over the erection and maintenance of poles, wires, and other facilities of electric suppliers in streets, alleys, and other public ways. (1965, c. 287, s. 1; 1971, c. 698, s. 1.)

§§ 160A-339 through 160A-340. Reserved for future codification purposes.

Article 16A.

Provision of Communications Service by Cities.

§ 160A-340. Definitions.

The following definitions apply in this Article:

(1) City-owned communications service provider. - A city that provides communications service using a communications network, whether directly, indirectly, or through an interlocal agreement or a joint agency.

(2) Communications network. - A wired or wireless network for the provision of communications service.

(3) Communications service. - The provision of cable, video programming, telecommunications, broadband, or high-speed Internet access service to the public, or any sector of the public, for a fee, regardless of the technology used to deliver the service. The terms "cable service," "telecommunications service," and "video programming service" have the same meanings as in G.S. 105-164.3. The following is not considered the provision of communications service:

a. The sharing of data or voice between governmental entities for internal governmental purposes.

b. The remote reading or polling of data from utility or parking meters, or the provisioning of energy demand reduction or smart grid services for an electric, water, or sewer system.

c. The provision of free services to the public or a subset thereof.

(4) High-speed Internet access service. - Internet access service with transmission speeds that are equal to or greater than the requirements for basic broadband tier 1 service as defined by the Federal Communications Commission for broadband data gathering and reporting.

(5) Interlocal agreement. - An agreement between units of local government as authorized by Part 1 of Article 20 of Chapter 160A of the General Statutes.

(6) Joint agency. - A joint agency created under Part 1 of Article 20 of Chapter 160A of the General Statutes. (2011-84, s. 1(a).)

§ 160A-340.1. City-owned communications service provider requirements.

(a)   A city-owned communications service provider shall meet all of the following requirements:

(1)   Comply in its provision of communications service with all local, State, and federal laws, regulations, or other requirements applicable to the provision of the communications service if provided by a private communications service provider.

(2)   In accordance with the provisions of Chapter 159 of the General Statutes, the Local Government Finance Act, establish one or more separate enterprise funds for the provision of communications service, use the enterprise funds to separately account for revenues, expenses, property, and source of investment dollars associated with the provision of communications service, and prepare and publish an independent annual report and audit in accordance with generally accepted accounting principles that reflect the fully allocated cost of providing the communications service, including all direct and indirect costs. An annual independent audit conducted under G.S. 159-34 and submitted to the Local Government Commission satisfies the audit requirement of this subdivision.

(3)   Limit the provision of communications service to within the corporate limits of the city providing the communications service.

(4)   Shall not, directly or indirectly, under the powers of a city, exercise power or authority in any area, including zoning or land-use regulation, or exercise power to withhold or delay the provision of monopoly utility service, to require any person, including residents of a particular development, to use or subscribe to any communications service provided by the city-owned communications service provider.

(5)   Shall provide nondiscriminatory access to private communications service providers on a first-come, first-served basis to rights-of-way, poles, or conduits owned, leased, or operated by the city unless the facilities have insufficient capacity for the access and additional capacity cannot reasonably be added to the facilities. For purposes of this subdivision, the term "nondiscriminatory access" means that, at a minimum, access shall be granted on the same terms and conditions as that given to a city-owned communications service provider.

(6) Shall not air advertisements or other promotions for the city-owned communications service on a public, educational, or governmental access channel if the city requires another communications service provider to carry the channel. The city shall not use city resources that are not allocated for cost accounting purposes to the city-owned communications service to promote city-owned communications service in comparison to private services or, directly or indirectly, require city employees, officers, or contractors to purchase city services.

(7) Shall not subsidize the provision of communications service with funds from any other noncommunications service, operation, or other revenue source, including any funds or revenue generated from electric, gas, water, sewer, or garbage services.

(8) Shall not price any communications service below the cost of providing the service, including any direct or indirect subsidies received by the city-owned communications service provider and allocation of costs associated with any shared use of buildings, equipment, vehicles, and personnel with other city departments. The city shall, in calculating the costs of providing the communications service, impute (i) the cost of the capital component that is equivalent to the cost of capital available to private communications service providers in the same locality and (ii) an amount equal to all taxes, including property taxes, licenses, fees, and other assessments that would apply to a private communications service provider, including federal, State, and local taxes; rights-of-way, franchise, consent, or administrative fees; and pole attachment fees. In calculating the costs of the service the city may amortize the capital assets of the communications system over the useful life of the assets in accordance with generally accepted principles of governmental accounting.

(9) The city shall annually remit to the general fund of the city an amount equivalent to all taxes or fees a private communications service provider would be required to pay the city or county in which the city is located, including any applicable tax refunds received by the city-owned communications service provider because of its government status and a sum equal to the amount of property tax that would have been due if the city-owned communications service provider were a private communications service provider.

(b) A city-owned communications service provider shall not be required to obtain voter approval under G.S. 160A-321 prior to the sale or discontinuance of the city's communications network. (2011-84, s. 1(a).)

§ 160A-340.2. Exemptions.

(a)   The provisions of G.S. 160A-340.1, 160A-340.4, 160A-340.5, and 160A-340.6 do not apply to the purchase, lease, construction, or operation of facilities by a city to provide communications service within the city's corporate limits for the city's internal governmental purposes, including the sharing of data or voice between governmental entities for internal governmental purposes, or within the corporate limits of another unit of local government that is a party with the city to an interlocal agreement under Part 1 of Article 20 of Chapter 160A of the General Statutes for the provision of internal government services.

(b)   The provisions of G.S. 160A-340.1, 160A-340.4, and 160A-340.5 do not apply to the provision of communications service in an unserved area. A city seeking to provide communications service in an unserved area shall petition the North Carolina Utilities Commission for a determination that an area is unserved. The petition shall identify with specificity the geographic area for which the designation is sought. Any private communications service provider, or any other interested party, may, within a time established by order of the Commission, which time shall be no fewer than 30 days, file with the Commission an objection to the designation on the grounds that one or more areas designated in the petition is not an unserved area or that the city is not otherwise eligible to provide the service. For purposes of this subsection, the term "unserved area" means a census block, as designated by the most recent census of the U.S. Census Bureau, in which at least fifty percent (50%) of households either have no access to high-speed Internet service or have access to high-speed Internet service only from a satellite provider. A city may petition the Commission to serve multiple contiguous unserved areas in the same proceeding.

(c)   The provisions of G.S. 160A-340.1, 160A-340.3, 160A-340.4, 160A-340.5, and 160A-340.6 do not apply to a city or joint agency providing communications service as of January 1, 2011, provided the city or joint agency limits the provision of communications service to any one or more of the following:

(1)   Persons within the corporate limits of the city providing the communications service. For the purposes of this subsection, corporate limits shall mean the corporate limits of the city as of April 1, 2011, or as expanded through annexation.

(2) Existing customers of the communications service as of April 1, 2011. Service to a customer outside the service area of the city or joint agency who is also a public entity must comply with the open bidding procedures of G.S. 143-129.8 upon the expiration or termination of the existing service contract.

(3) The following service areas:

a. For the joint agency operated by the cities of Davidson and Mooresville, the service area is the combined areas of the city of Cornelius; the town of Troutman; the town of Huntersville; the unincorporated areas of Mecklenburg County north of a line beginning at Highway 16 along the west boundary of the county, extending eastward along Highway 16, continuing east along Interstate 485, and continuing eastward to the eastern boundary of the county along Eastfield Road; and the unincorporated areas of Iredell County south of Interstate 40, excluding Statesville and the extraterritorial jurisdiction of Statesville.

b. For the city of Salisbury, the service area is the municipalities of Salisbury, Spencer, East Spencer, Granite Quarry, Rockwell, Faith, Cleveland, China Grove, Landis and the corridors between those cities. The service area also includes the economic development sites, public safety facilities, governmental facilities, and educational schools and colleges located outside the municipalities and the corridors between the municipalities and these sites, facilities, schools, and colleges. The corridors between Salisbury and these municipalities and these sites, facilities, schools, and colleges includes only the area necessary to provide service to these municipalities and these sites, facilities, schools, and colleges and shall not be wider than 300 feet. The elected bodies of Spencer, East Spencer, Granite Quarry, Rockwell, Faith, Cleveland, China Grove, and Landis shall vote to approve the service extension into each respective municipality before Salisbury can provide service to that municipality. The Rowan County Board of County Commissioners shall vote to approve service extension to any governmental economic development site, governmental facility, school, or college owned by Rowan County. The Rowan Salisbury School Board shall also vote to approve service extension to schools.

c. For the city of Wilson, the service area is the county limits of Wilson County, including the incorporated areas within the County.

d. For all other cities or joint agencies offering communications service, the service area is the area designated in the map filed as part of the initial notice of franchise with the Secretary of State as of January 1, 2011.

(d) The exemptions provided in this section do not exempt a city or joint agency from laws and rules of general applicability to governmental services, including nondiscriminatory obligations.

(e) In the event a city subject to the exemption set forth in subsection (c) of this section provides communications service to a customer outside the limits set forth in that subsection, the city shall have 30 days from the date of notice or discovery to cease providing service to the customer without loss of the exemption. (2011-84, s. 1(a).)

§ 160A-340.3. Notice; public hearing.

A city or joint agency that proposes to provide communications service shall hold not fewer than two public hearings, which shall be held not less than 30 days apart, for the purpose of gathering information and comment. Notice of the hearings shall be published at least once a week for four consecutive weeks in the predominant newspaper of general circulation in the area in which the city is located. The notice shall also be provided to the North Carolina Utilities Commission, which shall post the notice on its Web site, and to all companies that have requested service of the notices from the city clerk. The city shall deposit the notice in the U.S. mail to companies that have requested notice at least 45 days prior to the hearing subject to the notice. Private communications service providers shall be permitted to participate fully in the public hearings by presenting testimony and documentation relevant to their service offerings and the city's plans. Any feasibility study, business plan, or public survey conducted or prepared by the city in connection with the proposed communications service project is a public record as defined by G.S. 132-1 and shall be made available to the public prior to the public hearings required by this section. This section does not apply to the repair, rebuilding, replacement, or improvement of an existing communications network, or equipment relating thereto. (2011-84, s. 1(a).)

§ 160A-340.4. Financing.

(a) A city or joint agency subject to the provisions of G.S. 160A-340.1 shall not enter into a contract under G.S. 160A-19 or G.S. 160A-20 to purchase or to finance the purchase of property for use in a communications network or to finance the construction of fixtures or improvements for use in a communications network unless it complies with subsection (b) of this section.

The provisions of this section shall not apply to the repair, rebuilding, replacement, or improvement of an existing communications network, or equipment relating thereto.

(b)   A city shall not incur debt for the purpose of constructing a communications system without first holding a special election under G.S. 163-287 on the question of whether the city may provide communications service. If a majority of the votes cast in the special election are for the city providing communications service, the city may incur the debt for the service. If a majority of the votes cast in the special election are against the city providing communications service, the city shall not incur the debt. However, nothing in this section shall prohibit a city from revising its plan to offer communications service and calling another special election on the question prior to providing or offering to provide the service. A special election required under Chapter 159 of the General Statutes as a condition to the issuance of bonds shall satisfy the requirements of this section. (2011-84, s. 1(a).)

§ 160A-340.5. Taxes; payments in lieu of taxes.

(a)   A communications network owned or operated by a city or joint agency shall be exempt from property taxes. However, each city possessing an ownership share of a communications network and a joint agency owning a communications network shall, in lieu of property taxes, pay to any county authorized to levy property taxes the amount which would be assessed as taxes on real and personal property if the communications network were otherwise subject to valuation and assessment. Any payments in lieu of taxes shall be due and shall bear interest, if unpaid, as in the case of taxes on other property.

(b)   A city-owned communications service provider shall pay to the State, on an annual basis, an amount in lieu of taxes that would otherwise be due the State if the communications service was provided by a private communications service provider, including State income, franchise, vehicle, motor fuel, and other similar taxes. The amount of the payment in lieu of taxes shall be set annually by the Department of Revenue and shall approximate the taxes that would be due if the communications service was undertaken by a private communications service provider. A city-owned communications service provider must provide information requested by the Secretary of Revenue necessary for calculation of the assessment. The Department must inform each city-owned communications service provider of the amount of the assessment by January 1 of each year. The assessment is due by March 15 of each year. If the assessment is unpaid, the State may withhold the amount due, including interest on late payments, from distributions otherwise due the city under G.S. 105-164.44I.

(c) A city-owned communications service provider or a joint agency that provides communications service shall not be eligible for a refund under G.S. 105-164.14(c) for sales and use taxes paid on purchases of tangible personal property and services related to the provision of communications service, except to the extent a private communications service provider would be exempt from taxation. (2011-84, s. 1(a).)

§ 160A-340.6. Public-private partnerships for communications service.

(a) Prior to undertaking to construct a communications network for the provision of communications service, a city shall first solicit proposals from private business in accordance with the procedures of this section.

(b) The city shall issue requests for proposals that specify the nature and scope of the requested communications service, the area in which it is to be provided, any specifications and performance standards, and information as to the city's proposed participation in providing equipment, infrastructure, or other aspects of the service. The city may prescribe the form and content of proposals and may require that proposals contain sufficiently detailed information to allow for an objective evaluation of proposals using the factors stated in subsection (d) of this section. Each proposal shall at minimum contain all of the following:

(1) Information regarding the proposer's experience and qualifications to perform the requirements of the proposal.

(2) Information demonstrating the proposer's ability to secure financing needed to perform the requirements of the proposal.

(3) Information demonstrating the proposer's ability to provide staffing, implement work tasks, and carry out all other responsibilities necessary to perform the requirements of the proposal.

(4) Information clearly identifying and specifying all elements of cost of the proposal for the term of the proposed contract, including the cost of the purchase or lease of equipment and supplies, design, installation, operation, management, and maintenance of any system, and any proposed services.

(5) Any other information the city determines has a material bearing on its ability to evaluate the proposal.

(c) The city shall provide notice that it is requesting proposals in accordance with this subsection. The notice shall state the time and place where plans and specifications for the proposed service may be obtained and the time and place for opening proposals. Any notice given under this subsection shall reserve to the city the right to reject any or all proposals. Notice of request for proposals shall be given by all of the following methods:

(1) By mailing a notice of request for proposals to each firm that has obtained a license or permit to use the public rights-of-way in the city to provide a communications service within the city by depositing such notices in the U.S. mail at least 30 days prior to the date specified for the opening of proposals. In identifying firms, the city may rely upon lists provided by the Office of the Secretary of State and the North Carolina Utilities Commission.

(2) By posting a notice of request for proposals on the city's Web site at least 30 days before the time specified for the opening of proposals.

(3) By publishing a notice of request for proposals in a newspaper of general circulation in the county in which the city is predominantly located at least 30 days before the time specified for the opening of proposals.

(d) In evaluating proposals, the city may consider any relevant factors, including system design, system reliability, operational experience, operational costs, compatibility with existing systems and equipment, and emerging technology. The city may negotiate aspects of any proposal with any responsible proposer with regard to these factors to determine which proposal is the most responsive. A determination of most responsive proposer by the city shall be final.

(e) The city may negotiate a contract with the most responsive proposer for the performance of communications service specified in the request for proposals. All contracts entered into pursuant to this section shall be approved and awarded by the governing body of the city.

(f) If the city is unable to successfully negotiate the terms of a contract with the most responsive proposer within 60 days of the opening of the proposals, the city may proceed to negotiate with the firm determined to be the next most responsive proposer if such a proposer exists. If the city is unable to successfully negotiate the terms of a contract with the next most responsive proposer within 60 days, it may proceed under this Article to provide communications service.

(g) All proposals shall be sealed and shall be opened in public. Provided, that trade secrets shall remain confidential as provided under G.S. 132-1.2. (2011-84, s. 1(a).)

Article 17.

Cemeteries.

§ 160A-341. Authority to establish and operate cemeteries.

A city shall have authority to establish, operate, and maintain cemeteries either inside or outside its corporate limits, may acquire and hold real and personal property for cemetery purposes by gift, purchase, or (for real property) by exercise of the power of eminent domain, may devote any property owned by the city to use as a cemetery, may prohibit burials at any place within the city other than city cemeteries, and may regulate the manner of burial in city cemeteries. Nothing in this section shall confer upon any city authority to prohibit or regulate burials in cemeteries licensed by the State Burial Association Commissioner, or in church cemeteries.

As used in this Article "cemetery" includes columbariums and facilities for cremation. (1917, c. 136, subch. 5, s. 1; 1919, cc. 136, 237; C.S., s. 2787; 1969, c. 402; 1971, c. 698, s. 1.)

§ 160A-342. Authority to transfer cemeteries.

A city may transfer and convey any city cemetery property, together with any accumulated perpetual care trust funds set aside for the maintenance of the cemetery, to any religious organization or cemetery licensed by the State Burial Association Commissioner, upon condition that the transferee will continue use of the property as a cemetery, will perpetually maintain it, and will apply any perpetual care trust funds so transferred only for maintenance of the cemetery. (1917, c. 136, subch. 5, s. 1; 1919, cc. 136, 237; C.S., s. 2787; 1969, c. 402; 1971, c. 698, s. 1.)

§ 160A-343. Authority to abandon cemeteries.

A city shall have authority to abandon any cemetery that has not been used for interment purposes within 10 years. Upon abandonment, all monuments, tombstones, and the contents of all graves within the cemetery shall be transferred at city expense to another city cemetery, or to a cemetery licensed by the State Burial Association Commissioner. After the transfer of monuments, tombstones, and the contents of graves, the city may take possession of, convey, or use the former cemetery property for any lawful purpose. (1917, c. 136, subch. 5, s. 1; 1919, cc. 136, 237; C.S., s. 2787; 1969, c. 402; 1971, c. 698, s. 1.)

§ 160A-344. Authority to assume control of abandoned cemeteries.

(a) Whenever property not under the control or in the possession of any church or religious organization in any city has been heretofore set aside or used for cemetery purposes, and the trustees or owners named in the deed or deeds for the property have died, or are unknown, or the deeds of conveyance have been lost or misplaced and no record of title thereto has been found, and the property has been occupied and used for burial purposes for a time sufficient to identify its use as cemetery property, the city in which the cemetery is located is authorized to take possession of the land and any adjoining land not held by known claimants of title, have the property surveyed and lines established, and to designate and appropriate the property as a city cemetery.

(b) The city may have the land subdivided and laid off into family burial plots, may sell any of the unused lots so laid off to any person for burial purposes, and may use the proceeds of the sale for the improvement and upkeep of the cemetery.

(c) The city may appropriate and use funds for the improvement and maintenance of the cemetery, and all laws and ordinances applicable to city cemeteries shall apply to the cemetery from and after the date that the city assumes control of it. (1971, c. 698, s. 1.)

§ 160A-345. Authority to condemn cemeteries.

A city shall have authority to acquire title in fee simple by purchase or exercise of the power of eminent domain to any cemetery, graveyard, or burial place within the city and to operate and maintain the property so acquired as a city cemetery. This section shall not apply to a cemetery licensed by the North Carolina State Burial Association Commissioner, nor to property owned or controlled by any church or religious organization, unless the owner of the property consents to the acquisition. (1951, c. 385, s. 1; 1971, c. 698, s. 1.)

§ 160A-346. Authority to condemn easements for perpetual care.

A city shall have authority to acquire an easement for perpetual care by gift, grant, purchase, or exercise of the power of eminent domain in any cemetery, graveyard, or burial place within the city. When a perpetual care easement is acquired under this section, all city ordinances concerning the care and upkeep of city cemeteries shall be applicable to the cemetery, and the income from city perpetual care trust funds may be used to care for and maintain the cemetery. This section shall not apply to a cemetery licensed by the North Carolina State Burial Association Commissioner or to property owned or controlled by any church or religious organization unless the owner of the property consents to the acquisition. (1951, c. 385, s. 2; 1971, c. 698, s. 1.)

§ 160A-347. Perpetual care trust funds.

(a) A city is authorized to create a perpetual care trust fund for any cemeteries under its ownership or control, to accept gifts, grants, and devises on behalf of the perpetual care trust fund, to deposit any revenues realized from the sale of lots in or the operation of city cemeteries in the perpetual care trust fund, and to hold and administer the trust fund for the purpose of perpetually caring for and beautifying the city's cemeteries. The city may make contracts with the owners of plots in city cemeteries obligating the city to maintain the plots in perpetuity upon payment of such sums as the council may fix.

(b) The principal of perpetual care trust funds shall be held intact, and the income from such funds shall be used to carry out contracts with plot owners for the perpetual care of the plots, and to maintain and perpetually care for the cemetery.

(c) Perpetual care trust funds shall be kept separate and apart from all other city funds, and shall in no case be appropriated by, lent to, or in any manner used by the city for any purpose other than the perpetual care of city cemeteries. (1917, c. 136, subch. 9, s. 1; C.S., ss. 2810, 2811, 2812; 1927, c. 254; 1971, c. 698, s. 1; 2011-284, s. 113.)

§ 160A-348. Regulation of city cemeteries.

A city may by ordinance adopt rules and regulations concerning the opening of graves, the erection of tombstones and monuments, the building of walls and fences, the hours of opening and closing and all other matters concerning the use, operation, and maintenance of city cemeteries. The ordinance may impose a schedule of prices for lots and fees for the opening of graves in the cemetery, but it may not require the owners of plots to purchase monuments, vaults, or other items from the city. (1971, c. 698, s. 1.)

§ 160A-349. Reserved for future codification purposes.

Article 17A.

Cemetery Trustees.

§ 160A-349.1. Creation of board authorized; official title; terms of office; vacancies.

The governing body of any municipal corporation which now owns or shall hereafter own a cemetery is authorized, if it is deemed proper, to create a board composed of not less than three nor more than five persons, to be known as "Cemetery Trustees of the Town or City of_____, North Carolina"; shall fix the term of office of each member, in no case to exceed five years, and in case of any vacancy by death, resignation or otherwise, elect a successor. (Pub. Loc. 1923, c. 583, s. 1.)

§ 160A-349.2. Members to meet and organize; meetings; bond of secretary and treasurer; record of proceedings.

The members of said board, when properly elected, shall within 30 days after notice of their election convene and designate one of their number chairman, one secretary and treasurer, and provide for regular meetings at such times as the said board shall fix; it shall also fix the bond to be given by the secretary and treasurer, conditioned for the faithful accounting of all moneys which shall come into his hands; shall provide for special meetings, and shall cause the secretary to keep a record of its proceedings. (Pub. Loc. 1923, c. 583, s. 2.)

§ 160A-349.3. Property vested.

Upon the creation of such board the title to all property held by the town or city and used for cemetery purposes shall pass to and vest in said board, subject to the same limitations, conditions and restrictions as it was held by the town or city; provided, that the governing body of the town or city may at any time by resolution direct that title to such property shall pass to and vest in the town or city itself, and in such event it shall be the duty of the board and its officers to execute all necessary documents to effect such transfer and vesting. (Pub. Loc. 1923, c. 583, s. 3; 1979, 2nd Sess., c. 1247, s. 30.)

§ 160A-349.4. Control and management; superintendent and assistants; enumeration of powers.

The said board shall have the exclusive control and management of such cemetery; shall have the power to employ a superintendent and such assistants as may be needed, and may do any and all things pertaining to the control, maintenance, management and upkeep of the cemetery which the governing body of the town or city could have done, or which by law the governing body of the town or city shall hereafter be authorized to do. (Pub. Loc. 1923, c. 583, s. 4.)

§ 160A-349.5. Rules continued in force.

All rules and regulations heretofore adopted by the town or city for the control, upkeep, management, and maintenance, as well as policing of the cemetery, shall continue in force and effect until and after the said board shall have changed the same as herein provided for. (Pub. Loc. 1923, c. 583, s. 5.)

§ 160A-349.6. Rules for maintaining order and policing; force of rules; copy to governing body; publication.

The said board shall have power to adopt rules and regulations for maintaining order in the cemetery and policing the same, and such rules and regulations, when adopted, shall have the same force and effect as ordinances adopted and passed by the governing body of the town or city. When any such rules and regulations shall be adopted the secretary of the board shall transmit a copy thereof to the governing body of the town or city, and shall cause a copy to be published in some newspaper published in the town or city, and the said rules and regulations shall be in force and effect 10 days after their publication. (Pub. Loc. 1923, c. 583, s. 6.)

§ 160A-349.7. Presentation of budget; details of budget; appropriation; payment to board.

Thirty days prior to the adoption of the annual budget by the governing body of the town or city, the said trustees shall present to such governing body a budget for the ensuing year, in which said budget there shall be set out in detail an accurate account of the receipts and expenditures of the board for the previous year, the estimated expense for the ensuing year, the estimated source of income from all sources, other than appropriation by the governing body of the town or city, any balance on hand, and such other information as the said trustees may think proper; and the said governing body of the town or city shall in the annual budget include such appropriation as it deems proper for the care and maintenance of the said cemetery for the ensuing year, which shall be paid over to the board of trustees in monthly installments.

For purposes of the Local Government Budget and Fiscal Control Act (Chapter 159, Subchapter III), the board of trustees of a cemetery is a board of the municipal corporation establishing the board of trustees and is not a public authority as defined by G.S. 159-7. (Pub. Loc. 1923, c. 583, s. 7; 1971, c. 780, s. 37.3; 1973, c. 474, s. 31; 1979, 2nd Sess., c. 1247, s. 31.)

§ 160A-349.8. Commissioners to obtain maps, plats and deeds; list of lots sold and owners; surveys and plats to be made; additional lots, streets, walks and parkways; price of lots; regulation of sale of lots.

The board of trustees shall obtain from the governing body all maps, plats, deeds and other evidences relating to the lands, lots and property of the cemetery; they shall also obtain from the governing body of the town or city, as nearly as possible, an accurate list of the lots theretofore sold, together with the names of the owners thereof. The said board of trustees shall from time to time cause surveys to be made, maps and plats prepared, laying out additional lots, streets, paths, walks and parkways; shall fix a price at which such lots shall be sold, which price may from time to time, in the discretion of the board, be changed; shall adopt rules and regulations as to the sale of said lots and deliver to the purchaser or purchasers deed or evidences of title thereto. (Pub. Loc. 1923, c. 583, s. 8.)

§ 160A-349.9. Power to acquire land; adjacent property; disposal of money from lot sales; investments; income from investment.

The said board shall have the power to acquire additional lands for cemetery purposes, either by purchase or otherwise. In making such additional acquisitions of property, if possible, they shall acquire adjacent property; all moneys received from the sale of lots shall be held by the board of trustees intact and used for the purchase of additional lands; to beautify and otherwise maintain and keep the present property and the future acquired property. The board may, if it seems best to it, invest the said money in good, interest-bearing securities, payable to the said board, and the income derived therefrom shall be by the board used in the beautifying, maintenance and upkeep of the cemetery or cemeteries under its control. (Pub. Loc. 1923, c. 583, s. 9.)

§ 160A-349.10. Power to condemn land; procedure for condemnation; board incorporated.

If it becomes necessary to acquire additional lands for cemetery purposes and the board cannot agree with the owners upon the price thereof, the board shall have the power to condemn the lands for cemetery purposes, and in so doing the provisions of Chapter 40A of the General Statutes shall be followed as nearly as possible, and to that end, and for that purpose, the board of trustees of any cemetery acquired under this Article shall be deemed and considered a corporation and a body politic. (Pub. Loc. 1923, c. 583, s. 10; 2001-487, s. 38(i).)

§ 160A-349.11. Price of lands included in budget.

If any lands are acquired by purchase or condemnation for cemetery purposes and the board of trustees shall not have sufficient funds with which to pay for the same, the amount necessary shall be included in their budget request, and the governing body of any town or city may make an appropriation to complete the purchase. (Pub. Loc. 1923, c. 583, s. 11; 1979, 2nd Sess., c. 1247, s. 32.)

§ 160A-349.12. Power to accept gifts; exclusive use of gifts.

The board of trustees of any cemetery shall have the power to accept gifts, either by devise or otherwise, and hold the same for the purposes expressed in the gift, and any monies coming into the hands of such board by devise or otherwise shall be by the board used exclusively for the purposes for which it is given. (Pub. Loc. 1923, c. 583, s. 12; 2011-284, s. 114.)

§ 160A-349.13. Sale of unnecessary property.

The board of trustees of any cemetery, created pursuant to this Article, shall have the power to sell at public auction, as provided by G.S. 160-59, any real property, title to which is held by it, which it shall determine to be unfit or unnecessary for cemetery purposes, except when such sale would violate the terms of any deed, gift or trust pursuant to which the property proposed to be sold was acquired. Any such sales and conveyances heretofore made by any such board of trustees are hereby validated. (1951, c. 87.)

§ 160A-349.14. Exercise of powers subject to approval.

The board may not act to acquire or sell land pursuant to G.S. 160A-349.9, G.S. 160A-349.10, or G.S. 160A-349.13 unless such action was approved in advance by the governing body of the town or city. (1979, 2nd Sess., c. 1247, s. 33.)

§ 160A-349.15. Termination.

The governing body of the town or city shall have the authority to terminate the existence of the board at any time. In the event of such termination, all property and assets of the board shall automatically become the property of the town or city and the town or city shall succeed to all rights, obligations and liabilities of the board. Further, in the event of such termination, it shall be the duty of the board and its officers to execute all necessary documents to effect the transfer of property and assets to the town or city. (1979, 2nd Sess., c. 1247, s. 34.)

Article 18.

Parks and Recreation.

§ 160A-350. Short title.

This Article shall be known and may be cited as the "Recreation Enabling Law." (1945, c. 1052; 1971, c. 698, s. 1.)

§ 160A-351. Declaration of State policy.

The lack of adequate recreational programs and facilities is a menace to the morals, happiness, and welfare of the people of this State. Making available recreational opportunities for citizens of all ages is a subject of general interest and concern, and a function requiring appropriate action by both State and local government. The General Assembly therefore declares that the public good and the general welfare of the citizens of this State require adequate recreation programs, that the creation, establishment, and operation of parks and recreation programs is a proper governmental function, and that it is the policy of North Carolina to forever encourage, foster, and provide these facilities and programs for all its citizens. (1945, c. 1052; 1971, c. 698, s. 1.)

§ 160A-352. Recreation defined.

"Recreation" means activities that are diversionary in character and aid in promoting entertainment, pleasure, relaxation, instruction, and other physical, mental, and cultural development and leisure time experiences. (1945, c. 1052; 1971, c. 698, s. 1.)

§ 160A-353. Powers.

In addition to any other powers it may possess to provide for the general welfare of its citizens, each county and city in this State shall have authority to:

(1)   Establish and conduct a system of supervised recreation;

(2)   Set apart lands and buildings for parks, playgrounds, recreational centers, and other recreational programs and facilities;

(3)   Acquire real property, either within or without the corporate limits of the city or the boundaries of the county, including water and air rights, for parks and recreation programs and facilities by gift, grant, purchase, lease, exercise of the power of eminent domain, or any other lawful method.

(4)   Provide, acquire, construct, equip, operate, and maintain parks, playgrounds, recreation centers, and recreation facilities, including all buildings, structures, and equipment necessary or useful in connection therewith;

(5)   Appropriate funds to carry out the provisions of this Article;

(6)   Accept any gift, grant, lease, loan, or devise of real or personal property for parks and recreation programs. Devises and gifts may be accepted and held subject to such terms and conditions as may be imposed by the grantor or trustor, except that no county or city may accept or administer any terms that require it to discriminate among its citizens on the basis of race, sex, or religion. (1945, c. 1052; 1971, c. 698, s. 1; 1973, c. 426, s. 55; 2011-284, s. 115.)

§ 160A-354. Administration of parks and recreation programs.

A city or county may operate a parks and recreation system as a line department, or it may create a parks and recreation commission and vest in it authority to operate the parks and recreation system. (1945, c. 1052; 1971, c. 698, s. 1.)

§ 160A-355. Joint parks and recreation systems.

Any two or more units of local government may cooperate in establishing parks and recreation systems as authorized in Article 20, Part 1, of this Chapter. (1945, c. 1052; 1967, c. 1228; 1971, c. 698, s. 1.)

§ 160A-356. Financing parks and recreation.

Each county and city is authorized to expend for its parks and recreation system any of its revenues not otherwise limited as to use by law. (1945, c. 1052; 1971, c. 698, s. 1; 1975, c. 664, s. 12.)

§ 160A-357. Repealed by Session Laws 1975, c. 664, s. 13.

§ 160A-358. Reserved for future codification purposes.

§ 160A-359. Reserved for future codification purposes.

Article 19.

Planning and Regulation of Development.

Part 1. General Provisions.

§ 160A-360. Territorial jurisdiction.

(a)   All of the powers granted by this Article may be exercised by any city within its corporate limits. In addition, any city may exercise these powers within a defined area extending not more than one mile beyond its limits. With the approval of the board or boards of county commissioners with jurisdiction over the area, a city of 10,000 or more population but less than 25,000 may exercise these powers over an area extending not more than two miles beyond its limits and a city of 25,000 or more population may exercise these powers over an area extending not more than three miles beyond its limits. The boundaries of the city's extraterritorial jurisdiction shall be the same for all powers conferred in this Article. No city may exercise extraterritorially any power conferred by this Article that it is not exercising within its corporate limits. In determining the population of a city for the purposes of this Article, the city council and the board of county commissioners may use the most recent annual estimate of population as certified by the Secretary of the North Carolina Department of Administration.

(a1)   Any municipality planning to exercise extraterritorial jurisdiction under this Article shall notify the owners of all parcels of land proposed for addition to the area of extraterritorial jurisdiction, as shown on the county tax records. The notice shall be sent by first-class mail to the last addresses listed for affected property owners in the county tax records. The notice shall inform the landowner of the effect of the extension of extraterritorial jurisdiction, of the landowner's right to participate in a public hearing prior to adoption of any ordinance extending the area of extraterritorial jurisdiction, as provided in G.S. 160A-364, and the right of all residents of the area to apply to the board of county commissioners to serve as a representative on the planning board and the board of adjustment, as provided in G.S. 160A-362. The notice shall be mailed at least four weeks prior to the public hearing. The person or persons mailing the notices shall certify to the city council that the notices were sent by first-class mail, and the certificate shall be deemed conclusive in the absence of fraud.

(b)   Any council wishing to exercise extraterritorial jurisdiction under this Article shall adopt, and may amend from time to time, an ordinance specifying the areas to be included based upon existing or projected urban development and areas of critical concern to the city, as evidenced by officially adopted plans for its development. Boundaries shall be defined, to the extent feasible, in terms of geographical features identifiable on the ground. A council may, in its discretion, exclude from its extraterritorial jurisdiction areas lying in another county, areas separated from the city by barriers to urban growth, or areas whose projected development will have minimal impact on the city. The boundaries specified in the ordinance shall at all times be drawn on a map, set forth in a written description, or shown by a combination of these techniques. This delineation shall be maintained in the manner provided in G.S. 160A-22 for the delineation of the corporate limits, and shall be recorded in the office of the register of deeds of each county in which any portion of the area lies.

(c)   Where the extraterritorial jurisdiction of two or more cities overlaps, the jurisdictional boundary between them shall be a line connecting the midway points of the overlapping area unless the city councils agree to another boundary line within the overlapping area based upon existing or projected patterns of development.

(d)   If a city fails to adopt an ordinance specifying the boundaries of its extraterritorial jurisdiction, the county of which it is a part shall be authorized to exercise the powers granted by this Article in any area beyond the city's corporate limits. The county may also, on request of the city council, exercise any or all these powers in any or all areas lying within the city's corporate limits or within the city's specified area of extraterritorial jurisdiction.

(e)   No city may hereafter extend its extraterritorial powers under this Article into any area for which the county at that time has adopted and is enforcing a zoning ordinance and subdivision regulations and within which it is enforcing the State Building Code. However, the city may do so where the county is not exercising all three of these powers, or when the city and the county have agreed upon the area within which each will exercise the powers conferred by this Article.

(f)   When a city annexes, or a new city is incorporated in, or a city extends its jurisdiction to include, an area that is currently being regulated by the county, the county regulations and powers of enforcement shall remain in effect until (i) the city has adopted such regulations, or (ii) a period of 60 days has elapsed following the annexation, extension or incorporation, whichever is sooner. During this period the city may hold hearings and take any other measures that may be required in order to adopt its regulations for the area.

(f1)   When a city relinquishes jurisdiction over an area that it is regulating under this Article to a county, the city regulations and powers of enforcement shall remain in effect until (i) the county has adopted this regulation or (ii) a period of 60 days has elapsed following the action by which the city relinquished jurisdiction, whichever is sooner. During this period the county may hold hearings and take other measures that may be required in order to adopt its regulations for the area.

(g)   When a local government is granted powers by this section subject to the request, approval, or agreement of another local government, the request, approval, or agreement shall be evidenced by a formally adopted resolution of that government's legislative body. Any such request, approval, or agreement can be rescinded upon two years' written notice to the other legislative bodies concerned by repealing the resolution. The resolution may be modified at any time by mutual agreement of the legislative bodies concerned.

(h)   Nothing in this section shall repeal, modify, or amend any local act which defines the boundaries of a city's extraterritorial jurisdiction by metes and bounds or courses and distances.

(i)   Whenever a city or county, pursuant to this section, acquires jurisdiction over a territory that theretofore has been subject to the jurisdiction of another local government, any person who has acquired vested rights under a permit, certificate, or other evidence of compliance issued by the local government surrendering jurisdiction may exercise those rights as if no change of jurisdiction had occurred. The city or county acquiring jurisdiction may take any action regarding such a permit, certificate, or other evidence of compliance that could have been taken by the local government surrendering jurisdiction pursuant to its ordinances and regulations. Except as provided in this subsection, any building, structure, or other land use in a territory over which a city or county has acquired jurisdiction is subject to the ordinances and regulations of the city or county.

(j)   Repealed by Session Laws 1973, c. 669, s. 1.

(k)   As used in this subsection, "bona fide farm purposes" is as described in G.S. 153A-340. As used in this subsection, "property" means a single tract of property or an identifiable portion of a single tract. Property that is located in the geographic area of a municipality's extraterritorial jurisdiction and that is used for bona fide farm purposes is exempt from exercise of the municipality's extraterritorial jurisdiction under this Article. Property that is located in the geographic area of a municipality's extraterritorial jurisdiction and that ceases to be used for bona fide farm purposes shall become subject to exercise of the municipality's extraterritorial jurisdiction under this Article.

(l)   A municipality may provide in its zoning ordinance that an accessory building of a "bona fide farm" as defined by G.S. 153A-340(b) has the same exemption from the building code as it would have under county zoning as provided by Part 3 of Article 18 of Chapter 153A of the General Statutes.

This subsection applies only to the City of Raleigh and the Towns of Apex, Cary, Fuquay-Varina, Garner, Holly Springs, Knightdale, Morrisville, Rolesville, Wake Forest, Wendell, and Zebulon. (1959, c. 1204; 1961, c. 103; c. 548, ss. 1, 13/4; c. 1217; 1963, cc. 519, 889, 1076, 1105; 1965, c. 121; c. 348, s. 2; c. 450, s. 1; c. 864, ss. 3-6; 1967, cc. 15, 22, 149; c. 197, s. 2; cc. 246, 685; c. 1208, s. 3; 1969, cc. 11, 53; c. 1010, s. 5; c. 1099; 1971, c. 698, s. 1; c. 1076, s. 3; 1973, c. 426, s. 56; c. 525; c. 669, s. 1; 1977, c. 882; c. 912, ss. 2, 4; 1995 (Reg. Sess., 1996), c. 746, s. 1; 2005-418, s. 10; 2011-34, ss. 1, 2; 2011-363, s. 4.)

§ 160A-361. Planning boards.

(a)   Any city may by ordinance create or designate one or more boards or commissions to perform the following duties:

(1)   Make studies of the area within its jurisdiction and surrounding areas;

(2)   Determine objectives to be sought in the development of the study area;

(3) Prepare and adopt plans for achieving these objectives;

(4) Develop and recommend policies, ordinances, administrative procedures, and other means for carrying out plans in a coordinated and efficient manner;

(5) Advise the council concerning the use and amendment of means for carrying out plans;

(6) Exercise any functions in the administration and enforcement of various means for carrying out plans that the council may direct;

(7) Perform any other related duties that the council may direct.

(b) A board or commission created or designated pursuant to this section may include, but shall not be limited to, one or more of the following:

(1) A planning board or commission of any size (with not fewer than three members) or composition deemed appropriate, organized in any manner deemed appropriate;

(2) A joint planning board created by two or more local governments pursuant to Article 20, Part 1, of this Chapter. (1919, c. 23, s. 1; C.S., s. 2643; 1945, c. 1040, s. 2; 1955, cc. 489, 1252; 1959, c. 327, s. 2; c. 390; 1971, c. 698, s. 1; 1973, c. 426, s. 57; 1979, 2nd Sess., c. 1247, s. 35; 1997-309, s. 7; 1997-456, s. 27; 2004-199, s. 41(a).)

§ 160A-362. Extraterritorial representation.

When a city elects to exercise extraterritorial zoning or subdivision-regulation powers under G.S. 160A-360, it shall in the ordinance creating or designating its planning board provide a means of proportional representation based on population for residents of the extraterritorial area to be regulated. Representation shall be provided by appointing at least one resident of the entire extraterritorial zoning and subdivision regulation area to the planning board and the board of adjustment that makes recommendations or grants relief in these matters. For purposes of this section, an additional member must be appointed to the planning board or board of adjustment to achieve proportional representation only when the population of the entire extraterritorial zoning and subdivision area constitutes a full fraction of the municipality's population divided by the total membership of the planning board or board of adjustment. Membership of joint municipal county planning agencies or boards of adjustment may be appointed as agreed by counties and municipalities. Any advisory board established prior to July 1, 1983, to provide the required extraterritorial representation shall constitute compliance with this section until the board is abolished by ordinance of the city. The representatives on the planning board and the board of adjustment shall be appointed by the board of county commissioners with jurisdiction over the area. When selecting a new representative to the planning board or to the board of adjustment as a result of an extension of the extraterritorial jurisdiction, the board of county commissioners shall hold a public hearing on the selection. A notice of the hearing shall be given once a week for two successive calendar weeks in a newspaper having general circulation in the area. The board of county commissioners shall select appointees only from those who apply at or before the public hearing. The county shall make the appointments within 45 days following the public hearing. Once a city provides proportional representation, no power available to a city under G.S. 160A-360 shall be ineffective in its extraterritorial area solely because county appointments have not yet been made. If there is an insufficient number of qualified residents of the area to meet membership requirements, the board of county commissioners may appoint as many other residents of the county as necessary to make up the requisite number. When the extraterritorial area extends into two or more counties, each board of county commissioners concerned shall appoint representatives from its portion of the area, as specified in the ordinance. If a board of county commissioners fails to make these appointments within 90 days after receiving a resolution from the city council requesting that they be made, the city council may make them. If the ordinance so provides, the outside representatives may have equal rights, privileges, and duties with the other members of the board to which they are appointed, regardless of whether the matters at issue arise within the city or within the extraterritorial area; otherwise they shall function only with respect to matters within the extraterritorial area. (1959, c. 1204; 1961, c. 103; c. 548, ss. 1, 13/4; c. 1217; 1963, cc. 519, 889, 1076, 1105; 1965, c. 121; c. 348, s. 2; c. 450, s. 1; c. 864, ss. 3-6; 1967, cc. 15, 22, 149; c. 197, s. 2; cc. 246, 685; c. 1208, s. 3; 1969, cc. 11, 53; c. 1010, s. 5; c. 1099; 1971, c. 698, s. 1; 1983, c. 584, ss. 1-4; 1995 (Reg. Sess., 1996), c. 746, s. 2; 2005-418, s. 11.)

§ 160A-363. Supplemental powers.

(a) A city or its designated planning board may accept, receive, and disburse in furtherance of its functions any funds, grants, and services made available by the federal government and its agencies, the State government and its agencies, any local government and its agencies, and any private and civic sources. Any city, or its designated planning board with the concurrence of the council, may enter into and carry out contracts with the State and federal governments or any agencies thereof under which financial or other planning assistance is made available to the city and may agree to and comply with any reasonable conditions that are imposed upon such assistance.

(b) Any city, or its designated planning board with the concurrence of the council, may enter into and carry out contracts with any other city, county, or regional council or planning agency under which it agrees to furnish technical planning assistance to the other local government or planning agency. Any city, or its designated planning board with the concurrence of its council, may enter into and carry out contracts with any other city, county, or regional council or planning agency under which it agrees to pay the other local government or planning board for technical planning assistance.

(c) Any city council is authorized to make any appropriations that may be necessary to carry out any activities or contracts authorized by this Article or to support, and compensate members of, any planning board that it may create pursuant to this Article, and to levy taxes for these purposes as a necessary expense.

(d) A city may elect to combine any of the ordinances authorized by this Article into a unified ordinance. Unless expressly provided otherwise, a city may apply any of the definitions and procedures authorized by law to any or all aspects of the unified ordinance and may employ any organizational structure, board, commission, or staffing arrangement authorized by law to any or all aspects of the ordinance.

(e) If the city is found to have illegally exacted a tax, fee, or monetary contribution for development or a development permit not specifically authorized by law, the city shall return the tax, fee, or monetary contribution plus interest of six percent (6%) per annum. (1919, c. 23, s. 1; C.S., s. 2643; 1945, c. 1040, s. 2; 1955, cc. 489, 1252; 1959, c. 327, s. 2; c. 390; 1971, c. 698, s. 1; 1983, c. 377, s. 9; 2004-199, s. 41(b); 2005-418, s. 1(a); 2007-371, s. 2.)

§ 160A-364. Procedure for adopting, amending, or repealing ordinances under Article.

(a) Before adopting, amending, or repealing any ordinance authorized by this Article, the city council shall hold a public hearing on it. A notice of the public hearing shall be given once a week for two successive calendar weeks in a newspaper having general circulation in the area. The notice shall be published the first time not less than 10 days nor more than 25 days before the date fixed for the hearing. In computing such period, the day of publication is not to be included but the day of the hearing shall be included.

(b) If the adoption or modification of the ordinance would result in any of the changes listed in this subsection and those changes would be located five miles or less from the perimeter boundary of a military base, the governing body of the local government shall provide written notice of the proposed changes by certified mail, or by any other written means reasonably designed to provide actual notice, to the commander of the military base or the commander's designee not less than 10 days nor more than 25 days before the date fixed for the public hearing. Prior to the date of the public hearing, the military may provide comments or analysis to the board [governing body of the local government] regarding the compatibility of the proposed changes with military operations at the base. If the board [governing body of the local government] does not receive a response within 30 days of the notice, the military is deemed to waive the comment period. If the military provides comments or analysis regarding the compatibility of the proposed ordinance or amendment with military operations at the base, the governing body of the local government shall take the comments and analysis into consideration before making a final determination on the ordinance. The proposed changes requiring notice are:

(1) Changes to the zoning map.

(2) Changes that affect the permitted uses of land.

(3) Changes relating to telecommunications towers or windmills.

(4) Changes to proposed new major subdivision preliminary plats.

(5) An increase in the size of an approved subdivision by more than fifty percent (50%) of the subdivision's total land area including developed and undeveloped land. (1923, c. 250, s. 4; C.S., s. 2776(u); 1927, c. 90; 1955, c. 1334, s. 1; 1971, c. 698, s. 1; 1973, c. 426, s. 58; 1977, c. 912, s. 5; 1979, 2nd

Sess., c. 1247, s. 36; 1981, c. 891, s. 1; 2004-75, s. 2; 2005-426, s. 1(a); 2013-59, s. 2.)

§ 160A-364.1. Statute of limitations.

(a) A cause of action as to the validity of any ordinance adopting or amending a zoning map or approving a special use, conditional use, or conditional zoning district request adopted under this Article or other applicable law shall accrue upon adoption of such ordinance and shall be brought within two months as provided in G.S. 1-54.1.

(b) Except as otherwise provided in subsection (a) of this section, an action challenging the validity of any zoning or unified development ordinance or any provision thereof adopted under this Article or other applicable law shall be brought within one year of the accrual of such action. Such an action accrues when the party bringing such action first has standing to challenge the ordinance. A challenge to an ordinance on the basis of an alleged defect in the adoption process shall be brought within three years after the adoption of the ordinance.

(c) Nothing in this section or in G.S. 1-54(10) or G.S. 1-54.1 shall bar a party in an action involving the enforcement of a zoning or unified development ordinance from raising as a defense to such enforcement action the invalidity of the ordinance. Nothing in this section or in G.S. 1-54(10) or G.S. 1-54.1 shall bar a party who files a timely appeal from an order, requirement, decision, or determination made by an administrative official contending that such party is in violation of a zoning or unified development ordinance from raising in the appeal the invalidity of such ordinance as a defense to such order, requirement, decision, or determination. A party in an enforcement action or appeal may not assert the invalidity of the ordinance on the basis of an alleged defect in the adoption process unless the defense is formally raised within three years of the adoption of the challenged ordinance.

(d) When a use constituting a violation of a zoning or unified development ordinance is in existence prior to adoption of the zoning or unified development ordinance creating the violation, and that use is grandfathered and subsequently terminated for any reason, a city shall bring an enforcement action within 10 years of the date of the termination of the grandfathered status, unless the violation poses an imminent hazard to health or public safety. (1981, c. 891, s.

3; 1995 (Reg. Sess., 1996), c. 746, s. 7; 2011-326, s. 22(b); 2011-384, s. 4; 2013-413, s. 5(b).)

§ 160A-365. Enforcement of ordinances.

Subject to the provisions of the ordinance, any ordinance adopted pursuant to authority conferred by this Article may be enforced by any remedy provided by G.S. 160A-175. (1971, c. 698, s. 1.)

§ 160A-366. Validation of ordinance.

Any city ordinance regularly adopted before January 1, 1972, under authority of general laws revised and reenacted in Chapter 160A, Article 19, or under authority of any city charter or local act concerning the same subject matter, is validated with respect to its application within the corporate limits of the city and as to its application within the extraterritorial jurisdiction of the city. Such an ordinance, and any city ordinance adopted since January 1, 1972, under authority of general laws revised and reenacted in Chapter 160A, Article 19, are hereby validated, notwithstanding the fact that such ordinances were not recorded pursuant to G.S. 160A-360(b) or 160A-364 and notwithstanding the fact that the adopting city council did not also adopt an ordinance defining or delineating by specific description the areas within its extraterritorial jurisdiction pursuant to G.S. 160A-360; provided that this act shall be deemed to validate ordinances of cities in Mecklenburg County only with respect to their application within the corporate limits of such cities. (1973, c. 669, s. 2.)

§§ 160A-367 through 160A-370. Reserved for future codification purposes.

Part 2. Subdivision Regulation.

§ 160A-371. Subdivision regulation.

A city may by ordinance regulate the subdivision of land within its territorial jurisdiction. In addition to final plat approval, the ordinance may include provisions for review and approval of sketch plans and preliminary plats. The ordinance may provide for different review procedures for differing classes of subdivisions. The ordinance may be adopted as part of a unified development ordinance or as a separate subdivision ordinance. Decisions on approval or denial of preliminary or final plats may be made only on the basis of standards explicitly set forth in the subdivision or unified development ordinance. Whenever the ordinance includes criteria for decision that require application of judgment, those criteria must provide adequate guiding standards for the entity charged with plat approval. (1955, c. 1334, s. 1; 1971, c. 698, s. 1; 2005-418, s. 2(a).)

§ 160A-372. Contents and requirements of ordinance.

(a)   A subdivision control ordinance may provide for the orderly growth and development of the city; for the coordination of transportation networks and utilities within proposed subdivisions with existing or planned streets and highways and with other public facilities; for the dedication or reservation of recreation areas serving residents of the immediate neighborhood within the subdivision or, alternatively, for provision of funds to be used to acquire recreation areas serving residents of the development or subdivision or more than one subdivision or development within the immediate area, and rights-of-way or easements for street and utility purposes including the dedication of rights-of-way pursuant to G.S. 136-66.10 or G.S. 136-66.11; and for the distribution of population and traffic in a manner that will avoid congestion and overcrowding and will create conditions that substantially promote public health, safety, and the general welfare.

(b)   The ordinance may require a plat be prepared, approved, and recorded pursuant to the provisions of the ordinance whenever any subdivision of land takes place. The ordinance may include requirements that plats show sufficient data to determine readily and reproduce accurately on the ground the location, bearing, and length of every street and alley line, lot line, easement boundary line, and other property boundaries, including the radius and other data for curved property lines, to an appropriate accuracy and in conformance with good surveying practice.

(c)   The ordinance may provide for the more orderly development of subdivisions by requiring the construction of community service facilities in accordance with municipal plans, policies, and standards. To assure compliance with these and other ordinance requirements, the ordinance may provide for performance guarantees to assure successful completion of required improvements. If a performance guarantee is required, the city shall provide a range of options of types of performance guarantees, including, but not limited to, surety bonds or letters of credit, from which the developer may choose. For any specific development, the type of performance guarantee from the range specified by the city shall be at the election of the developer.

The ordinance may provide for the reservation of school sites in accordance with comprehensive land use plans approved by the council or the planning board. In order for this authorization to become effective, before approving such plans the council or planning board and the board of education with jurisdiction over the area shall jointly determine the specific location and size of any school sites to be reserved, which information shall appear in the comprehensive land use plan. Whenever a subdivision is submitted for approval which includes part or all of a school site to be reserved under the plan, the council or planning board shall immediately notify the board of education and the board of education shall promptly decide whether it still wishes the site to be reserved. If the board of education does not wish to reserve the site, it shall so notify the council or planning board and no site shall be reserved. If the board of education does wish to reserve the site, the subdivision shall not be approved without such reservation. The board of education shall then have 18 months beginning on the date of final approval of the subdivision within which to acquire the site by purchase or by initiating condemnation proceedings. If the board of education has not purchased or begun proceedings to condemn the site within 18 months, the subdivider may treat the land as freed of the reservation.

The ordinance may provide that a developer may provide funds to the city whereby the city may acquire recreational land or areas to serve the development or subdivision, including the purchase of land that may be used to serve more than one subdivision or development within the immediate area. All funds received by the city pursuant to this paragraph shall be used only for the acquisition or development of recreation, park, or open space sites. Any formula enacted to determine the amount of funds that are to be provided under this paragraph shall be based on the value of the development or subdivision for property tax purposes. The ordinance may allow a combination or partial payment of funds and partial dedication of land when the governing body of the city determines that this combination is in the best interests of the citizens of the area to be served.

The ordinance may provide that in lieu of required street construction, a developer may be required to provide funds that the city may use for the construction of roads to serve the occupants, residents, or invitees of the subdivision or development and these funds may be used for roads which serve more than one subdivision or development within the area. All funds received by the city pursuant to this paragraph shall be used only for development of roads, including design, land acquisition, and construction. However, a city may undertake these activities in conjunction with the Department of Transportation under an agreement between the city and the Department of Transportation. Any formula adopted to determine the amount of funds the developer is to pay in lieu of required street construction shall be based on the trips generated from the subdivision or development. The ordinance may require a combination of partial payment of funds and partial dedication of constructed streets when the governing body of the city determines that a combination is in the best interests of the citizens of the area to be served. (1955, c. 1334, s. 1; 1961, c. 1168; 1971, c. 698, s. 1; 1973, c. 426, s. 59; 1985, c. 146, ss. 1, 2; 1987, c. 747, ss. 9, 18; 1989 (Reg. Sess., 1990), c. 1024, s. 39; 2005-426, s. 2(a).)

§ 160A-373. Ordinance to contain procedure for plat approval; approval prerequisite to plat recordation; statement by owner.

Any subdivision ordinance adopted pursuant to this Part shall contain provisions setting forth the procedures to be followed in granting or denying approval of a subdivision plat prior to its registration.

The ordinance may provide that final decisions on preliminary plats and final plats are to be made by:

(1)   The city council,

(2)   The city council on recommendation of a designated body, or

(3)   A designated planning board, technical review committee, or other designated body or staff person.

From and after the effective date of a subdivision ordinance that is adopted by the city, no subdivision plat of land within the city's jurisdiction shall be filed or recorded until it shall have been submitted to and approved by the council or appropriate agency, as specified in the subdivision ordinance, and until this approval shall have been entered on the face of the plat in writing by an authorized representative of the city. The Review Officer, pursuant to G.S. 47-30.2, shall not certify a plat of a subdivision of land located within the territorial jurisdiction of a city that has not been approved in accordance with these provisions, nor shall the clerk of superior court order or direct the recording of a plat if the recording would be in conflict with this section. (1955, c. 1334, s. 1; 1971, c. 698, s. 1; 1973, c. 426, s. 60; 1997-309, s. 8; 2005-418, s. 3(a).)

§ 160A-374. Effect of plat approval on dedications.

The approval of a plat shall not be deemed to constitute or effect the acceptance by the city or public of the dedication of any street or other ground, public utility line, or other public facility shown on the plat. However, any city council may by resolution accept any dedication made to the public of lands or facilities for streets, parks, public utility lines, or other public purposes, when the lands or facilities are located within its subdivision-regulation jurisdiction. Acceptance of dedication of lands or facilities located within the subdivision-regulation jurisdiction but outside the corporate limits of a city shall not place on the city any duty to open, operate, repair, or maintain any street, utility line, or other land or facility, and a city shall in no event be held to answer in any civil action or proceeding for failure to open, repair, or maintain any street located outside its corporate limits. Unless a city, county or other public entity operating a water system shall have agreed to begin operation and maintenance of the water system or water system facilities within one year of the time of issuance of a certificate of occupancy for the first unit of housing in the subdivision, a city or county shall not, as part of its subdivision regulation applied to facilities or land outside the corporate limits of a city, require dedication of water systems or facilities as a condition for subdivision approval. (1955, c. 1334, s. 1; 1971, c. 698, s. 1; 1983 (Reg. Sess., 1984), c. 1080; 1985, c. 635.)

§ 160A-375. Penalties for transferring lots in unapproved subdivisions.

(a)   If a city adopts an ordinance regulating the subdivision of land as authorized herein, any person who, being the owner or agent of the owner of any land located within the jurisdiction of that city, thereafter subdivides his land in violation of the ordinance or transfers or sells land by reference to, exhibition of, or any other use of a plat showing a subdivision of the land before the plat has been properly approved under such ordinance and recorded in the office of the appropriate register of deeds, shall be guilty of a Class 1 misdemeanor. The description by metes and bounds in the instrument of transfer or other document used in the process of selling or transferring land shall not exempt the transaction from this penalty. The city may bring an action for injunction of any illegal subdivision, transfer, conveyance, or sale of land, and the court shall, upon appropriate findings, issue an injunction and order requiring the offending party to comply with the subdivision ordinance. Building permits required pursuant to G.S. 160A-417 may be denied for lots that have been illegally subdivided. In addition to other remedies, a city may institute any appropriate action or proceedings to prevent the unlawful subdivision of land, to restrain, correct, or abate the violation, or to prevent any illegal act or conduct.

(b) The provisions of this section shall not prohibit any owner or its agent from entering into contracts to sell or lease by reference to an approved preliminary plat for which a final plat has not yet been properly approved under the subdivision ordinance or recorded with the register of deeds, provided the contract does all of the following:

(1) Incorporates as an attachment a copy of the preliminary plat referenced in the contract and obligates the owner to deliver to the buyer a copy of the recorded plat prior to closing and conveyance.

(2) Plainly and conspicuously notifies the prospective buyer or lessee that a final subdivision plat has not been approved or recorded at the time of the contract, that no governmental body will incur any obligation to the prospective buyer or lessee with respect to the approval of the final subdivision plat, that changes between the preliminary and final plats are possible, and that the contract or lease may be terminated without breach by the buyer or lessee if the final recorded plat differs in any material respect from the preliminary plat.

(3) Provides that if the approved and recorded final plat does not differ in any material respect from the plat referred to in the contract, the buyer or lessee may not be required by the seller or lessor to close any earlier than five days after the delivery of a copy of the final recorded plat.

(4) Provides that if the approved and recorded final plat differs in any material respect from the preliminary plat referred to in the contract, the buyer or lessee may not be required by the seller or lessor to close any earlier than 15 days after the delivery of the final recorded plat, during which 15-day period the buyer or lessee may terminate the contract without breach or any further obligation and may receive a refund of all earnest money or prepaid purchase price.

(c) The provisions of this section shall not prohibit any owner or its agent from entering into contracts to sell or lease land by reference to an approved preliminary plat for which a final plat has not been properly approved under the subdivision ordinance or recorded with the register of deeds where the buyer or lessee is any person who has contracted to acquire or lease the land for the purpose of engaging in the business of construction of residential, commercial, or industrial buildings on the land, or for the purpose of resale or lease of the land to persons engaged in that kind of business, provided that no conveyance of that land may occur and no contract to lease it may become effective until after the final plat has been properly approved under the subdivision ordinance and recorded with the register of deeds. (1955, c. 1334, s. 1; 1971, c. 698, s. 1; 1977, c. 820, s. 2; 1993, c. 539, s. 1087; 1994, Ex. Sess., c. 24, s. 14(c); 2005-426, s. 3(a).)

§ 160A-376. Definition.

(a)   For the purpose of this Part, "subdivision" means all divisions of a tract or parcel of land into two or more lots, building sites, or other divisions when any one or more of those divisions is created for the purpose of sale or building development (whether immediate or future) and shall include all divisions of land involving the dedication of a new street or a change in existing streets; but the following shall not be included within this definition nor be subject to the regulations authorized by this Part:

(1)   The combination or recombination of portions of previously subdivided and recorded lots where the total number of lots is not increased and the resultant lots are equal to or exceed the standards of the municipality as shown in its subdivision regulations.

(2)   The division of land into parcels greater than 10 acres where no street right-of-way dedication is involved.

(3)   The public acquisition by purchase of strips of land for the widening or opening of streets or for public transportation system corridors.

(4)   The division of a tract in single ownership whose entire area is no greater than two acres into not more than three lots, where no street right-of-way dedication is involved and where the resultant lots are equal to or exceed the standards of the municipality, as shown in its subdivision regulations.

(b)   A city may provide for expedited review of specified classes of subdivisions. (1955, c. 1334, s. 1; 1971, c. 698, s. 1; 1973, c. 426, s. 61; 1977, c. 912, s. 6; 2003-284, s. 29.23(a); 2005-426, s. 4(a).)

§ 160A-377. Appeals of decisions on subdivision plats.

(a) When a subdivision ordinance adopted under this Part provides that the decision whether to approve or deny a preliminary or final subdivision plat is to be made by a city council or a planning board, other than a planning board comprised solely of members of a city planning staff, and the ordinance authorizes the council or planning board to make a quasi-judicial decision in deciding whether to approve the subdivision plat, then that quasi-judicial decision of the council or planning board shall be subject to review by the superior court by proceedings in the nature of certiorari. The provisions of G.S. 160A-381(c), 160A-388(e2)(2), and 160A-393 shall apply to those appeals.

(b) When a subdivision ordinance adopted under this Part provides that a city council, planning board, or staff member is authorized to make only an administrative or ministerial decision in deciding whether to approve a preliminary or final subdivision plat, then any party aggrieved by that administrative or ministerial decision may seek to have the decision reviewed by filing an action in superior court seeking appropriate declaratory or equitable relief. Such an action must be filed within the time frame specified in G.S. 160A-381(c) for petitions in the nature of certiorari.

(c) For purposes of this section, an ordinance shall be deemed to authorize a quasi-judicial decision if the city council or planning board is authorized to decide whether to approve or deny the plat based not only upon whether the application complies with the specific requirements set forth in the ordinance, but also on whether the application complies with one or more generally stated standards requiring a discretionary decision to be made by the city council or planning board. (2009-421, s. 2(a); 2013-126, s. 12.)

§ 160A-378. Reserved for future codification purposes.

§ 160A-379. Reserved for future codification purposes.

§ 160A-380. Reserved for future codification purposes.

Part 3. Zoning.

§ 160A-381. Grant of power.

(a) For the purpose of promoting health, safety, morals, or the general welfare of the community, any city may adopt zoning and development regulation ordinances. These ordinances may be adopted as part of a unified development ordinance or as a separate ordinance. A zoning ordinance may regulate and restrict the height, number of stories and size of buildings and other structures, the percentage of lots that may be occupied, the size of yards, courts and other open spaces, the density of population, the location and use of buildings, structures and land. The ordinance may provide density credits or severable development rights for dedicated rights-of-way pursuant to G.S. 136-66.10 or G.S. 136-66.11.

(b) Expired.

(b1) These regulations may provide that a board of adjustment may determine and vary their application in harmony with their general purpose and intent and in accordance with general or specific rules therein contained, provided no change in permitted uses may be authorized by variance.

(c) The regulations may also provide that the board of adjustment, the planning board, or the city council may issue special use permits or conditional use permits in the classes of cases or situations and in accordance with the principles, conditions, safeguards, and procedures specified therein and may impose reasonable and appropriate conditions and safeguards upon these permits. When deciding special use permits or conditional use permits, the city council or planning board shall follow quasi-judicial procedures. Notice of hearings on special or conditional use permit applications shall be as provided in G.S. 160A-388(a2). No vote greater than a majority vote shall be required for the city council or planning board to issue such permits. For the purposes of this section, vacant positions on the board and members who are disqualified from voting on a quasi-judicial matter shall not be considered "members of the board" for calculation of the requisite majority. Every such decision of the city council or planning board shall be subject to review of the superior court in the nature of certiorari in accordance with G.S. 160A-388.

Where appropriate, such conditions may include requirements that street and utility rights-of-way be dedicated to the public and that provision be made of recreational space and facilities.

(d) A city council member shall not vote on any zoning map or text amendment where the outcome of the matter being considered is reasonably likely to have a direct, substantial, and readily identifiable financial impact on the member. Members of appointed boards providing advice to the city council shall not vote on recommendations regarding any zoning map or text amendment where the outcome of the matter being considered is reasonably likely to have a direct, substantial, and readily identifiable financial impact on the member.

(e) As provided in this subsection, cities may adopt temporary moratoria on any city development approval required by law, except for the purpose of developing and adopting new or amended plans or ordinances as to residential uses. The duration of any moratorium shall be reasonable in light of the specific conditions that warrant imposition of the moratorium and may not exceed the period of time necessary to correct, modify, or resolve such conditions. Except in cases of imminent and substantial threat to public health or safety, before adopting an ordinance imposing a development moratorium with a duration of 60 days or any shorter period, the governing board shall hold a public hearing and shall publish a notice of the hearing in a newspaper having general circulation in the area not less than seven days before the date set for the hearing. A development moratorium with a duration of 61 days or longer, and any extension of a moratorium so that the total duration is 61 days or longer, is subject to the notice and hearing requirements of G.S. 160A-364. Absent an imminent threat to public health or safety, a development moratorium adopted pursuant to this section shall not apply to any project for which a valid building permit issued pursuant to G.S. 160A-417 is outstanding, to any project for which a conditional use permit application or special use permit application has been accepted, to development set forth in a site-specific or phased development plan approved pursuant to G.S. 160A-385.1, to development for which substantial expenditures have already been made in good faith reliance on a prior valid administrative or quasi-judicial permit or approval, or to preliminary or final subdivision plats that have been accepted for review by the city prior to the call for public hearing to adopt the moratorium. Any preliminary subdivision plat accepted for review by the city prior to the call for public hearing, if subsequently approved, shall be allowed to proceed to final plat approval without being subject to the moratorium.

Any ordinance establishing a development moratorium must expressly include at the time of adoption each of the following:

(1) A clear statement of the problems or conditions necessitating the moratorium and what courses of action, alternative to a moratorium, were considered by the city and why those alternative courses of action were not deemed adequate.

(2) A clear statement of the development approvals subject to the moratorium and how a moratorium on those approvals will address the problems or conditions leading to imposition of the moratorium.

(3) An express date for termination of the moratorium and a statement setting forth why that duration is reasonably necessary to address the problems or conditions leading to imposition of the moratorium.

(4) A clear statement of the actions, and the schedule for those actions, proposed to be taken by the city during the duration of the moratorium to address the problems or conditions leading to imposition of the moratorium.

No moratorium may be subsequently renewed or extended for any additional period unless the city shall have taken all reasonable and feasible steps proposed to be taken by the city in its ordinance establishing the moratorium to address the problems or conditions leading to imposition of the moratorium and unless new facts and conditions warrant an extension. Any ordinance renewing or extending a development moratorium must expressly include, at the time of adoption, the findings set forth in subdivisions (1) through (4) of this subsection, including what new facts or conditions warrant the extension.

Any person aggrieved by the imposition of a moratorium on development approvals required by law may apply to the appropriate division of the General Court of Justice for an order enjoining the enforcement of the moratorium, and the court shall have jurisdiction to issue that order. Actions brought pursuant to this section shall be set down for immediate hearing, and subsequent proceedings in those actions shall be accorded priority by the trial and appellate courts. In any such action, the city shall have the burden of showing compliance with the procedural requirements of this subsection.

(f) In order to encourage construction that uses sustainable design principles and to improve energy efficiency in buildings, a city may charge reduced building permit fees or provide partial rebates of building permit fees for buildings that are constructed or renovated using design principles that conform to or exceed one or more of the following certifications or ratings:

(1) Leadership in Energy and Environmental Design (LEED) certification or higher rating under certification standards adopted by the U.S. Green Building Council.

(2) A One Globe or higher rating under the Green Globes program standards adopted by the Green Building Initiative.

(3) A certification or rating by another nationally recognized certification or rating system that is equivalent or greater than those listed in subdivisions (1) and (2) of this subsection.

(g) A zoning or unified development ordinance may not differentiate in terms of the regulations applicable to fraternities or sororities between those fraternities or sororities that are approved or recognized by a college or university and those that are not. (1923, c. 250, s. 1; C.S., s. 2776(r); 1967, c. 1208, s. 1; 1971, c. 698, s. 1; 1981, c. 891, s. 5; 1985, c. 442, s. 1; 1987, c. 747, s. 11; 1995, c. 357, s. 1; 2005-426, s. 5(a); 2007-381, s. 2; 2011-286, s. 2; 2013-126, s. 4; 2013-413, s. 6(b).)

Vision Books Order Form

Fax Orders:	1-980-299-5965
Phone Orders:	1-704-898-0770
E-mail Orders:	www.visionbooks.org
Mail Orders:	Vision Books, LLC P.O. Box 42406 Charlotte, NC 28215

Shipp To:
Name_____
Address_____
City_____State_____Zip_____
Phone_____Fax_____
Email_____@_____

Bill To: We can bill a third party on your behalf.
Name_____
Address_____
City_____State_____Zip_____
Phone___(_____)_____Fax_____
Email_____@_____

Pamphlet Number ($15.00 Each)	Qty	Total Cost
_____	_____	_____
_____	_____	_____
_____	_____	_____
_____	_____	_____
_____	_____	_____
_____	_____	_____
_____	_____	_____
<u>Full Volume Set 1-92</u>	<u>92 Pamphlets</u>	<u>1,380.00</u>

Free Shipping & Handling on Full Volume Orders
Add $1.00 Shipping & Handling Per Pamphlet $_____

Total Cost $_____

Thank you for your support. Management!

DID YOU ENJOY THIS BOOK?

Vision Books, LLC would like to hear from you! If you or someone you know has been fasely imprisoned, we would like to hear your story. If the 'North Carolina Criminal Law and Procedure' has had an effect in your life or if you have suggestions, we would like to hear from you. Send your letters to:

Vision Books, LLC
Attn: Staff Writers
P.O. Box 42406
Charlotte, NC 28215
Email: staff@visionbooks.org

Order Additional Copies:

Fax Orders: 1-980-299-5965

Phone Orders: 1-704-898-0770

E-mail Orders: www.visionbooks.org

Mail Orders: Vision Books, LLC
                      P.O. Box 42406
                      Charlotte, NC 28215

www.ingramcontent.com/pod-product-compliance
Lightning Source LLC
Chambersburg PA
CBHW051632170526
45167CB00001B/152